THE
POLE

D1462400

WITHDRAWN

BOOKS BY P. J. CAPELOTTI

Author

Explorers Air Yacht: The Sikorsky S-38 Flying Boat

The Wellman Polar Airship Expeditions at Virgohamna, Danskøya, Svalbard

By Airship to the North Pole: An Archaeology of Human Exploration

Editor

Our Man in the Crimea: Commander Hugo Koehler and the Russian Civil War

Spitsbergen: The American Military and Political Geographies, 1941–1950

Before the Airships Came: E. B. Baldwin's Journal of the Wellman Polar Expedition to Franz Josef Land, 1898–1899

General Editor

U.S. Army Heraldic Crests

BY AIRSHIP TO THE NORTH POLE

An Archaeology of Human Exploration

P. J. CAPELOTTI

Rutgers University Press
New Brunswick, New Jersey, and London

Library of Congress Cataloging-in-Publication Data

Capelotti, P. J. (Peter Joseph), 1960–

    By airship to North Pole : an archaeology of human exploration /
P. J. Capelotti.
      p.   cm.
    Includes bibliographical references and index.
    ISBN 0-8135-2633-7 (cloth : alk. paper)
    1. Polar regions—Discovery and exploration.   2. North Pole—
Discovery and exploration.   3. Airship. I. Title.
    G587.C36   1999
    910′.91632—dc21   98-37615
                                                           CIP

British Cataloging-in-Publication data for this book is
available from the British Library

Frontispiece photo courtesy of the Norwegian Polar Institute archives.

Copyright © 1999 by P. J. Capelotti
All rights reserved
No part of this book may be reproduced or utilized in any form or by any means,
electronic or mechanical, or by any information storage and retrieval system, without
written permission from the publisher. Please contact Rutgers University Press, 100
Joyce Kilmer Avenue, Piscataway, NJ 08854–8099. The only exception to this prohibi-
tion is "fair use" as defined by U.S. copyright law.

Manufactured in the United States of America

For Professor Wynne Caldwell

Contents

Illustrations

On a balloon journey toward the North Pole more than a century ago, a Swedish balloonist and his crew released several carrier pigeons at various points en route. In the summer of 1897, these birds were still the quickest way to send a message through the Arctic to civilization in the south, and they carried messages for the expedition's sponsoring newspaper, *Aftonbladet,* in Stockholm.

The Swedish engineer who sought the North Pole with two companions in 1897 was named Salomon August Andrée (1856–1897). In his hydrogen balloon *Eagle* (*Örnen*), Andrée drifted toward the Pole from a circular wooden shed constructed on the north shore of Danes Island in the Spitsbergen archipelago.

If they reached the Pole, the crew of *Eagle* would release a specially designed cork buoy. This buoy was equipped with a trigger that, upon hitting the ice, extracted a small Union flag of Sweden. If the aeronauts never regained land, if they perished on the ice, the buoy would drift atop the circulating ice surrounding the North Pole until, in three or four years' time, it drifted out of the ice and washed onto some civilized shore, where the news of their polar triumph could be hand-carried to Stockholm.

But Salomon Andrée would never see his goal. Two hundred miles north of Danes Island, the escape of gas through the fabric of the balloon and the weight of mist and ice on the gasbag forced the *Eagle* onto the polar ice pack, still four hundred cold miles short of the North Pole. After abandoning their balloon, Andrée and his crew struggled south on foot, reaching White Island (Kvitøya), the northeasternmost of the islands in the Spitsbergen archipelago. There they made camp and waited. For more than thirty years, the world would wonder what became of them.

Among those who wondered most intently was a remarkable and optimistic journalist from Chicago named Walter Wellman (1858–1934). Between 1894 and 1909, Wellman organized and led five of his own expeditions in search of the North Pole. He launched his most ambitious undertaking in 1906, when he constructed an extensive base camp, complete with an airship hangar, on the northern shore of Danes Island. On the same rocky shoreline where Andrée had launched his balloon nearly a decade earlier, Wellman built his camp in plain view of the ruins of Andrée's balloon shed. As the American journalist wrote in one of his many newspaper and magazine dispatches from Danes Island, "Our decision to occupy the very spot marked by that tragedy of exploration may be taken as evidence that, whatever else we may be, we are not superstitious."

As a seasoned reporter, Walter Wellman believed carrier pigeons simply would not do. If *he* reached the Pole, *he* would use an early wireless set installed on board his airship, the *America*. Broadcasting at the limits of the transmitter's capabilities, Wellman would send the word six hundred miles south to Danes Island, that he and his companions had become the first humans to reach the geographic North Pole, the Holy Grail of centuries of failed expeditions to the Arctic.

Wellman's receiving station at Danes Island would then broadcast the news to Hammerfest in northern Norway, which would pass the word down the coast to Tromsø, which would send it via the transatlantic cable to Chicago. There, Wellman's sponsoring newspaper, the *Chicago Record-Herald,* would publish the news in time for Chicagoans to ponder it over their breakfast of bacon and sausage cut and ground from the Chicago slaughterhouses. The instantaneous transmission of the news, as much as the journey itself, was to be one of the triumphs of the age.

In 1907 and 1909, Wellman's two revolutionary flights in the *America* marked the first voyages by a motorized airship in the Arctic. In September 1909, the same month he learned of the competing polar claims of the American explorers Robert E. Peary and Frederick A. Cook, Wellman abandoned his camp on Danes Island, abandoned his polar dream, and turned his aeronautical ambitions instead to crossing the Atlantic Ocean. This equally audacious airship expedition captured the headlines of the world in the fall of 1910, when *America* drifted for more than one thousand miles before Wellman and his crew finally abandoned ship near Bermuda.

In 1926, the famous Norwegian polar explorer Roald Amundsen sailed over the North Pole in an Italian airship piloted by its Italian designer, Umberto Nobile. After their triumph, both men paid handsome tributes to the Arctic balloon pioneer Salomon Andrée, whose fate was still unknown but who by the time of Amundsen's flight had attained a status somewhere between tragic hero and brave martyr for science, especially in his native Sweden. Neither man mentioned Walter Wellman, who, though still very much alive and retired in New York City, had been long forgotten.

The aerial expeditions of Andrée and Wellman were remarkable in their day and seem only to grow more so with the passage of time. To launch a balloon or airship toward the North Pole from Danes Island more than a century ago seemed so remarkable to me that I felt compelled to journey to the island myself. I needed to find out what, if anything, these men had left behind. As an archaeologist, I believed it just might tell us something new about the Swedish saint and the American failure. More, I thought I might learn something about where we as humans had once been, and where we might be going.

—P. J. Capelotti
Abington, Pennsylvania
October 1, 1998

A Select Chronology of Northern Expeditions and Events

YEAR	EVENT
1194	Icelandic Sagas report a land of "cold coasts," or "Svalbard," four days' sailing from Iceland.
1596	Seeking a polar route to China, two Dutch ships piloted by Willem Barentsz sail along the coast of what they call "Spitsbergen," the Svalbard of the Viking Sagas.
1607	Henry Hudson of Britain's Muscovy Company seeks a passage over the North Pole to Asia, only to be stopped by the wall of permanent ice north of Spitsbergen.
1773	Constantine John Phipps leads HMS *Racehorse* and *Carcass* to the Seven Islands, the northernmost islands in the Spitsbergen archipelago.
1818	Captain David Buchan and Lieutenant John Franklin lead the ships *Trent* and *Dorothea* in an exploration of northwestern Spitsbergen that finds no simple sea route to the North Pole.
1827	William Parry and several dozen British sailors drag two heavy boats north of the Seven Islands to a new Farthest North mark of 82°45'.
1853	Philadelphia doctor Elisha Kent Kane tries to reach the North Pole by sailing between Greenland and Ellesmere Island, and is stopped by ice in the Kennedy Channel.
1854	Salomon August Andrée is born in Gränna, Sweden.

1858   Walter Wellman is born in Mentor, Ohio.

1860   American surgeon Isaac Israel Hayes sails the ship *United States* into the Kennedy Channel but returns in 1861 without proceeding much farther north than Kane.

1868   Swedish explorer Adolf Erik Nordenskiöld sails his ship *Sofia* to 81°42' north of Svalbard.

1871   American Charles Francis Hall on board the ship *Polaris* beats Adolf Erik Nordenskiöld's mark and reaches the Farthest North yet for a surface vessel, but dies under mysterious circumstances in October 1871, before he can launch a planned sledge expedition toward the Pole in the spring of 1872.

1872/ 1874   Austrians Karl Weyprecht and Julius von Payer on board the *Tegetthoff* mount an expedition toward the Pole that discovers instead a previously unknown Arctic archipelago they name Franz Josef Land in honor of their emperor.

1875/ 1876   Royal Navy captain George S. Nares leads HMS *Alert* up the Kennedy Channel to still another Farthest North for a surface vessel: 82°28'. In the spring of 1876, the British try to drag two sledges north to the Pole. After several weeks, they establish a new Farthest North but are still four hundred miles from the Pole. The sledging parties retreat, leaving three dead and several nearly dead from exhaustion and scurvy.

1879/ 1881   U.S. Navy captain George Washington DeLong, sponsored by the *New York Herald,* enters the Arctic on board the *Jeanette.* The expedition ends in disaster when the *Jeanette* is crushed by ice and the crew starves while retreating toward the coast of Siberia.

1881/ 1884   U.S. Army officer Adolphus Greely leads a team establishing a weather station on Ellesmere Island. In the spring of 1882, Lieutenant James Lockwood and Sergeant D. L. Brainard sledge to Greenland and beat the Farthest North mark set by the Nares expedition. The margin of victory, however, is slight, and overshadowed when successive relief expeditions fail to relieve Greely and his men. When rescue arrives at last in 1884, nineteen of Greely's original twenty-six men are dead.

1886   American engineer Robert Edwin Peary tries and fails to walk across Greenland from west to east.

1888   Norwegian scientist Fridtjof Nansen leads an expedition that skis across Greenland from east to west.

1893 /   Nansen places *Fram,* a vessel specially built for
1896   Arctic ice, into the polar ice pack north of Siberia. Three years later, *Fram,* now captained by Otto Sverdrup, drifts out of the ice near Danes Island, Svalbard. In March of 1895, Nansen and Hjalmar Johansen, a lieutenant in the Norwegian Navy Reserve, had left *Fram* at about 84° N and skied with sledges to 86°13'06", a new northernmost mark by almost three degrees (about 180 miles). After a perilous return journey, Nansen and Johansen are rescued by a British expedition in Franz Josef Land.

1894   Swedish engineer Salomon Andrée announces his intention to drift to the North Pole in a hydrogen balloon.

1894   Chicago journalist Walter Wellman on board the Norwegian ship *Ragnvald Jarl* reaches Walden Island north of Spitsbergen where the ship is pinned by ice and sinks.

1896   Andrée builds a hangar on the north shore of Danes Island and inflates the hydrogen balloon *Örnen* (*Eagle*), but a lack of wind from the south makes it impossible to launch toward the Pole. Andrée meets Sverdrup and the crew of *Fram* as they return from their three-year polar drift.

1897   With two companions, Andrée on July 11 launches *Eagle* toward the North Pole. Save for a few notes found on carrier pigeons, no trace of the expedition is found for more than thirty-three years.

1898 /   Walter Wellman leads his second north polar
1899   expedition, reaching the northern edge of the Franz Josef Land archipelago before slipping on the ice and fracturing his leg. One of the Norwegian members of the expedition, Bernt Bentzen, dies.

1899/   Luigi Amadeo de Savoy, an Italian duke, leads an
1900   expedition to Franz Josef Land that reaches 86°34' N, beating Nansen's Farthest North by twenty-three miles.

1900   A German named Oskar Bauendahl journeys to Danes Island. There he salvages wood from Andrée's hangar and builds a raft. His projected polar expedition ends with the raft aground south of Danes Island at Prinz Karl Foreland.

1902   Using pickaxes to hack a path through the pack ice, Robert Peary reaches 84°17' N on April 21 when exhaustion and an open impasse of water force him to retreat.

1906   Claiming sledging speeds across the pack ice that have never been duplicated, Peary declares that hehas reached 87°06' on April 21, beating the Abruzzi expedition's Farthest North by thirty-six miles.

1906   Walter Wellman brings the first powered airship into the Arctic, to his old camp on Danes Island, but the motors are so flawed that Wellman doesn't bother to inflate, much less fly the airship.

1907   Wellman returns to Danes Island with a new airship built by Melvin Vaniman, and manages a late-season flight of approximately fifteen miles. It is the first flight of a motorized airship in the Arctic.

1908   Dr. Frederick Cook, an American physician and Arctic explorer, asserting remarkable sledging distances of seventeen miles per day, claims to have reached the North Pole on April 21.

1909   Claiming even more stunning distances over the ice of twenty-five to forty-three miles a day, Robert Peary announces that he reached the North Pole on April 6. (By comparison, a *snowmobile* expedition to the Pole in 1968 made good an average of eleven miles per day.)

1909   Wellman, in his most successful (and final) Arctic flight, pilots his airship approximately forty miles north of Danes Island before mechanical failures force him back.

1910   An expedition of Count von Zeppelin investigates Spitsbergen as a possible base for a Zeppelin expedition to the Pole.

1920   Due in part to Nansen's diplomacy, Norway gains sovereignty over the Spitsbergen archipelago.

1925   Norwegian explorer Captain Roald Amundsen flies to 88° N in two Dornier-Wal seaplanes before the aircraft are forced down on the ice and Amundsen is forced to evacuate both air crews on board a single plane.

1926   In May, U.S. Navy officer Richard Evelyn Byrd leaves Ny-Ålesund (King's Bay), Spitsbergen, with his pilot, Floyd Bennett, and claims to have become the first to fly to the Pole, but his accomplishment is doubted by most polar historians.

1926   Also in May, Amundsen leads the airship *Norge* in an expedition across the Pole and on to a landing in Teller, Alaska.

1928   Italian air force general Umberto Nobile, who designed and built the airship *Norge,* builds a second similar airship, *Italia,* and pilots it to the Pole. *Italia* crashes on its return from the Pole, setting off a massive international rescue effort. During the long rescue process, the fifty-seven-year-old Amundsen is lost at sea while flying a French seaplane to Nobile's rescue.

1930   Fridtjof Nansen dies on May 13, at the age of sixty-eight. Three months later, the remains of Andrée's last camp are discovered on White Island by a Norwegian sealing ship. The spectacular finds create an international media sensation.

1934   Walter Wellman dies of liver cancer in New York City at the age of seventy-five.

1978   Umberto Nobile dies in Rome at the age of ninety-three.

A Note on Norwegian Geography

*T*he modern Norwegian name for Danes Island is Danskøya. Virgo Harbor is, in Norwegian, Virgohamna. The area bounded by White Island (Kvitøya) on the northeast, Bear Island (Bjørnøya) on the south, and Danes Island and Amsterdam Island (Amsterdamøya) on the northwest is called Svalbard, not Spitsbergen, although Northwest Spitsbergen is still used for the main island of the archipelago. The capital of Svalbard is Longyearbyen (Longyear City), named for the American venture capitalist John Munro Longyear, who founded the Arctic Coal Company there in 1905. The Norwegian *Sysselmann* (governor) of the islands has his offices in Longyearbyen, on a hill overlooking the small northern mining town.

For this North American edition, I have retained the names Danes Island and Spitsbergen, for two reasons. First, these were the names used in S. A. Andrée's and Walter Wellman's day, and, second, they are still the names most Americans associate with this remote group of Arctic islands. I apologize to my few American friends and all my Norwegian friends who live, love, or do their research in what we all know as Svalbard.

BY AIRSHIP TO THE
NORTH POLE

Introduction

On a remote and uninhabited fortress of an island in the Spitsbergen archipelago called Danes Island lies the icy anchorage of Virgo Harbor. The initial attempts to reach the North Pole by air were launched from this small harbor, around the turn of the century. First to depart was a Swedish expedition led by engineer Salomon A. Andrée, followed by an American attempt directed by journalist Walter Wellman. Nearly a century later, in the summer of 1993, I lived on the shoreline of Virgo Harbor, within sight of the ruins of those early aeronautical expeditions, studying their archaeological remains.

This book is about those two expeditions. It is also about the capacity of archaeological remains to cast both the expeditions and the men who led them in a very different light from that thrown upon them by traditional history. The few written accounts of these expeditions generally consider one man a lunatic and the other a fraud.

I was particularly interested in the latter, because he was the American, and the United States possesses a distinct and distressing lineage of polar fakery. Recent research and revelations had seriously undermined American claims to the discovery of the North Pole, claims made by the most famous polar explorers in U.S. history: Robert E. Peary, Richard E. Byrd, and Frederick A. Cook. Was there some inherent flaw in the American character that, like a bad gene, caused its polar explorers to be found so wanting?

I did not want to believe it of this American, maybe because he was a journalist who became a world explorer and eventually captained his own airship on daring attempts to reach the North Pole and cross the Atlantic. As such, he struck me as a true-life character who had somehow stepped straight from the prophetic pages of Jules Verne. I too started out as a journalist, and now, as a professional archaeologist, I use a small blimp to take aerial photographs of archaeological sites.

So I had a reservoir of sympathy for this American, as I did for any individual who tried to adapt, as early as 1900, to all of the new technologies increasingly required to live in the modern world. Explorers in particular faced the challenge of using advanced technology to answer scientific questions without becoming mere technicians in the process.

Yet, despite his modern—for 1909—airship, the written record had long found this American a buffoon. And most people believe, as Hemingway remarked, that paper doesn't bleed. In other words, books and newspapers and letters do not lie. I believed this myself as I made the transition from college journalist to postgraduate historian.

In the late 1980s, my view changed when I heard a lecture by the famous anthropologist Richard A. Gould. Gould spoke of his historical archaeology research on the forts and shipwrecks of Bermuda and demonstrated with vivid clarity that paper most certainly does bleed. What was more, paper all but hemorrhages: it is full of contradictions, lies, and a myriad of differences in nuance, interpretation, and style.

According to Gould, all of these differences, embedded within the written accounts of human events, present a glorious field of opportunity for archaeologists, who, like scientists in a laboratory, can use them as competing hypotheses, or questions, to be asked of human history. But how can one ever evaluate these hypotheses? Sort them out? See which ones hold up under scientific scrutiny?

That is where archaeology comes in. Archaeology uses the material things people create—from stone tools to spacecraft—to examine both the mind and the matter of human existence. Archaeologists who study human groups before the invention of writing must develop their hypotheses exclusively from material evidence, including human bones, stone tools, the remains of meals of plants and animals, and geological strata.

Archaeologists with access to a written record, on the other hand, have the advantage of being able to study more than just the material debris people leave around themselves as they move through their lives. These archaeologists—historical archaeologists—can read and study what people write about themselves, their contemporaries, their rivals and friends; how they justify their actions; what they decide to leave in their autobiographies and, maybe more significant, what they choose to leave out. Historical archaeology, Gould said, provides the means not only to fill in many of the missing gaps in the autobiography of the human race, but also to test one person's version of events against another's, or even a single individual's many different versions.

Gould had a final message: the world outside ourselves *is* knowable, objective archaeological tests of the written record *are* possible, despite a sea of postmodern writings arguing just the opposite. In a constantly shifting academic world, where each morning seems to bring a new rush to the -ism du jour, Gould offered a rational positivist philosophy to hang one's hat on.

A few years later, I was presented with the opportunity to go to Virgo Harbor. I had always wanted to write about the early aeronautical polar expeditions that originated there. The accounts I had read were all unsatisfying, and I knew why. Most mentioned these attempted Arctic flights only in passing, but more frustrating was that no author had actually visited the launch sites themselves. I felt my writings would be incomplete until I had seen Virgo Harbor with my own eyes.

But seeing a place with my own eyes hardly constituted a rationale for the expense and danger of traveling four thousand miles to an impossibly remote island in the Arctic. I did not have the slightest interest in merely visiting a historic site, snapping a few pictures, and returning home. I had to travel with a purpose; I needed to bring home not just new pictures but new knowledge as well. For these expeditions, in my view, were the very first to attempt to lift the human species off the ground, not merely to see if it could be done, but deliberately, in order to explore unknown, remote, and hostile territories from the air.

So I had long thought it vital to travel to this shoreline and examine the remains of these intrepid pioneer explorers. And as I contemplated the approach of the twenty-first century and the likely human exploration of Mars, I felt that studying the base camps of these early explorers might tell us something about ourselves that we could never learn from books, journals, or newspapers.

It was the work of Gould, which he had by then expounded upon in his brilliant 1990 book *Recovering the Past,* that provided a scientific basis for my journey, and the many historical details of these expeditions that furnished a bagful of hypotheses to test. And so I found myself on the morning of July 20, 1993, in a dense fog that obscured visibility much beyond fifty feet, stepping off a rubber Zodiac inflatable boat and onto the stony shore of Virgo Harbor for a month of archaeological research.

Tourists and trappers and the occasional geologist visit Virgo Harbor, but my month-long stay was likely the first time since 1909 that anyone had remained there for more than a few hours or days. Although Danish and Norwegian archaeologists had visited the island to study the sites of early whaling activity, no one had considered the remains of the two aeronautical North Pole expeditions worth their time.

The crew and Z-boats of the Norwegian icebreaker *Polarsyssel* placed my British guide Lucy Gilbert and me ashore at some distance to the east of the area of historic ruins, since Norwegian historic preservation rules permit no camps or fires within three hundred feet of cultural remains in the Spitsbergen islands. As quickly as I could break away from setting up our camp, I hiked westward along the shore, toward the small amphitheater of crumbling rock that encloses the Swedish and American airship base camps. Along the way I gazed up at the heights of those ancient cliffs to see a chronicle of Arctic graffiti partially obscured behind the lofting fog:

Meteor
1964

Irma
1925

Lingen
1961

Skule
(date obscured)

Ships and expeditions had preceded us and left their marks in ten-foot-high letters on the cliff face, testaments to a human need to record our passages, even—perhaps especially—in places where almost no one will ever see them again.

Danes Island received its name from Danish whalers who hunted their catch in Kobbefjorden on the west coast of the island in 1631. In 1773 HMS *Carcass,* part of an expedition under Constantine Phipps that later reached the Seven Islands (Sjuøyane) farther north and east, moored off Danes Island. One of the crew members on board the *Carcass* was fourteen-year-old midshipman Horatio Nelson, who stole from the ship one night to hunt the polar bear that nearly killed the future admiral and hero of Trafalgar.

Geographic names on maps of the island reflect its place in the history of polar and aeronautical exploration: Luftskipodden (Airship Point), on the west coast; and Ballongkollen (Balloon Hill), a knob on the southwest corner of the island. Virgo Harbor itself was named for the Swedish freighter *Virgo,* which carried Salomon A. Andrée and his hydrogen balloon to the protected anchorage in 1896. Then there was Wellmankollen (Wellman Hill), a small knob on the northeast of the island just south of Virgo Harbor, and the only geographic spot in the world named for Walter Wellman, the Chicago reporter who tried to reach the North Pole five times, on each succeeding expedition seemingly finding new and more spectacular ways to fail.

The shoreline of Virgo Harbor holds a crowded archaeological assemblage. In addition to Wellman's base camp, there are the remnants of a house that British sportsman Arnold Pike used to overwinter on the island in 1888. Pike's hut was later commandeered by Wellman during his first Arctic expedition, an attempt to reach the North Pole by ship and sledge in 1894. The remains of Andrée's circular balloon shed are also there. From this spot Andrée launched his balloon *Eagle* toward the North Pole in the summer of 1897.

Wellman would return to Danes Island three more times, in 1906, 1907, and 1909, building an enormous hangar in which he inflated the first motorized airship ever flown in the Arctic. These relatively modern remains are bracketed by the moundlike ruins of three Dutch whaling ovens and at least eight graves of whalers dating from the early seventeenth century.

Danes Island today is only one of many frozen islands in both the Arctic and the Antarctic under the sovereignty of the maritime nation of Norway. In Scandinavia, many people believe that Viking longships reached the Spitsbergen islands eight hundred years ago. Icelandic annals as early as 1194 record that a place called Svalbard—the land of the cold coast—was discovered that year, and give its location as a four-day sail from the north coast of Iceland. That Icelanders, of all people, should name anywhere on earth "cold," and be so specific about its location, seems to indicate that Spitsbergen was not unknown to the medieval imagination.

Perhaps the heavy keel of a Viking ship even touched upon the shoreline of Virgo Harbor. It would not have been unnatural for the Vikings to voyage so far north. They apparently thought that their newly found cold coast was part of Greenland, for it fit neatly with their certain view that the world was circular, like a gigantic dinner plate, with a round coastal landmass surrounding a great inland sea.

What is certain is that Danes Island, gray and enshrouded on most days behind thick curtains of mist and fog, was one of the first far northern places discovered as mercantile explorers of the 1500s set out to find a trade route across the North Pole. In the decades after the expeditions of Columbus, as the Spanish and Portuguese consolidated their grip on the great southern sea routes to the Spice Islands of the East Indies and the trading ports of India and China, the British, the Dutch, the Danes, and later the French were left to fight over whatever possible northern routes to Asia might exist for their own trading fleets.

When the Dutch navigator Willem Barentsz led an expedition north in the summer of 1596, looking for a quick route across the North Pole to China, he became the first person to see the cold coast since the Vikings. He called it Spitsbergen, the place of sharp mountains. But Barentsz and those who followed him north soon found their way to China blocked by an impenetrable polar sea full of fractured and drifting ice. Their wooden ships were no match for this polar ice cap. Nearly four more centuries would pass before a ship—the Soviet nuclear icebreaker *Arktis*—was built with enough strength to cleave its way through the ten-foot-thick ice pack and reach the Pole.

Still, Barentsz and his fellow mercantile explorers of the northern sea did not sail home empty-handed. In looking for a route across the Pole to China, they inadvertently stumbled instead upon one of the richest whaling grounds anywhere in the world's oceans. The place-names that would be attached to the shorelines of this area in the decades to follow tell the economic tale of the cities and countries that fought over access to the oil of the whales: English Bay, Hamburg Bay, Amsterdam Island, Holland Point, Danes Island.

It took the whalers of these European nations little more than thirty years to slaughter the entire population of the coastal whales of northern Spitsbergen. That accomplished, the whaling fleets moved offshore, where they continued their relentless hunt for another three centuries. The shore-based whaling stations of the many competing nations were dismantled and the shorelines abandoned, passing from history into the realm of archaeology, where they were rediscovered and excavated by Danish and Norwegian archaeologists in the late 1970s.

In 1993, walking around the ruins of the Dutch whaling station on the sandy spit of land at Smeerenburg, on Amsterdam Island, a mile away from Virgo Harbor, I came across an enormous whale vertebra. Gray and decayed, it rested in a shallow lagoon, an ancient faunal testament. I stared at that piece of broken backbone for a long while, absorbing its evidence of a seemingly timeless human capacity to overexploit natural resources, even here. Six hundred miles from the North Pole.

The whalers, however, would never sail that final six hundred miles. The line of ice would shift somewhat in summer, at times crushing down upon Danes Island and the other islets of northwest Spitsbergen, at times moving offshore and leaving an ice-free corridor from Danes Island to the Seven Islands. But every summer, no matter the slight seasonal variation, the line of impassable ice would still be there.

These seasonal variations, noted in detail by the thousands of whaling expeditions to the waters around Spitsbergen in the 1600s and 1700s, were used by some to argue that it was only a matter of pushing a bit farther north before an ice-free corridor was located that would allow ships to sail all the way to the Pole. One true believer, a strange British dilettante by the name of Daines Barrington, strung together a series of thirdhand sailors' yarns and persuaded both the Royal Society and the British Admiralty to mount a polar expedition north from Spitsbergen. (This was the Phipps Expedition of 1773.) The Admiralty should have known better; a century and a half of whaling logbooks showed nothing but a wall of ice north of Spitsbergen. Although Phipps and his crew reached the Seven Islands, they were stopped there, confirming that no simple sea route to the Pole existed.

For the better part of the next half century, little attention was paid to the North Pole. By now it was clear to most that no sea route to China could pass over the Pole, so polar exploration soon lost whatever economic value it might once have possessed. And revolutions in North America and France drew the men and ships of the Royal Navy elsewhere.

By 1820, after the British had deposited Napoleon on St. Helena and lost two naval wars with the Americans, the Royal Navy found itself with too many sailors and too few missions. John Barrow, secretary of the Admiralty, who had visited Spitsbergen on board a whaler, thought he had one. Barrow set in motion a series of naval expeditions in search of a northwest passage to China that would pass between the many islands of Arctic Canada. This search would not end until the disastrous expedition of Sir John Franklin in 1845 and the many futile rescue missions sent in search of Franklin's two ships. To this day, though many have looked, neither Franklin's remains nor his lost vessels have been seen again.

Barrow also revived another bizarre notion of Daines Barrington, who once wrote of a polar sea, free of ice, that existed just beyond the ice barrier north of Spitsbergen. Disregarding what was now more than two centuries of whaling reports, Barrow sent an expedition under Captain David Buchan to Spitsbergen in 1818 to discover what the Admiralty already knew: sailing vessels could not reach the North Pole.

That serious naval officers could make the same mistake so many times over seems incredible, but as polar historian Clive Holland writes, "In matters concerning the North Pole, and especially the

'Open Polar Sea' beyond it, the ability of otherwise rational men to delude themselves was remarkable."[1] Buchan's expedition finally convinced Barrow that no such thing as an "Open Polar Sea" existed.

Still, Barrow now believed that the attainment of the Pole would be valuable for scientific reasons, and this scientific curiosity justified further exploration by the Royal Navy. Since it was now clear that the only way to reach the Pole was on foot, Barrow in 1827 dispatched an expedition under William Parry to the ice pack north of Spitsbergen.

Parry had with him several dozen men and two enormous boats mounted on steel sledge runners. Parry's men dragged these sledge-boats north for a month, by which time their supplies were half gone and the North Pole was still four hundred miles away. Worse, as Parry had known for some time but did not tell his men, ocean currents had been carrying the ice—and his men—*south,* faster than they were pulling their heavy sledge-boats north. Realizing the futility of the situation, Parry ordered his men to turn around. Parry's failure discouraged explorers for many years from undertaking any more such drudgery in the Arctic, and his Farthest North mark of 82°45' would not be bested for another half century.

It was a Philadelphia doctor, Elisha Kent Kane, who took up the polar challenge. In 1853, under the guise of looking for the remnants of the lost Franklin expedition, Kane sailed north into Baffin Bay, the body of water that separates Greenland from Ellesmere Island, Canada. Kane's discovery of a frozen waterway between Greenland and Ellesmere, which he named Kennedy Channel, led him to the belief that at the end of this waterway the fabled Open Polar Sea would be found at last.

Kane and his fellow American explorers chose to ignore the experiences of Phipps, Buchan, and Parry, and began instead to force ship after ship up the Kennedy Channel toward the grail of the Open Polar Sea. The ice that crushed down upon Spitsbergen and Greenland, they argued, was merely a belt. Once beyond it, a ship could sail on open water to the Pole. That such a notion could withstand for a century all the evidence thrown against it, elevates the Open Polar Sea almost to the status of an El Dorado. Another mystical idea, that in the middle of this open sea stood a soaring volcanic mountain, seemed only to intensify the ardor of these explorers to break through the Kennedy Channel.

The experiences of Charles Francis Hall, the most remarkable explorer, perhaps, in all of American history, also fed this fever. Throughout the years of the U.S. Civil War, Hall had lived with Eskimos in Arctic Canada. In 1871, Hall was placed in command of a

U.S.-sponsored vessel called *Polaris,* with the express mission of reaching the Pole. Unlike Kane, Hall breezed through Kennedy Channel to a wider basin beyond, which he named after himself. Hall and *Polaris* eventually reached the northern shores of Greenland, the northernmost point attained by any ocean vessel to that date. An experienced Arctic traveler, Hall was poised to strike for the Pole in the spring of 1872.

What happened next went unexplained for nearly a century. Hall was taken violently ill, complained that he was being poisoned by, among others, the Smithsonian Institution scientist on board,[2] and died in October 1871. In 1968, a Dartmouth College English professor and biographer of Hall's, Chauncey Loomis, received permission to exhume Hall's body from the frozen shoreline of Polaris Harbor, where the explorer had been buried.

Loomis had tests run on small clippings of Hall's hair and fingernails. Hall had indeed been poisoned. But was it the evil Dr. Emil Bessels of the Smithsonian (in the salon, with the arsenic)? Or the master of the *Polaris,* Sidney Budington? Or any of the crew, frightened by the intensity of Hall's mad dream of a springtime dash to the North Pole? Or had Hall simply overdosed on the arsenic that was used at the time as both medicine and poison? No one will ever know for certain.

Hall's "Farthest North" by a ship inspired others to follow his Kennedy Channel route. Twenty-five years later, Robert E. Peary would refer to it as "the American Route" to the Pole. (What he really meant was the *Peary* Route. When others, American or not, used it, Peary used all his considerable talents to discredit them.)

Two summers after Hall's death, an Austrian expedition, one of the last expeditions to believe in the Open Polar Sea, sailed north from Europe and discovered a series of islands to the east of Spitsbergen, an archipelago they named after their emperor, Franz Josef. The following year, 1875, the British mounted their first polar attempt since Parry. The next spring, as with Parry, the British began dragging two heavy boats toward the Pole, and they succeeded in besting Hall's Farthest North for a ship. But the expedition ended prematurely, through scurvy, exhaustion, and death, and so discouraged the British that they turned away from the North Pole once and for all. Soon they would begin dragging their heavy sledges toward the South Pole instead, leaving several more Royal Navy sailors dead in the snow, and again without result.

The next attempt on the Pole, in 1879, was also the first to be sponsored by a newspaper. James Gordon Bennett, publisher of the most influential newspaper in the United States, the *New York Herald,*[2] was fascinated with such faraway places as the Arctic and Africa. In 1869, he had ordered his reporter Henry Morton Stanley to Africa to "find" the British missionary Dr. David Livingstone, whom many presumed to be dead. When Stanley found Livingstone, alive and well, in 1871, his dispatches from Africa triggered a rise in the circulation of the *Herald*, just as Bennett had hoped they would. Bennett had found a formula for gaining readership for his newspaper, and in succeeding years he used it again and again.

In 1873, Bennett sent two of his reporters on board a vessel that went to look for the survivors of Hall's expedition. Five years later, Bennett assigned a reporter to accompany an American Geographic Society expedition to King William Island in the Canadian Arctic, where rumor had it that John Franklin's diary could be found. No diary was recovered, but the expedition did retrieve several relics and skeletal remains of Franklin's sailors who had died on the island. Once again, *Herald* circulation received a boost from the stories published about these finds.

In 1879, Bennett sponsored his greatest venture in the Arctic, an attempt by U.S. Navy captain George Washington DeLong to reach the Pole in a vessel called *Jeanette*, after Bennett's sister. DeLong and Bennett were both influenced by the ideas of a German geographer, August Petermann, who argued for the existence of—yes!—the Open Polar Sea, surrounded by a suitably scientific-sounding ring of ice Petermann called the "Paleocrystic Sea." The way to reach the open water was not via Spitsbergen or Greenland, Petermann theorized, but through the Bering Strait that separates Alaska from Russia. A warm Pacific Ocean current flowing north from Japan would carve a path north through the ice and meet with the warm waters of the Gulf Stream, flowing north between Greenland and Spitsbergen. Where these two currents met, at the top of the world, there, at long last, DeLong would find the Open Polar Sea. The captain and many of his unfortunate U.S. Navy sailors would die bitter deaths disproving this theory. That the U.S. Navy agreed to man the ship, while Bennett paid for the expedition and issued what amounted to orders to the secretary of the navy, speaks to the enormous power that a newspaper publisher could command when the subject was geographic exploration in the late nineteenth century.

The Swedish explorer Adolf Erik Nordenskiöld was searching for a Northeast Passage across the top of Russia at the time, and when a few months passed without word from him, Bennett decided that Nordenskiöld, like Livingstone, was in dire need of rescue. In this scenario, DeLong would play the part of Henry Morton Stanley. DeLong sailed from San Francisco in the summer of 1879, but before the

Jeanette even reached the Arctic, Nordenskiöld and his ship *Vega* broke through the ice and reached the Bering Sea. With no dramatic rescue to report, DeLong turned north toward the Pole and Petermann's open sea. The expedition would become a colossal catastrophe for the navy—and another boost for the *Herald*'s circulation.

Two months out from San Francisco, *Jeanette* was stuck in the ice north of Siberia, ice which never loosened its grip. Two years later, this same ice pack crushed DeLong's ship once and for all. He and his men took to their small boats and made a desperate retreat to the Siberian coast. One of the three boats reached safety; one vanished with all hands; and DeLong's own small boat made it to shore, where DeLong and all but two of his men starved to death as they waited in vain for relief.

To intensify the disaster, a U.S. Navy vessel sent to find DeLong was itself a casualty; after catching fire, it sank in the Arctic. The mercurial Bennett used the double disaster for all the dramatic publicity value it held, then sent his reporters off to cover stories in more favorable—and warmer—climes.

The U.S. Army fared no better (and many would say much worse) in the Arctic. In 1882, during the First International Polar Year, several nations established meteorological stations in the Arctic to record weather observations for a full year. A U.S. Army officer, Adolphus Greely, led the American contingent, which camped on Ellesmere Island in Canada and sent out a flying expedition consisting of Lieutenant James Lockwood and Sergeant D. L. Brainard to Greenland in the spring of 1882. By a minute margin, Lockwood and Brainard beat the British Farthest North record set in 1876, but from there the expedition met with disaster. Relief ships sent to retrieve Greely and his men failed to reach them in 1882 *or 1883*. When a relief ship finally made contact in 1884, Greely and Brainard and five others were still alive, but Lockwood and eighteen other men were dead.

The public and congressional outcries over the failures of DeLong and Greely would have a far-reaching impact for future American polar explorers. Not until the strategic value of the Arctic was rediscovered during World War II would any significant public money be spent on its exploration or exploitation. Until then, American explorers like Walter Wellman and many others would have to rely on their own wits to secure private donations, along with newspaper sponsorships, advertising tie-ins, and the backing of newly formed special interest organizations like the National Geographic Society and the Explorers Club, to fund their expeditions. This lack of public funding would, in turn, lead many to question both their methods and their motives.

On the other hand, one country that did continue to support polar exploration was Norway. And when wreckage from the *Jeanette* washed ashore in Greenland and was authenticated and reported in the press, a young Norwegian oceanographer named Fridtjof Nansen was paying keen attention. Nansen would one day become much more than a world-class scientist. He would earn high distinction as a diplomat when Norway became independent from Sweden after the turn of the century, and as a humanitarian after the First World War, when he organized the repatriation of nearly half a million prisoners of war and received the Nobel Peace Prize. But in the 1880s he was a young, serious scientist in his midtwenties, in search of new ways to explore old questions about the ice surrounding the North Pole.

In 1888, Nansen led an expedition that skied across Greenland from east to west, an accomplishment that particularly perturbed an American naval engineer named Robert Peary, who had failed to do the same thing in the opposite direction two years earlier. Nansen then proposed the most audacious expedition to that point in polar history. He speculated that if the wreckage of a ship could be carried from one side of the Arctic to another, why not an entire ship, intact and with its crew safe and warm on board?

Nansen's scientific credibility and his Greenland crossing enabled him to raise the funds necessary to build *Fram* (*Forward*), a specially designed Arctic vessel with soft rounded chines that could resist the squeeze of ice by riding on top of it, just as a watermelon seed pinched between two fingers would be propelled through the air. To test his polar drift hypothesis, Nansen in 1893 placed *Fram* into the ice not far from the spot where DeLong was beset fourteen years earlier. Nansen and his special ship then vanished for several years, their fate a complete mystery. On a shelf in *Fram's* library was a copy of one of the crew's favorite stories—and one of the best-selling books in the world—Jules Verne's *Five Weeks in a Balloon*.

The popularity of the stories of Jules Verne, combined with Bennett's proven formula for increasing newspaper circulation through stories of expeditions to far-off locales, made it easier for explorers to fund their expeditions, and demonstrated the extent of the late-nineteenth-century appetite for dramatic geographic explorations.[3] Verne himself followed these expeditions closely, and his early stories and novels, like *A Winter amid the Ice* (1855), *The English at the North Pole* (1864), and *The Field of Ice* (1866), reveal a serious student of contemporary expedition narratives. Who but Jules Verne would have a submarine captain, upon arriving at the South Pole, place his

1. *The Pole as nationalistic race. Jules Verne's Captain Hatteras, whose "customary disdain of the Englishman for the Yankee [had] turned to hatred . . . ; he made up his mind, at any price, to beat his bold [American] rival, and to reach the Pole itself." Hatteras's ship was named* Forward, *a name Nansen would use in its Norwegian form two decades later for his polar vessel:* Fram. *(From Verne's 1875 novel* The Voyages and Adventures of Captain Hatteras, *p. 95, in the author's collection.)*

hand on the shoulder of his scientific companion and almost casually remark:

> "Professor, in 1600 the Dutchman Gheritk, driven by currents and storms, reached latitude 64° south and discovered the South Shetland Islands. On January 17, 1773, the illustrious Captain Cook, following the 38th meridian, reached latitude 67° 30'; and on January 30, 1774, via the 109th meridian, he got so far as 71° 15'. In 1819 the Russian Bellinghausen reached the 69th parallel and two years later, the 66th at longitude 111° west. In 1820 the Englishman Bransfield could not get past 65°. That same year the American Morrel, whose reports are dubious, went along the 42nd meridian and claims he discovered open sea at latitude 70°14'. In 1825 the Englishman Powell . . ."[4]

Only a Jules Verne could get away with such a learned monologue, which has the speaker continuing on through another twenty years and seven more Antarctic expeditions. This typical Vernian passage also demonstrates the exceptionally high level of geographic literacy on the part of the readers of popular literature in Verne's day, who would slog through such miniature exploration histories and keep coming back for more.

In all likelihood, the first two explorers who sought to reach the North Pole by air grew up reading about the adventures of Captain Nemo, Phileas Fogg, and Michel Strogoff. Salomon Andrée, born in Gränna, Sweden, in 1854, would have been nine years old when *Five Weeks in a Balloon* was published in 1863. Walter Wellman, born in Mentor, Ohio, in 1858, would have been five. Verne published *20,000 Leagues under the Sea* in 1870, when Andrée was an impressionable sixteen-year-old, Wellman a school lad of twelve. And when Phileas Fogg departed the Reform Club in London in 1872, on a bet that he could go around the world in only eighty days, an eighteen-year-old Andrée was beginning to dream of wind currents that might carry balloons just as ocean currents carry ships, and a fourteen-year-old Wellman was in business as an editor of the weekly newspaper in Sutton, Nebraska, which he ran with his nineteen-year-old brother. Later in life, when these progressive, educated men conducted experiments with aeronautical technology in the polar regions, these experiments must have seemed to them not so far-fetched when compared with those of Verne's fictional heroes.

The year after Nansen and his science fiction library disappeared into the northern mists was a momentous one for both Andrée and Wellman. Wellman, now thirty-six, would organize his first attempt to reach the North Pole, an expedition that would venture into the same icy waters once sailed by Phipps and Nelson, Buchan and Parry.

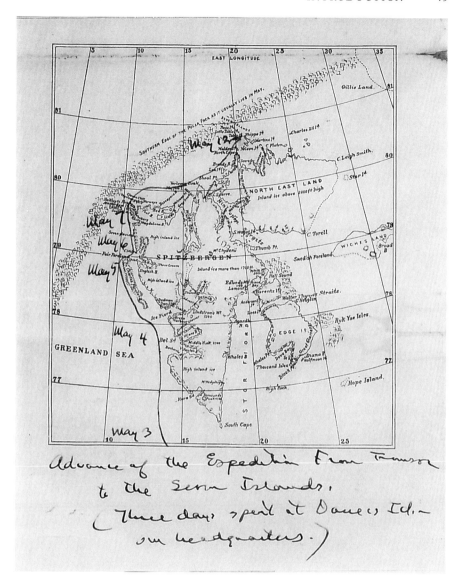

2. *Wellman's annotated chart of "Spitzbergen" from his 1894 attempt on the Pole. The dates run from May 3 to May 12, and the note at the bottom reads: "Advance of the Expedition from Tromsoe to the Seven Islands. (Three days spent at Dane's Id.—our headquarters.)" (Courtesy of the Chicago Historical Society.)*

And Andrée, just turned forty, would stun the geographic world when he announced his plan to drift to the Pole in a hydrogen balloon, a balloon equipped with enough strange and miraculous mechanical devices to make even Jules Verne himself envious.

As their headquarters, both men would use a remote and fogbound port in far northwestern Spitsbergen: Virgo Harbor.

PART ONE

HISTORY:

*The Aerial Polar Expeditions of
Salomon A. Andrée and Walter Wellman,
1896–1909*

Is it not a little strange to be floating here above the Polar Sea?
To be the first that have floated here in a balloon. How soon, I
wonder, shall we have successors? Shall we be thought mad or
will our example be followed? I cannot deny that all three of us
are dominated by a feeling of pride. We think we can well face
death, having done what we have done. Isn't it all, perhaps, the
expression of an extremely strong sense of individuality which
cannot bear the thought of living and dying like a man in the
ranks, forgotten by coming generations? Is this ambition?

—*Salomon A. Andrée, during his balloon attempt
on the North Pole, July 1897*

Millions are spent for telescopes with which to make maps
of Mars, and there are endless regions of our own sphere
which are not mapped. One cannot imagine a better way to
make geographical investigations than from an airship car.

—*geographer Ernest De Koven Leffingwell,
commenting on the announcement of the
Wellman polar airship expedition, January 6, 1906*

CHAPTER ONE

Saint of the Swedes:
The Implacable Mr. Andrée

O n Sunday afternoon, July 11, 1897, the second week of a miners' strike in the United States forced up the price of coal eighty cents a ton. Lack of coal at the pumping stations threatened Chicago with a water cutoff. When scabs arrived to take the jobs of striking miners in Newburg, Ohio, riots broke out.

New York City, on that Sunday in July, sweltered through 98 percent humidity and temperatures in the high 80s. At the U.S. Naval Academy in Annapolis, thirty-seven cadets cooled off in the brig after refusing to turn in the cadet(s) responsible for firing an errant torpedo during a drunken Fourth of July celebration. A passing tornado blew down oil derricks in Lima, Ohio.

Andrew Carnegie's retirement as the richest man in the world was still four years away, the first heavier-than-air flight six years away. Even though a major war seemed unthinkable, the first "peace conference" would convene at The Hague in two years.

It was a restless, optimistic time. Technology shortened distances and increased the tempo of everyday life, and people believed they stood on the verge of conquering the final mysteries of nature and geography.

Nowhere was this belief more apparent than on Danes Island in the Arctic archipelago of Spitsbergen, a lonely outpost seven hundred miles from the North Pole. On that Sunday a century ago, on that rocky wind-blasted ice-fouled shoreline just shy of 80° North of the equator, workers, engineers, and sailors from Sweden loosened the guy wires and chipped away the top levels of Salomon August Andrée's wooden balloon house, the most northern airport ever constructed. They prepared to release Andrée's balloon *Eagle* (*Örnen*) into a strong south wind. *Eagle* was set to ride that wind all the way to the North Pole, a remote blank spot on the charts, and one which no one had ever seen. Yet seemingly everywhere there existed a belief that the attainment of the North Pole would confer a special magic upon its discoverer, his nation, and, some even thought, on the whole of the human race.

*A*t 1:15 p.m., Andrée and his two companions, engineer Knut Fraenkel and photographer Nils Strindberg, climbed into the car of *Eagle*. The other members of the expedition cheered. Andrée uncharacteristically hesitated. Perhaps the enormity of what he was about to attempt finally dawned on him, and he experienced a momentary stricture of nerve. Or perhaps, at the penultimate moment, he was seized by a spasm of common sense.

Just as quickly, after consultation with (and, no doubt, fortification from) Strindberg and Fraenkel, the hesitation vanished. At 1:46 p.m., Andrée bellowed through a megaphone, "Cut away everywhere!"[1] *Eagle* began to rise.

The aerial race to the North Pole, a race that would start and finish in Spitsbergen and would not be won for thirty years, had begun.

*T*hough begun on October 18, 1854, the remarkable existence of Salomon August Andrée never actually came to an end. An engineer with a seemingly unlimited faith in technology, Andrée stoutly tethered his life to the common ambition that he not be buried a cipher. The result of his reliance on machinery was that his marvelous story—especially the chapter on the manner of his demise—was for thirty-three years locked in the frozen time capsule of a remote island of the high Arctic, awaiting more than an armchair theorist to come and find it.

Andrée loathed questions of the spirit. He was a consummate nineteenth-century agnostic technocrat, and it would be difficult to find a man more formidably equipped by temperament and training to cheat the combined spirits of Death, God, and Time.

"[He was] an uncommonly big and strong child, and . . . [h]is questions were very often difficult to answer," wrote his mother. "If . . . treated unjustly by any companion . . . he spared no effort to pay him back."[2] In rustic Gränna, Sweden, he grew up in a family of four brothers and two sisters. A disciple of both scientific and social Darwinism, Andrée liked the out-of-doors less than he looked forward to the subjugation of Nature through scientific laws. During his college years at Sweden's Royal Institute of Technology, he conducted an experiment in which he dressed as a workman, wandered to laborers' eating-houses, and chatted with the patrons. A restless intellectual impatient with schools, which he felt had nothing to offer, Andrée would have abandoned his education if not for his father's skilled persuasion.

At twenty-two, Andrée visited the United States, where he begged for and received a janitor's job in the Swedish section of Philadelphia's Centennial Exposition. He swept the floors and studied the exhibits, and on one of his days off he tracked down and introduced himself to American balloonist John Wise. Andrée had developed an interest in aeronautics, and Wise gave him a notebook full of techniques developed in the course of four hundred ascents. After reading C.F.E. Bjorling's *Laws of the Winds,* Andrée decided that trade winds could push cargo and passenger balloons along regular air routes. Wise invited Andrée on a flight, but the balloon they were to use burst while being filled and Andrée lost the chance.

After six months in the United States, Andrée returned to Sweden and held a couple of mechanical jobs: assistant to a mechanical engineer, co-owner of a machine shop. Then a professor with whom he had studied in college offered him an assistantship. His faith in science ("everything is subject to law") solidified.[3]

In 1882, while the Americans James Lockwood and D. L. Brainard of the Greely expedition were reaching their Farthest North, eleven nations established twelve meteorological stations in the Arctic and two more in the Antarctic as part of the First International Polar Year. Sweden anchored its effort in Spitsbergen. Nils Ekholm of the Meteorological Institute of Stockholm led the Swedish expedition. Andrée found his way into the position of procurer of technical equipment and would also take atmospheric and electrical observations at the Swede's base camp at Cape Thordsen.

With characteristic thoroughness, Andrée found a way to keep water in a measuring device fluid, even at -22° F, and took fifteen thousand observations when most of the other international expeditions came to a halt as temperatures dropped far below freezing. For a month, he shut himself into a dark hut to determine whether the yellow-green color that skin takes on during polar darkness is just a visual reaction to the long polar night. He emerged into the sunlight to discover that it is not. With all the frustrations of the applied scientist, he wrote of the Spitsbergen experiments, "As usual, much work and little result."[4]

Back in Stockholm, Andrée noted his thirtieth birthday and strode toward midlife as chief engineer of the Swedish Patent Office. Marriage was out of the question for him. With a woman, he wrote, "one has to deal with factors which cannot be arranged according to a plan. It is altogether too great a risk to bind oneself to a condition of things where another individual would be fully entitled . . . to demand the same place in my life that I myself occupied."[5] This last was the essence of Andrée, of Andrée's time, and on through much of the time since. Humanity's salvation lay not in humanity (especially in the form of the notoriously "unplannable" woman), but in the Machine, which could be imagined, drawn, built, and programmed, all according to plan.

Or so Andrée thought.

*T*hree and a half hours past midnight on July 15, 1893, Andrée left the surface of the earth in a balloon for the first time. In the spring he had applied for and been awarded a grant from a Swedish foundation to obtain a balloon. The basis of his application was, of course, applied science. There would be no suffusion of adventure, no pretensions to aeronautical glory; Andrée was, after all, a practical scientist, and seriousness followed him like a cold front. His balloon would be used for scientific observations only, observations like temperature and humidity at various altitudes, the pathways of air currents, and anything else his instruments could record.

Andrée's first balloon, though christened *Svea* (*Sweden*), was built in France. With a volume of over thirty-seven thousand cubic feet, it stood at about one-seventh the volume of current Goodyear blimps. It was—despite Andrée's expressed wish that it would act as a mere platform for bland scientific observations—destined for memorable adventures.

Swedish territory sank beneath *Svea* on its first flight, falling away until the balloon and its sole crewman soared to an altitude of almost three miles. All was silence. From that great height, Andrée heard dogs bark with the clarity of sounds in the night. He made what observations he could, but he felt put upon. He needed more time for observation. He scribbled a note that in later flights he would try to leave the piloting to someone else and perhaps have a third assistant along to record his measurements, leaving himself as a pure observer. How he would have loved the laptop computer!

Near 6 a.m., he landed twenty-six miles from his starting point.

Three weeks later, he lifted off again, and again alone. *Svea* this day carried its pilot-scientist an entire degree on the map in seven hours, a slow nine-miles-per-hour drift. Andrée took his measurements and had time to begin experiments with aerial photography. One of the photographs resulting from this nascent remote sensing even corrected an existing map. He learned, too, that *Svea* descended when in the shadow of a cloud, and watched the expansion of the gas-bag and the gain of height when the envelope saw sunlight.

When Andrée went aloft again, two months later, at 9 a.m. on October 19, it was nearly his last flight. A slight breeze at liftoff turned gusty and carried *Svea* not inland but toward the Baltic Sea. By the time he had made his observations, it was too late to land; *Svea* was on its way to Finland. A long guide-rope, designed to prevent just such a mishap by making the spherical free balloon somewhat dirigible, or controllable, trailed through the water, faster than Andrée had supposed it could be pulled by the balloon. Leaning over the edge of the basket, he lowered an anchor on another rope, but the balloon continued unchecked. Rather ingeniously sizing up the situation, Andrée lowered two empty sacks attached to a third rope into the sea below. The sacks opened in *Svea*'s direction, forming what were surely history's first aerial sea anchors.

A steamer hove into view, and Andrée changed the angle of *Svea*'s sails and maneuvered toward it. His first thought was to catch his three trailing lines in the rigging of the ship, until he made a visual equation of the steamer's funnel and the thirty-seven thousand cubic feet of highly inflammable hydrogen above his head. He steered *Svea* clear of the steamer. The only choice short of letting out all the gas and ditching in the sea was to make for Finland. He tried to haul in the sea anchors to increase speed, but when they would not budge he cut them loose. *Svea* leaped to a speed of eighteen miles per hour. Andrée waved off more passing ships and then cut the anchor free to gain still more speed. *Svea* finally descended onto a remote Baltic island at 7:18 p.m., a moment fixed in history only because the jolt of landing stopped Andrée's watch.

He endured a cold night alone before he was spotted and plucked off the island the next morning. Throughout that long night, he went back over his Baltic adventure: he had been airborne over ten hours, and *Svea* had carried him 170 miles. Impressed by his own skillful employment of guide-lines—draglines which allowed him to steer the balloon a few points off the wind—Andrée wrote later that his guide-roped balloon could *"traverse greater distances than a free balloon of equal dimensions."*[6] A free balloon, he thought, would lose gas every time it ascended more than a few hundred feet. His balloon, kept in contact with the earth through the use of the guide-ropes, would not.

The guide-ropes performed another service, as well. He began to believe he was close to overcoming the greatest flaw of a free balloon—its utter lack of dirigibility. It was a prescient thought. Andrée believed he was the first explorer who ever experimented with the use of guide-ropes to steer a hydrogen balloon over water (he was in fact the second). At that moment, Andrée ceased being merely a technological tinkerer and began to glimmer horizons far more vast.

"*I* scarcely need to point out," Andrée wrote, perhaps as he sat amid his crumpled gear during his solitary night on that coastal Finland islet, "*what extreme importance this is* for the possibility of making long balloon flights for geographical purposes."[7] It is conceivable that on that night, after only his third flight, Andrée brooded about making the greatest flight of them all: a voyage to the North Pole in a controlled balloon. It does not seem to have bothered him that in the crash landing he had lost a group of aerial photographs and all of his scientific instruments had been smashed.

Andrée returned home and did not make another ascent until February 26, 1894. *Svea* on that flight traveled eighty-nine miles, and Andrée braked the end of its flight by throwing an anchor over the side. When the anchor finally caught on the ground, Andrée and his ship were pulled down and thrown into a tree.

During his sixth flight, in midsummer 1894, Andrée added a sail which he could reposition to catch the wind, and a guide-rope which trailed from *Svea* and which followed a design derived from his experiences during the inadvertent Baltic flight. Manipulating the guide-rope and sail, Andrée found he could veer the balloon almost thirty degrees off the direction of the wind. En route, he tossed postcards overboard. When they were mailed to him later by their finders on the ground, Andrée was able to map his route. He thought that if his minor navigating feat could somehow be regulated—and he believed he was well on his way toward accomplishing just that—then long, controlled flights along major belts of wind were within the realm of possibility.

In November of 1894, *Svea* carried Andrée from Gothenburg to Gotland, and at the end of the flight he used a rip-valve that opened a huge rent in the fabric of the balloon to bring the expedition back to earth on more or less the spot he wanted. By releasing some gas, he saved himself the indignity of being dragged across hedge and tree until the anchor held, as had been his bad luck on the first seven flights.

His final ascent in *Svea* came in March of 1895. Total mileage on his nine experimental flights amounted to some nine hundred miles, flown in under forty hours; average speed: twenty-two and half miles per hour. Within these forty hours aloft, he'd recorded four hundred observations while piloting his balloon. These were all most impressive records, and Andrée was soon recognized as one of the premier balloonists of Europe. But, for the flights he envisioned, it was far from enough.

*H*ow to point a balloon off the wind had been the great mystery of aeronautical design and error for two hundred years. Wind currents blow in huge loping circular patterns and can reverse their field entirely. Balloonists therefore were liable to be blown back to the point from which they had embarked. Overcast skies shrank the volume of gas in a balloon's envelope and forced the aeronaut to jettison ballast. But sunlight the next moment could expand the gasbag, and if the following rise was not checked with sufficient ballast, the balloon ultimately would sail to "pressure-height," the altitude at which gas pressure could rupture the envelope and send the airship crashing back to earth.

In 1670, a Brescian Jesuit named Francesco de Lana proposed a scheme for maneuvering a balloon with sails and ballast. Although his scheme was never tested, clearly it would not have worked; the balloon he designed was to be lifted by four copper globes sealed to create a vacuum, and that vacuum would not have budged.

History's first manned ascent was not made until Messieurs Laurent and Pilatre de Rozier lifted off in a small hot-air balloon on the afternoon of November 21, 1783, in Paris. Their craft was a fleur-de-lis-decorated balloon built by the brothers Montgolfier. Little more than a week later, J.A.C. Charles and M. N. Robert ascended from the Tuileries Gardens in *La Charliere,* one of the first hydrogen balloons. Charles's balloon flew twenty-seven miles before landing safely at Nesle.

In the years and decades after these first flights, geographic barriers began to recede before the voyages of floating ships. On January 7, 1785, John Jeffries and Jean-Pierre Blanchard crossed the English Channel in a boat-shaped car slung underneath a small balloon. A half century later, aeronaut Charles Green piloted the *Nassau* from London to Wellburg, Germany, 480 miles in eighteen hours. Thirteen years after Green, in September 1849, balloonist François Arban crossed the Alps. And ten years after Arban—when S. A. Andrée was five years old—John Wise flew with John La Mountain in the *Atlantic* from St. Louis to Jefferson County, New York, at the not inconsiderable speed of forty miles per hour. The 810 miles (or, put another way, a bit more than the distance from Spitsbergen to the North Pole) were covered in nineteen hours and fifty minutes. The poet Victor

Hugo watched a balloon ascend into the clouds during this same year of 1859, and wrote that the machine represented "the great elan of progress toward the heavens."

> Toward the divine, pure future, toward virtue,
> Toward beckoning science,
> Toward the end of evil, toward generous forgiveness,
> Toward abundance, peace and laughter, and a happy Mankind.[8]

Hugo notwithstanding, for the foreseeable future balloons would move toward only those places favored by strong winds. Except for the flight of the *Nassau*, which, like Andrée's *Svea*, employed guide-ropes for steering, these early attempts were all free flights in unpowered, unsteerable balloons. Control was possible only in ascent and descent by skilled use of ballast. In the meantime, the cause of controlled horizontal flight in powered balloons had not been ignored.

The first true dirigible, designed in 1784 by Jean-Baptiste Meusnier, was a remarkably prescient craft, having many aspects of later airships: an oval gas envelope supporting a gondola with nets and rope, and three propellers and a rudder. Meusnier never built his craft because no compact, lightweight source of power existed to drive the props. The Swiss inventor Samuel Pauly built a fish-shaped dirigible and tested it in Paris in 1804, but the first actual dirigible was not built until 1852, when Henri Giffard piloted his 3-hp steam engine–driven airship seventeen miles from the Hippodrome in Paris to the town of Trappes. Giffard had finally gotten an airship under power, albeit underpowered. But he had yet to bring an airship under control. Attempts at control were made both in France and in the United States from 1859 to 1884, using everything from muscle power to electric engines as power plants. But the mystery was not solved until the twentieth century, and Salomon August Andrée was not destined to live that long.

*A*ndrée had found in his trial flights some limited success in the pursuit of dirigibility. Using lines that dragged the earth's surface in combination with properly set sails, he was able to steer *Svea* on a moderately windward course.

Another line, a ballast line several hundred feet long, kept the balloon in constant touch with the earth, preventing the risks of pressure-height and at the same time conserving the sand ballast attached to the car. Andrée tossed sand overboard only when the permeable envelope began to leak hydrogen, causing the balloon to sink.

Andrée's *Svea* leaked hydrogen more than he ever acknowledged. It would never be impermeable enough to remain aloft for as long as his purpose necessitated. One suspects that his acquired knowledge of technology was so refined that he must have recognized this weakness in his balloon. But once he had formulated his polar goal, and then announced it publicly, he would not be swerved. For perhaps the only time in his life, he subordinated his faith in engineer's calculus to what, even as he announced it, amounted to undeserved faith in an unproven airship. But once the first steps had been taken, the first balloon trials aimed at establishing a science of aerial navigation, how could he not become intoxicated with its possibilities? And since the proper motor-dirigible awaited the experiments of Alberto Santos-Dumont and Ferdinand von Zeppelin at the turn of the century, Andrée was virtually alone in inventing a field of theory and application, which, in the manner of the time, conferred upon him the status of aeronautical expert.

Andrée gave himself less than a year and a half to perfect his new science. On February 13, 1895, he announced to the world (in the assemblage of the Swedish Anthropological and Geographical Society) that he was mounting an expedition to sail to the North Pole in a balloon. And he wanted to be ready to lift off from the Spitsbergen archipelago by July 1, 1896.

*A*ccording to Andrée's theory—the only one the state of 1896 dirigible technology allowed him to formulate—guide-ropes seven hundred feet long would be used to control the actions of his balloon. This—again, in theory—was accomplished when the balloon dragged the lines across the ground. Thick and heavy, the lines consequently caused the balloon to sink. As it sank, longer and longer lengths of the guide-ropes lay on the ground. In this way the weight of the guide-ropes was transferred from the balloon to the ground, until a sort of equilibrium was reached. Ideally this happened about three hundred feet above the earth. Then, by positioning the sails properly, the pilot of the balloon could make it catch a favorable wind; trimming the sails enabled the balloon to reject an unfavorable wind.

"This is . . . not the dreamed-of, perfectly dirigible air balloon, so devoutly longed for, since we have not seen it yet," Andrée wrote, "but the air balloon which we already possess and which is regarded so unfavorably merely because attention is focused on its weak point. Such an air balloon is, however, capable of carrying the explorer to the Pole and home again in safety; with such a balloon the journey across the waste of ice can be carried out."[9]

Andrée proposed to dragline his way over the pack ice separating Spitsbergen from the Pole. He equipped the lines with points of weakness, so that in the event one of them became stuck in the ice pack it would automatically break away. If the weak point did not break the line off, an electrically activated explosive device, which Andrée had commissioned an engineer to build, would be lowered from the car and detonated at the desired point, cutting the line and once again setting the balloon free.

Still more novel technology accompanied Andrée north. Since any open flame in the cockpit threatened the hydrogen, Andrée had a special stove built that was lowered twenty-five feet overboard before dinner. A small lighter lit the flame from that distance, and within five minutes water boiled. A small mirror allowed the balloonists to check on the progress of the soup. After the meal was cooked, a puff of air into a long tube running from the cockpit to the stove extinguished the flame. A hot dinner could then be hauled back into the car.

Andrée could afford these devices because of the generosity of well-heeled patrons. When he announced his polar expedition, he also announced its unmet cost: $34,800. Less than three months after the announcement, the great inventor Alfred Nobel donated half the cost of the voyage. King Oscar of Sweden put in $8,000 of his own money. With such imprimaturs, Andrée raised the rest much more quickly. The ease of fund-raising aroused suspicions in the foreign press. "This Mr. Andrée," wrote one Austrian paper, "who wishes to go to the North Pole and back by means of an air balloon, is simply a fool or a swindler."[10]

He was neither, of course. But he did have an obsession that was as carefully calculated as it was unbalanced.

On June 7, 1896, Andrée and his expedition sailed from Gothenburg for Spitsbergen. A hundred boats followed the expedition ship, *Virgo,* from Gothenburg harbor, in a seaborne procession of Scandinavian pride. The polar balloon, stored in *Virgo's* hold, had been built under the watchful eyes of Messieurs Gaston Tissandier and Charles Renard, both of whom had built electrically powered (or, more precisely, electrically *under*powered) dirigibles in 1883 and 1884. Their designs would be successfully imitated twenty years later by Paul and Pierre Lebaudy, who by 1902 were able to mount adequate engines on their dirigibles, enabling them to maneuver against the wind.

The French balloon maker who constructed Andrée's craft, Henri Lachambre, was also on board *Virgo.* In his balloon works in Paris,

Lachambre had stitched together 3,360 pieces of Chinese pongee silk, and the resulting seams were over nine miles long. This highway of seams was then covered with strips of silk and varnished with vulcanized rubber.

Gabriel Yon, the French aeronaut who had built *Svea,* looked with disgust upon the seven or eight million stitches holding those nine miles of seams together. Millions of pinpricks from millions of stitches in a balloon designed to loft two thousand miles over the polar sea did not inspire confidence. But Alexis Machuron, Lachambre's young assistant and nephew, calculated that this new balloon, *Eagle,* could remain aloft for over a month.

The two men who would fly north with Andrée also embarked on *Virgo.* Nils Strindberg, a twenty-three-year-old physics teacher and photographer, a relative of the dramatist August Strindberg, possessed talents ranging from violin playing to geodetic mapping. After selection as a member of Andrée's team, he made six balloon ascents in Paris and conducted experiments on the permeability of *Eagle's* envelope.

The expedition's second man was Dr. Nils Ekholm, Andrée's leader from the earlier meteorological expedition on Spitsbergen. Looking at the results of Strindberg's permeability tests, Ekholm was not in the least convinced that there was better than an even chance of reaching the Pole. The balloon built to stay aloft for a month would not hold its hydrogen gas for more than a few days.

*L*achambre settled into his drawing room aboard *Virgo,* entertained and catered to, he wrote, by one "Charlotte, a complaisant Swede, wearing a coquettish little white toque of the comic opera type."[11] In *Virgo's* stateroom, introductions were made over brandy and whiskey, toasts delivered to the success of the flight, and speeches given in Andrée's honor. After dinner, Lachambre was served his coffee on deck. He pulled contentedly on a Havana. *Virgo* headed north.

"Gently cradled by the waves," wrote the self-fulfilled Lachambre, "I abandon[ed] myself to my reveries."[12]

*T*wo weeks later, feeling their way north along the western coast of the Spitsbergen archipelago with inadequate charts, the men on board the *Virgo* anchored their ship at a sheltered harbor on the north coast of Danes Island. High hills enclosed the harbor on three sides; the opening on the fourth side led directly north. Roughly six hundred miles in that fourth direction was a spot where the summer sun

3. *Andrée's wooden hangar, prefabricated in Sweden, is erected on the shore of Virgo Harbor in the summer of 1896. (Courtesy of the Andréemuseet, Gränna, Sweden.)*

circled the sky at a constant altitude, never setting or rising. If these explorers were to stand at that spot, and watch the sun orbit the earth without dipping or rising, they would know that they stood at the geographic North Pole—at the top of the world.

On the rock-strewn shore stood a small wooden house built by a Britisher named Arnold Pike, and Pike gave permission for its use as the expedition's headquarters. On Tuesday, June 23, 1896, the crewmen of *Virgo* began unloading the materials needed to build the prefabricated balloon shed; the balloon itself, and the hydrogen-generating plant, would be brought ashore as soon as the shed was complete. Ferrying the large crate that contained the balloon proved a difficult task, since it weighed more than a ton and had to be maneuvered around plates of ice in the harbor. The temperature hovered just above freezing, and Andrée felt an urgency in the fresh southwest wind.

Carpenters brought from Sweden assembled the balloon house, a wooden octagon structure sixty feet tall. Two staircases led to a balcony at the top, and guys were driven into the permafrost and into the granite hills to secure the balloon shed against the wind.

"The start will take place in the month of July as soon as the weather is favorable," wrote Andrée, "that is, at a moment when the air is sufficiently clear and when there is a fresh southerly or almost southerly wind blowing."[13] Unlike virtually every other balloon flight in history, launched in the most optimistic of dead calms, *Eagle* would be launched directly into the gusts of a southern gale. Without such a wind, the expedition would go nowhere.

"Such a wind," according to Andrée, "should be one of the chief conditions enabling the balloon to penetrate as quickly as possible far into the unknown regions, and in the direction of the Pole."[14] Andrée had noted the relative mild weather during his first journey to Spitsbergen. For the month of July, he had recorded an average low of 36° F and average high of 46.8° F. The visibility had been good, with occasional light rain or snowfall. It was another of the flaws in Andrée's applications of his science and technology that he counted on nature for an exact duplication of those earlier conditions in order to make a safe passage to the Pole. But *Eagle* would be flying not over the Spitsbergen landmass in summer but above the twisting pack of ice, where mists and an impenetrable fog would steal lift from the balloon, soak it through with moisture, and ultimately try to drive it down onto the pack.

Eagle was not inflated until July 27 and did not stand ready in its balloon shed until the first week in August. According to the terms of *Virgo*'s insurance policy, the ship would remain protected against ice damage only if it departed from Spitsbergen by August 20. A south wind had to arrive before then. During the wait, Andrée took meteorological observations and collected specimens of rock and moss. After leaving his watch on board *Virgo* at 2 a.m., he would on some nights go ashore and crawl into his small mat bunk in the car of *Eagle*. There he would read a volume taken from a small bookshelf near the bunk, and fall asleep as the car swayed in the northern breeze.

With Lachambre, Strindberg checked the permeability of the balloon after it was inflated. The results were discouraging. Since being inflated, the balloon had lost one hundred pounds of lift every twenty-four hours. Just when one seam was plugged and varnished, gas found a way to sneak out through another row of stitching. Ekholm was mortified.

Three weeks passed, with no trace of a south wind.

*E*arly in August, a flash of excitement broke the chill of the northern camp. The Norwegian oceanographer Fridtjof Nansen's sturdy ship *Fram* appeared in Virgo Harbor. Without Nansen, the ship was

4. *An Arctic harbor and the vessel it was named for. Andrée's balloon shed and Pike's house can be seen on shore as the Swedish vessel* Virgo *rides at anchor in the harbor that would later be named for it: Virgo Harbor. (Courtesy of the Andréemuseet, Gränna, Sweden.)*

returning home to Norway after its three-and-a-half-year drift through the polar sea. Many had long since given the small ship up for lost. It was as if a ghost ship had returned from the Pole.

As we have seen, Nansen had predicted that a ship constructed with rounded bilges could wedge itself into the ice pack of the Polar Sea and ride up on top of the pack when the ice squeezed its soft chine. The ship would then float on the prevailing currents of ice across the Arctic, with luck across the Pole itself. But, with the memory of the U.S. exploring ship *Jeanette* being crushed in the ice in 1881, many had scorned Nansen's theories of both shipbuilding and oceanography.

But wreckage from the *Jeanette,* which had been crushed near the New Siberian Islands, provided evidence for Nansen's theory when it was discovered three years later in Greenland, over three thousand miles away. Even so, when Nansen lodged *Fram* into the pack ice in September of 1893, and vanished into the polar night for three years of incommunicado exploring, he and his crew were presumed to be lost at sea.

But at Virgo Harbor in early August of 1896, *Fram* had reappeared. Nansen had been right: put the right ship into the ice on one edge of the polar sea, and, with time and tide, it would drift out of the pack somewhere on the other side.

Fram's crew had to explain the absence of Nansen himself to the anxious Swedes at Andrée's balloon camp. On March 14, 1895, Nansen and Lieutenant Hjalmar Johansen had left the ship at about 84° N for a dash to the Pole with ski, sledges, and twenty-eight dogs. Within a month, they had trod 170 miles closer to the North Pole than had anyone before them, attaining their now-famous latitude of 86°14' N. Then they began a long retreat south, wintering in an improvised shallow hut dug out of the shoreline of an island in the icy Franz Josef Land archipelago. *Fram* meanwhile had drifted out of the pack in midsummer 1896 and landed at Danes Island, where its Norwegian crew of eleven was startled by the sight of Andrée's balloon expedition. After so much time locked in the ice, the crew was understandably shocked that a Swedish balloon team proposed to cover in thirty days the distance they themselves had covered in three and a half years.

At about the same moment, unbeknownst to the crew on *Fram,* Nansen and Johansen were rescued from their hut in Franz Josef Land after a phenomenally lucky and unscheduled rendezvous with a British expedition that had been wintering in the archipelago.

"A few fathoms from the *Fram* Andrée and his companions raise a vigorous cheer in honor of Nansen," wrote Lachambre later. At Tromsø, in northern Norway, Nansen had landed while *Fram* was at Virgo Harbor, and the rest of the world broke into vigorous cheering for the vindicated explorer.[15]

"The small party [from *Fram* came] to visit our quarters," wrote Lachambre, "and the balloon, which is waiting in the shed. It is easy to imagine how greatly these men are astonished. Then the expedition came on board the *Virgo,* where champagne was soon foaming. . . . [Lieutenant Hansen of the *Fram*] put numerous questions to me concerning the events which had taken place in Europe for the last three years."[16]

In *Fram's* library Lachambre noticed a copy of Jules Verne's novel *Five Weeks in a Balloon.* Hansen told Lachambre the crew of *Fram* often daydreamed of a balloon expedition coming to their relief.

*A*ndrée woke early on Monday, August 17, and watched the clouds. They were drifting south. For three straight weeks they had drifted south. In three days *Virgo's* insurance would expire. He had built the most northern hangar in the world and inflated a large hydrogen balloon in four days. He was little more than six hundred miles from the North Pole. But he had arrived at his base camp too late.

There would be no balloon attempt on the Pole in 1896. Andrée ordered *Eagle*'s valves opened, and 4,500 cubic meters of hydrogen streamed free.

*W*hile Nansen returned to Norway to a tumultuous hero's welcome, the Andrée Polar Expedition of 1896 returned in ignominy and not a little embarrassment to Stockholm. Andrée was perhaps slightly comforted that the magnitude of Nansen's headlines overshadowed his own negative reviews.

With Nansen's triumph, cartographers added another circle around the North Pole, closer by 161 miles than the circle drawn after the 1882 trek of the Americans Lockwood and Brainard. And yet, spectacular as the Arctic drift and dash of Nansen and Johansen had been, the Pole still lay hidden in the fog, somewhere beyond the rim drawn by Nansen and *Fram*. No human had been closer to the Pole than 231.6 miles.

Andrée could still be first.

Andrée returned to the Swedish Patent Office. Absorbed in his duties there, he thought little of the Pole. Strindberg returned to his fiancée, determined to reach the Pole with Andrée at some future time. Ekholm, still in shock and furious at Andrée for concealing the permeability of the balloon, resigned from the expedition. Lachambre returned to Paris, and the polar balloon soon followed him. Andrée, stung by Ekholm's public criticisms of the balloon, requested that Lachambre add a new band of silk around the equator of the balloon. This increased the envelope's volume from 4,500 to 5,000 cubic meters, and increased its weight as well.

During the winter of 1896–1897, Ekholm's place in the Andrée balloon party was taken by a towering twenty-six-year-old engineer, Knut Fraenkel. In the spring, Fraenkel, and a fourth, alternate member of the expedition, Lieutenant G.V.E. Svedenborg, traveled from Stockholm to Paris to learn the art of balloon navigation from Lachambre.

In April 1897, Nansen and Johansen went to Stockholm to receive a medal from the Union (between Sweden and Norway) government. Per Olaf Sundman, in his documentary novel on Andrée's adventure, *The Flight of the Eagle,* re-created the scene at the banquet that followed presentation of the medals.

Andrée gave a speech in honor of Nansen. Nansen reciprocated,

5. The crew of Andrée's 1897 balloon expedition: Lieutenant G.V.E. Svedenborg (backup member), Nils Strindberg, Knut Fraenkel, and Salomon A. Andrée. (Courtesy of the Andréemuseet, Gränna, Sweden.)

lauding Andrée in high verbiage. When Nansen sat down, Albert Engström, a young author, chided Nansen for lying through his teeth.

"Calm down," Sundman has Nansen icily replying to Engström. "Banquets are banquets. Ceremonious and so forth. In any case, why shouldn't one encourage idiots?"[17]

*A*ndrée, Strindberg, Fraenkel, and Svedenborg sailed from Gothenburg harbor aboard the Swedish gunboat *Svenskund* on the evening of May 18, 1897. *Svenskund* joined *Virgo* as a second supply ship, and the two vessels entered the pack ice of Virgo Harbor less than two weeks later. Near a high bluff, two flagstaffs were sighted as the ships reached the harbor. They were signals that the balloon shed had survived the vicious winter storms. As soon as they disembarked, the explorers raised two Swedish flags over the shed.

After six feet of snow and ice were chipped away, the balloon was laid out on the floor of the shed, inflated with air, and the interior seams varnished. Following its reinflation with hydrogen, strips of linen soaked in acetate of lead were laid across the outer seams. If there was a leak, it would show as a dark blotch on the linen, the reaction of hydrogen with the acetate of lead. The varnishing and testing took most of June, so that *Eagle* was not ready to fly until July 1.

Svedenborg was ordered to go as far north as possible after the balloon was launched, and to lay in a depot of supplies that the polar fliers could head for in case of trouble. After these preparations, all that could be done was to wait for the strong southerly wind that had been so elusive the previous summer.

On July 6, a fierce gale sprang from the south, but Andrée guessed that it would not hold, and decided against a launch. Strindberg wrote letters home to his fiancée. Fraenkel walked around the retreating snowfields of Danes Island. Andrée collected moss and brooded. Another week passed.

Finally, at 3 a.m. on the morning of July 11, a fresh wind rose from the south. Andrée called everyone together and told Strindberg and Fraenkel to take care of any final personal correspondence. The wait was over.

By eight in the morning, occasional clouds were streaming from the south across an otherwise clear sky. The polar fliers, with Svedenborg and Alexis Machuron (a young balloon builder who joined the expedition when Lachambre declined a second summer at Spitsbergen), made last-minute checks of the balloon from the top balcony of the hangar. The wind rose. The explorers stood at the top of the shed, feeling it sway with each fresh gust.

"Shall we try it or not?" Andrée asked.

Fraenkel nodded.

"I think we ought to try it," said Strindberg.[18]

Andrée hesitated, but a veto was out of the question. He asked the captain of *Svenskund* to send a party ashore to dismantle the north wall of the balloon shed.

Alexis Machuron, the aeronautical specialist, wondered where the balloon might ultimately come to rest. "We need not fear," he wrote, "that the explorers will be lost in the glaciers of Greenland." The balloon, Machuron calculated, had a life span of fifty days. Even if the expedition became a disabled muddle, Andrée had told his colleagues, the balloon would still be afloat after a month, and the winds would ultimately blow them *somewhere.* "The chances seem to point most to Siberia," Machuron concluded, mainly because anyone looking at a map of the Arctic would immediately identify Siberia as the largest target.[19] Shoot for Paris, Lindbergh surmised in 1927, and you're bound to hit somewhere on the coastline of Europe. Alexis Machuron made a similar calculation thirty years earlier.

Next came Alaska, on a virtual 20° E rhumb line from Spitsbergen. If Andrée's three guide-ropes could point *Eagle* off the wind, the balloon could—in fifty days or considerably less—make for Alaska.

Greenland was unlikely since Machuron felt the ice cap there cooled the air, and hence the balloon, too much and so would not present the right atmosphere for a balloon. He did not seem to consider why the same conditions should not apply with equivalent results over the polar ice cap. "If, owing to some unforeseen cause, they should be obliged to descend to the ice-field," concluded Machuron, "they would have to return in the same way as did Dr. Nansen. After all, [Nansen had survived] for fifteen months on the ice-field with only three month's provisions."[20]

Andrée anticipated a forced landing on the pack, yet the specter of a long march did not seem to trouble him. The balloon carried two sledges and a prefabricated wood-and-canvas boat. But, like the guide-ropes, which were Andrée's navigational lifelines, the sledges and the boat remained stowed in the hold of *Svenskund* until launch hour arrived. While his gear sat untested, Andrée and his companions took depth soundings in Virgo Harbor, climbed and studied glaciers nearby, and took note of weather and wind. Andrée's backup equipment remained untouched.

The polar team did not put together the boat to see whether or not all its parts had been shipped; they made no tests with man-haul-ing the sledges to determine what they could or could not carry; they did not even inspect a critical primary system, comprising the three one-thousand-foot-long guide-ropes, upon which Andrée based his aeronautical theory (the guide-ropes now lay in coils on the shore of Virgo Harbor). These ropes had each been fitted in two places with metal screw couplings. If, as they dragged along the jagged pack ice, one of them became twisted and stuck fast, it could be unscrewed and left behind. This idea, without which the voyage would become a free-floating gamble, was brought to the edge of the polar sea without being tested anywhere but on the drawing board. No one knew how these lines would react under Arctic conditions, because no one knew how they performed under *any* conditions. Andrée's keystone was dubious indeed.

During that early morning of July 11, two Norwegian sailing ships, escaping the southern gale, anchored in Virgo Harbor, just in time to witness the launch. By 11 a.m., the south wind had been steady for over a third of a day. Andrée stalled, giving orders into the wind through a megaphone. The patent engineer who had reviewed so many sketches of new technology, drawings which made the conquest of nature seem so deceptively simple, now stood with his fragile balloon before seven hundred miles of implacable, unconquered ice. Perhaps he was not giving orders so much as orchestrating, maybe for dramatic effect, maybe hoping for a shift of wind to avoid a test of his technology against the force of nature. We will never know.

The balloon bumped against the sides of the shed, oscillating in the wind. It was losing gas, losing lift, each hour Andrée delayed. By noon, he'd reached the crossroads of his life. To go on, challenge nature in his balloon, invite death in the cause of science and history. Or return to the Stockholm Patent Office and die a cipher on pension. It is likely the technologist's life had reduced itself to this decision. The choice was obvious and through his own efforts unavoidable. Andrée had framed a set of improbable conditions for launch, which perhaps he hoped would never materialize. But at last his hour had struck. Even so, he equivocated.

"The departure is decided upon" was all he said.[21]

"*E*verywhere is feverish activity," wrote Machuron. "The preparations go on rapidly."[22]

It was a rare crystalline day on the almost perpetually fogbound island. Shreds of cloud continued to scud north on the south wind. Panel after numbered panel tumbled from the north face of the balloon shed; the balloon itself rose in small increments as bags of ballast were handed down from the netting. The wind became even stronger; the balloon oscillated more violently within its octagon shed.

Thirty-two carrier pigeons, which Andrée hoped would fly his dispatches back to his Stockholm newspaper, *Aftonbladet,* were placed in their baskets under the balloon's carrying-ring. It was also Andrée's idea to have Strindberg take aerial photographs of the Arctic landscape—the first experiment in remote sensing of the polar regions—and en route post them off to Stockholm via carrier pigeon.

The final ballast bags were removed so that the balloon was tethered by only three cables. The two-story, half-ton car, on which three men would live and navigate during the flight, was brought into the shed and attached with six cables to the carrying-ring. Strindberg circled the balloon shed, taking photographs of the last-minute preparations. Once the car was in place, ballast was attached to it for the flight. The final panels from the balloon house were let down, and the long guide-ropes and ballast lines with their metal screw couplings were laid down in coils in the short distance between the hangar and the harbor.

It was time to go.

"Strindberg and Fraenkel," yelled Andrée. "Are you ready to get into the car?"[23]

Strindberg went to his friend Machuron, gave him all his undeveloped film, then broke down while asking Machuron to deliver final letters to his fiancée.

"How many days," wrote Machuron, "how many months will she be anxiously waiting, and receiving no news? What anxiety, what suspense await that poor young girl!"[24]

Andrée handed a telegram to the captain of *Svenskund,* to be delivered to the king of Sweden.

> AT THE MOMENT OF THEIR DEPARTURE, THE MEMBERS OF THE EXPEDITION TO THE NORTH POLE BEG YOUR MAGESTY TO ACCEPT THEIR VERY HUMBLE SALUTATIONS AND THE ASSURANCE OF THEIR DEEPEST GRATITUDE.
>
> ANDRÉE[25]

Andrée posted another telegram to *Aftonbladet* and then took his place alongside Strindberg and Fraenkel in the car.

Armed with knives to cut the ballast bags, the crews of *Eagle* and *Svenskund* now awaited a brief moment of calm in the winds before lines were cut away. Three *Svenskund* sailors with swords stood ready

6. *Andrée's polar balloon* Eagle *stands ready to launch from Virgo Harbor, July 1897. (Courtesy of the Norwegian Polar Institute archives.)*

to cut the three cables holding the balloon captive. The wind from the south was still holding by 1 p.m. It howled through the shed and flapped the canvas spread at the top of the shed to protect the balloon; it died, howled again, then there was extended calm. The next sound was a yell from Andrée.

"Cut away everywhere!"[26]

At 1:45, *Eagle* slowly rose out of its hangar. At the top of the house, the sheets of canvas sheltered the balloon's rise from the downdraft of the cliff behind. Strindberg photographed the ascent from *Eagle's* car; on the ground, hurrahs arose from crew members of *Svenskund* and the Norwegian sealers anchored in Virgo Harbor.

Machuron rushed out of the balloon shed to grab his own camera, but as he snapped his first photographs of *Eagle's* first flight he saw the balloon carried down toward the harbor. After clearing the top of the shed, the balloon had been hit directly by the downdraft.

"It sweeps down from the summit and attacks the balloon," Machuron observed. "[The balloon] . . . descends rapidly towards the sea."[27] Sailors rushed to a steam launch, ready to assist the aeronauts if *Eagle* was forced into the water. On board the balloon, all three polar fliers dumped ballast overboard. Four hundred pounds of sand poured over the side. Still *Eagle* sank, though more slowly, and the bottom of the rounded wood-and-canvas car touched down on the surface of Virgo Harbor, then rose again, carried north on the wind.

Cheers went up again. Hardly noticed in the confusion were the three navigational lines, as they unwound from their coils. They had become unscrewed at their metal couplings, and two-thirds of their length was deposited inadvertently on shore. This meant, quite aside from an instantaneous loss of dirigibility, that over half a ton of ballast was left on shore. *Eagle* shot to 2,000 feet, and twenty minutes after launch it crossed Hollandar Naze, a spit of sand leaning into Smeerenburg Fjord from Amsterdam Island, a mile north of Virgo Harbor.

Strindberg had intended to toss a last letter to his fiancée onto the sands of Hollandar Naze, and he had instructed Machuron to find it there and deliver it. In the rush to refloat *Eagle,* however, he momentarily forgot the letter, but as *Eagle* soared to over 1,900 feet and passed over Vogelsang Island, a rocky whaleback of an island northeast of Danes Island, he dropped the tin containing the letter, the world's first polar air mail, onto Vogelsang. Not knowing this, Machuron later searched Hollandar Naze for the letter without success. He did not know to look on Vogelsang, and to this day the tin remains undiscovered somewhere on Vogelsang Island.

Eagle passed into a cloud and dropped to 150 feet. What remained of the guide-ropes touched down on the water. Andrée's rudders, as it were, had ended their journey to the Pole before they had even begun. Why he did not force-land his balloon after losing his navigation system and try to launch again is mystifying. For after the guide-ropes twisted free, *Eagle* was little better than a free balloon, that handicapped creation Andrée had never trusted. "The ropes were caught in some rocks on the shore and the screws for separating the parts worked," Machuron later wrote. "But Andrée is well provided against the loss."[28]

Andrée was not well provided against loss of the ropes. In fact, he and his companions were all but doomed if they did not immediately land. This is something the bright balloon maker Machuron should have seen at once. But he, like the other men on shore, was too transfixed to react. The extraordinary sight of a great balloon straining against a bleak Arctic landscape, a quixotic manifestation of human daring, overwhelmed the men.

Aboard *Eagle,* the three polar fliers looked down to see the now-three-hundred-foot-long guide-ropes slash through the water. Fraenkel adjusted *Eagle*'s sails to catch the south wind, and the balloon headed due north at around twenty-two miles per hour.

Far from being discouraged, Machuron was ecstatic. "If it keeps up this initial speed and direction, it will reach the Pole in less than two days."[29]

Eagle grew smaller across the harbor. Svedenborg set off for the Seven Islands, far to the northeast, to lay in the cache of supplies. An hour after launch, *Eagle* was no longer visible on the horizon.

"For one moment then," wrote Machuron, "between two hills we perceive a grey speck over the sea, very very far away, and then it finally disappears. . . . our friends . . . are now shrouded in mystery."[30]

Eagle and its three voyagers vanished into gray Arctic mist.

*F*our days after launch, one of Andrée's carrier pigeons was shot by the captain of the Norwegian fishing vessel *Alken*. The pigeon carried a note from Andrée reporting that, two days earlier, at 12.30 p.m., July 13, 1897, *Eagle* was at 82°02' N. In two days, *Eagle* had traveled about 150 miles toward the Pole, at an average speed of six miles per hour.

"Good speed to E," the note read in part. "All well on board. This is third pigeon-post."[31]

Eagle then fell into protracted silence.

Articles attempting to offer explanations of the fate of the explorers appeared regularly. "The Andrée polar balloon expedition disappeared into the Arctic regions and nothing has ever come in the way of definite news of its fate," began one such piece in 1899.

> Most Arctic experts have believed that the bodies of the explorer and his companions rest upon some ice cap, imbedded in the snows of two winters, and wrapped, perhaps, in the torn silk sheets of the wrecked balloon.
>
> The conclusion . . . has been that the balloon . . . accomplished nothing, and that Andrée, with his two companions . . . perished miserably very soon afterward.[32]

Such was the opinion of the day.

Two years after the launch, however, the captain of another Norwegian cutter, *Martha Larsask,* made a stunning find. On the coast of King Charles Land, an island in the southeast of the Spitsbergen group—and about one hundred miles from Andrée's balloon shed—he discovered Andrée's "polar buoy."[33] This buoy was to have been dropped from the car of *Eagle* as it passed over the North Pole. Like the other buoys designed by Andrée for the flight, it was a large hollow cork bulb enclosed in copper mesh, painted in Swedish blue and yellow. But, unique among the system of buoys, when it dropped

7. *A ghostly image rescued after thirty-three years on White Island. The polar balloon* Eagle *comes to rest on the polar ice pack two hundred miles northeast of Danes Island. Soon after this photograph was taken on July 14, 1897, Andrée and his two companions began their final march, south to White Island and death. (Courtesy of the Andréemuseet, Gränna, Sweden.)*

from the car and hit the ice, a small Swedish flag popped from its top. On ice and ocean current the buoy would drift until it washed up on some shore of distant civilization. Discovery of the polar buoy sparked a regeneration of Andrée polar fever. Had *Eagle* reached the Pole?

A year later, in August of 1900, another buoy was discovered, and another note. It was found to be the first buoy Andrée had deposited on the ice, at ten o'clock in the evening of July 11, 1897. The ghostly note read in part:

> Our journey has so far gone well. We are still moving on at a height of 800 feet. . . . Four carrier-pigeons were sent off at 5:40 pm. Greenwich time. They flew westerly. We are now in over the ice which is much broken up in all directions. Weather magnificent. In best of humours.
>
> Andrée
Strindberg
Fraenkel
Above the clouds since 7:45 G.M.T.[34]

MARCH OF EVENTS
The Washington Herald
SUNDAY, NOVEMBER 16, 1930.

WORLD TOPICS

NOTED WRITERS

ANDREE'S OWN STORY

Dramatic Diaries of Lost Polar Expedition

NILS STRINDBERG.

Andree's Foreboding of Catastrophe

KNUT FRAENKEL.

An Imperishable Saga of the Arctic

FIRST OFFICIAL NARRATIVE OF ARCTIC BALLOON FLIGHT AND ITS TRAGIC OUTCOME

Andree and Strindberg Records Found With Their Bodies on White Island Where Swedish Aeronauts Died Reveal How Quest Failed and Tell of Thrilling Battle for Life

By S. A. Andree and Nils Strindberg

As reconstructed from their diaries by Professor Hans W. Ahlmann, Professor of Geography, University of Stockholm.

Copyright, 1930, in the United States of America, by North Newspaper Alliance. Copyright throughout the world by Albert Bonnier Forlag. All Rights Reserved. Reproduction in whole or in part prohibited.

IT was only 3 o'clock in the morning on the 11th of July, 1897, when the water in Virgo Harbor, Dane's Island, which previously had been as smooth as a mirror, was ruffled by the first cats-paws from the south-southwest. By 4 the wind had grown quite fresh, with now and then a squall, while the clouds moved northwards at a good rate.

Everything pointed to the south wind being steadier on this occasion than before, and that this

*R*elief expeditions were sent north to look for Andrée and his crew, but no further trace was found. Search parties from Sweden and Germany combed the Spitsbergen and Franz Josef Land archipelagoes and the New Siberian Islands. An American polar expedition under the direction of a Chicago journalist named Walter Wellman looked for Andrée without success in Franz Josef Land as well.

The first balloon to drift over the polar sea was somewhere down on the pack, lost and silent.

*T*he last attempt to fly over the North Pole in a dirigible was made by General Umberto Nobile in the airship *Italia* in 1928. The flight reached the Pole successfully but ended in a tragic crash on the return journey. Several of the crew, along with the wreck of the dirigible hull, were never found. But, as newspapers were quick to remind their readers that summer, none of the intrepid 1897 crew of the *Eagle* had ever been found either.

*O*n August 5, 1930, a Norwegian sealer on its way from Spitsbergen to Franz Josef Land landed on White Island, a small island off the far northeastern coast of the Spitsbergen archipelago. On board the ship was a crew of scientists making routine surveys of the area. On August 6, two sealers from the ship went ashore and discovered the remains of a campsite. Soon after, the chief scientist of the expedition, Dr. Gunnar Horn, identified the remains of three bodies, as well as a boat whose prow was imprinted with the words *Andrée's polar exp.* Salomon August Andrée and his two companions had been found at last.

Horn identified as well the diaries of both Andrée and Strindberg, a meteorological log kept by Fraenkel, and many of the expedition's artifacts, including rifles, the sledge, and the wood-and-canvas boat. The diaries revealed that the flight had lasted three days, during which time the balloon was as much dragged as flew across the pack ice. After sixty-five and a half hours of flight, the crew decided to crash-land the balloon, three hundred miles northeast of Danes Island and four hundred miles short of the Pole. There followed a forced march southward over the pack. The men shot polar bears to eat, dragged

8. *(Opposite) When the remains of Andrée and his companions were located in August 1930, and Andrée's diaries published just three months later, they created an international sensation. (From the author's collection.)*

the boat on top of the sledge, and were drenched by repeated falls into the icy water. The ice pack drifted, and the men were forced to retrace their steps for mile after grueling mile.

Just when they had mounted an ice floe and constructed a camp for the winter, the floe broke and forced them ashore on White Island. There, as a detailed medical analysis of the journals later made clear, the cumulative effects of eating poorly cooked trichina-infected bear meat caught up with the three explorers, and one by one they expired.

Also found on White Island were several rolls of undeveloped film. After thirty-three years in the ice, Strindberg's film was excavated and taken to a laboratory in Sweden and developed with excruciating care. Even more than Andrée's diary, these ghostly images rescued from the grip of the ice showed both the glory of Andrée's conception and the misery of its execution. They remain some of the most eerily fascinating images in the history of exploration.

CHAPTER TWO

The Greatest Show in the Arctic: The Unsinkable Mr. Wellman

On New Year's Eve, 1905, Frank B. Noyes, editor and publisher of the *Chicago Record-Herald,* gave the following order to Walter Wellman, one of the *Record-Herald's* star reporters: "Build an airship and with it go find the North Pole."[1] The assignment thrilled Wellman, for he had brooded over just such a scenario for more than a decade. For over a year, he had lobbied the owner of the *Record-Herald,* Victor Lawson, to finance the incredible scheme. As Wellman wrote later: "They accepted [my] plan as one worth trying. They were interested in a great idea: here was an opportunity to attempt a big thing for the world and for science."[2]

The *Record-Herald*—make no mistake—was interested more in snappy headlines and circulation boosting than in either science or the world. But no matter. Noyes had just the person required for such a grandiose project. Walter Wellman was fashioning for himself one of the most extraordinary careers in the history of American journalism, all in pursuit of the big thing, the great idea. If the history of exploration was to reduce him to little more than a humorous footnote, in his day Wellman held the stage as both a premier adventure journalist and high-profile Washington correspondent.

Wellman had the luck to live during the great age of newspaper sponsorship of expeditions, when an owner could point to a blank spot on the map, untaxed profits would pour forth, and the paper's readership slept easy in the knowledge that a star reporter had been dispatched to trudge toward that spot in pith helmet or mukluks. In that sense, Wellman was the very embodiment of the America of Theodore Roosevelt and William Howard Taft: his overblown ideas, his drive not to leave bad enough alone, and, not least, his hyperventilated writing style were all as large as his considerable girth.

In 1891, purporting to have discovered the exact landing spot of Columbus in the New World, on Watling Island (San Salvador), Wellman cabled the news back to the *Herald,* and then, as if to confirm his findings, he erected a marker on the spot. Thus began his career in exploration.

*U*nlike Salomon Andrée, the visionary tinkerer, Wellman preferred, as he put it, "[to] watch the progress of the arts and mechanics to see if some better means than the primitive sledge could not be found for advancing upon the [North] Pole."[3]

Wellman founded a newspaper, the *Cincinnati Evening Post,* at the age of twenty-one. In 1884, he became the Washington correspondent and political reporter for the *Chicago Herald* and its successor, the *Chicago Record-Herald.* He remained as a Washington correspondent until 1911, but although he covered and knew presidents from Chester A. Arthur to William Howard Taft, Wellman's abiding passion was exploration, and it is not hard to imagine that he fancied himself an American Henry Morton Stanley.

But, unlike Stanley, the very model of outrageous tenacity sent by the *New York Herald* in 1871 to "find" Dr. David Livingstone in Africa—and simultaneously launch an era of fierce competition among newspapers to be sponsors of major geographic expeditions—Wellman consistently overreached himself. His journalist's instincts told him that only the "big" stories interested readers, and so, perforce, only big expeditions would satisfy both his personal and professional ambitions.

The year after his "discovery" of the Columbus site on Watling Island, Wellman turned his attention to an even grander geographic quest—the search for the North Pole—toward which the journalist directed five expeditions and more than half a million dollars over seventeen years, before he lost two men, two airships, and a steamer, and finally gave up after hearing the news of Cook's and Peary's competing claims to the Pole in 1909. Thereafter, in 1910, he attempted the first crossing of the Atlantic Ocean by airship, quitting only when his airship's engine failed near Bermuda, over one thousand circuitous miles from its launch point in Atlantic City, New Jersey.

These spectacular failures were in their own quixotic ways intensely interesting and prophetic expeditions. For lack of a better phrase, they were typically American, in the same sense that Ray Bradbury described Jules Verne as an "American" author because of Verne's fictional and technological explorations of and confrontations with the universe. From the advertising that promoted them, to the high-powered fund-raising that paid for them, to the quasi-scientific rhetoric Wellman used to justify them, to the nascent technology that both enabled and doomed them, even to the extent that his brother Arthur filmed them, Wellman's expeditions were originals, prototypes for almost every twentieth-century geographic expedition that would follow. From the polar airship expeditions of Roald Amundsen and Umberto Nobile, to Richard Byrd, Parker Cramer, and Bernt Balchen and their pioneering use of aircraft in the Arctic and Antarctic, to the multimedia, multitechnological oceanographic expeditions of Jacques-Yves Cousteau and Robert D. Ballard, to the successes and failures of the U.S. space program, all in some manner could trace their uniquely "American" can-do origins to the example of Walter Wellman.

It was in part Wellman's very genius for quasi-scientific self-justification that caused him his biggest problems, both with a doubting public and among his rivals in the press. One of those press rivals, observing Wellman's constantly delayed progress toward flying over the Atlantic in his airship, offered a devastating critique:

> Since August 1 [Wellman] has followed the Spartan regimen he set himself without complaint. As usual through the hard and trying period of preparation Mr. Wellman left his rough Louis XIV couch on the side of the Chalfonte that is entirely exposed to the uncouth and untamed ocean at 8 o'clock this morning. . . .
>
> At the breakfast table Mr. Wellman ate the frugal but sustaining meal which wide experience at the wildest hotels along Broadway and other channels of travel has taught him is best for adventurers. He rarely has more than steak, eggs, buckwheat cakes, potatoes, fruit, biscuits and coffee for breakfast.
>
> A pause in training might be expected here, but Mr. Wellman is made of sterner stuff. He returned to his room, got his strength together, and when a newspaperman called up and asked "when the old gas-bag was going up," Mr. Wellman told him to go where a gas-bag would explode. . . .
>
> All Mr. Wellman wants of the weather is a dead calm around the hangar and a brisk west wind blowing everywhere else . . . and as a deep student of meteorology . . . [he] would go when he was ready for the trip, and did not give a rump-de-dump whoop-de-doo for what other folks said about it.[4]

A workman laboring on Wellman's airship that fall of 1910 remembered sixty years later that "around the hangar . . . Mr. Wellman always seemed to antagonize workers. . . . I remember a French mechanic that I think would have hurt Mr. Wellman if he had not been stopped."[5] Paul Garber, late curator emeritus of the National Air & Space Museum and dean of all U.S. air museum curators, recalled being a ten-year-old nuisance running through Wellman's hangar in

w York Times.

THE WEATHER.

Fair to-day; increasing cloudiness, probably showers, Thursday.

WEDNESDAY, OCTOBER 19, 1910.—TWENTY PAGES.

ONE CENT, In Greater New York, Elsewhere Jersey City and Newark TWO CENT

WELLMAN AND CREW RESCUED AT SEA, AIRSHIP LOST
VOYAGERS PICKED UP BY TRENT, 400 MILES OFF HATTERAS
LEADER SENDS STORY OF DARING TRIP TO THE TIMI

RE
IENS

e Does
Ca-
.

OUTH

Appeal
pe Af-
ited.

n Ellis
wn that
accomo
reau al
ded by
esident,
to see
many
in New

in New
iveston,
re been
ert the
lent sa-
nrnment
rather
arrivals
on with
ne out-
k from
up his
ions at
id some
illowed.
at Ellis
s of en-
relieved
ora. Its
operation
gration
f Com-
ianoral
er Wil-
d t'agt
a mili-

igh the
abem i-
waiting
at over
st close

himself
ignasia
sums
in this
s of a
mental
to re-
ered a

appeal
to-lay,
jilty of
charge
it week
s sero
MRT,
ring of
action
re real

treesod
owing
ran fla-
rmun
waited
immila
Age al
and
arnton,
of his
in half
which
r men
om his
ves al
wbl-b
ind his
said
miner.
tera in

shut in
ery
looked
nent?"

ighten-
the of
th with
an for
n that
ith has
still all
g thl.
of his
Taft's
of so
about
s other
ict at
e age;
could
After
latter
ae had
be he
i threat
srd for
the
Taft
plenty
afted
emith
sident
a law
n Nex

b- the
serant
is hid
onking
missing

Winds Drove Him Far South in His
Flight for Europe Under the
Auspices of The Times.

BLAMES THE EQUILIBRATOR

Its Heavy Drag and Jump from
Wave to Wave Retarded Airship
and Disarranged Machinery.

1,000 MILES IN 71 HOURS

Broke All Records for Dirigibles—
When Europe Became Impos-
sible, Tried for Bermuda.

SIGHTED TRENT IN 69TH HOUR

Then Crew Took to Lifeboat and
the Dirigible Went Adrift—
Captain Tells of Rescue.

PILOT TELLS OF MISHAPS

Forced to Throw Away Valuable Bal-
last to Keep Above the Waves—
Almost Hit a Schooner in the
Fog Off Nantucket.

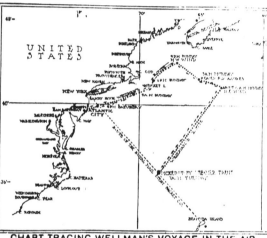

CHART TRACING WELLMAN'S VOYAGE IN THE AIR.

By WALTER WELLMAN.

By United Wireless to The New York Times.
Copyright, 1910, by The New York Times
Company. All rights reserved.

ON BOARD THE ROYAL
MAIL SS. TRENT AT SEA, Oct.
18.—The heroic Vaniman and
all my brave and loyal crew of
the dirigible balloon America, who
set sail with me from Atlantic City
at 8 o'clock last Saturday morning in an attempt to reach Europe through the air, are safe
on board the steamship Trent,
having been rescued from the
crippled balloon this morning
and taken on the ship some time
after 7 o'clock after more than
two hours of difficult manoeu-
vring.

When the America passed
Nantucket on Sunday morning,
as we reported at the time, conditions seemed favorable for the
completion of the journey across
the Atlantic. It was after we had
gone well past that point that the
conditions arose which finally
compelled the abandonment of
the balloon this morning and the
transfer of the men to the Trent.

After passing Nantucket Island
we went east-northeast for an estimated distance of 140 miles.
Our motors were not in use, as
the fresh westerly breeze we had
at Nantucket was still driving us
forward. Our only anxiety, a. I
said in a message at the time, lay
in the action of the equilibrator,
which had begun to jerk on the

end of it rode the heavy seas,
which had been kicked up by the
stiff breeze, it jerked shockingly
on the lines which held it to the
America. Under this stress the
ship set up a rolling motion, which
added to the strain and threatened
the entire destruction of the craft
if long continued.

It was a dreadful night for the
men aboard the ship. There was
much to be done to ease the strain,
and all did everything possible.

At times some would become
exhausted, and one by one the
men would sleep for a time. They
went to their hammocks expect-
ing that they would awake to find
themselves in the ocean, but all
they wanted was to sleep, and
they did so.

At no time, however, was there
any sign of faltering on their part.
At the worst moments they were
calm, and even cheerful.

As the seas grew in power and
pulled harder on the equilibrator
the America was drawn down almost to the level of the line of
whitecaps. Some of the waves
even struck the lifeboat, in which
lay our only hope of saving ourselves, and threatened at times to
carry it away.

Decided to Stick to the Ship.

At this point a consultation was
held to decide whether we should
abandon the ship and take to the
lifeboat. All hands agreed that
we should stick to the ship and, if
possible, on the other side of the
ocean. We threw over gasoline
to lighten her, and she rose above
the dangerous waves.

motor gasoline for the final effort
to reach a landing place.

All Monday we kept afloat with
difficulty. There was grave danger and a great strain on all, but
none thought of giving up. We
were resolved to hold to the ship
as long as possible and to give up
only when we saw that the task
was hopeless.

A fresh trouble came on Monday night. The weather turned
cold, and the change of temperature so affected the lifting power
of the gas in the great bag that
we found it necessary to jettison
more of the gasoline and part of
the machinery which had been
damaged in order to keep above
the waves.

We saw that it would be impossible to keep afloat another
night under such conditions, but
resolved to stay aboard the ship
during the day unless we should
meet a vessel. There was a doubt
whether this was wise, as there
was great danger that the equilibrator, with its constant jerking,
would pull us apart and we would
founder.

The lifeboat was finally
launched, with great difficulty, in
a high wind early this morning.
We had sighted the Trent coming toward us, two hours away,
and we realized that the only
course to take under the circumstances was to launch the boat
then, instead of waiting for the
night, when we would have to
take to it and no help would be
near.

The Trent Sighted.

It was 5:07 o'clock this morn-

a gust of wind whirled us aw
carrying the line out from
steamer.

Many times the line was lo
ered, and there was a scram
on board the Trent to make
fast. Each time the wind wo
catch us and push us away. Fin
ly the line was caught and ma
fast aboard the vessel, but a stro
gust of wind parted it and tore
away.

The Trent followed us, und
couraged, but it was evident th
this plan would not do. We ga
the signal to her to stand by
pick us up, for we would take
the lifeboat.

Launching the Lifeboat.

The operation of launching t
boat was performed with t
greatest skill. Vaniman broug
the airship down close to t
water and Simon directed t
springing of the hooks which i
leased the ropes to drop the bo
He was the last to get aboard t
boat, and he released the line
which set her free from t
America.

As we were getting away, ho
ever, the equilibrator, which h
done so much harm, alm
put an end to our efforts to lea
the ship. Under the impulse
the waves, it was lashing abo
and as the boat was in the wat
it struck a glancing blow th
almost smashed the little cra
As it was, the boat was half ca
sized. She was soon righted, ho
ever, and the oars were mann
and we pulled for the Trent, whi
had kept as close to us as possib

Ropes were thrown from t

Atlantic City, New Jersey, moving from place to place for the best view of the airship. "Wellman came over to me, lifted me up, and set me on top of a large crate, so high that I couldn't climb down," Garber recalled.[6]

*T*hroughout his seventy-six years, Wellman displayed a similar knack for lifting his problems out of the way. Because of obstinacy, fear, or the sincerity of his beliefs, Wellman could never be budged from a chosen position. He accused his colleagues in the media of pushing Andrée to certain death. "He [Andrée] realized his balloon was not fit for such a voyage. . . . But . . . if he failed to start, the yellow press would hound him into his grave, and he preferred death in the Arctics. I know from men who were with him that Andrée said, just before he sailed . . . that he was committing suicide."[7]

There were threads of truth in this, but only threads. Andrée certainly knew his balloon was flawed, but Andrée was also forty-three (the same age as Umberto Nobile when his airship crashed in 1928 not far from the site of *Eagle*'s touchdown in 1897), and he knew that the generation of practical motor-driven dirigibles might be two decades away. (It was.) Andrée drifted north in his balloon as much in fear of the actuarial tables as of either the ice pack or the newspapers. Perhaps Andrée even had the glimmerings of a death wish. But despite his failure to shake down his equipment in Spitsbergen, Andrée had attempted a balloon flight to the Pole with the best gear of his day—much of it designed by Andrée himself.

But set aside such considerations for a larger one: Andrée's polar buoy. This buoy, which he was to have dropped if his ship reached the Pole, was found in 1899. At the least, no explorer could thereafter attempt the Pole in absolute certainty Andrée had not been there first. It was not, as Wellman wrote, "pretty well settled that within thirty or forty hours Andrée's balloon came down in the ice-strewn Barents Sea to the east of Spitsbergen," though this was, with hindsight, remarkable prophecy, temporally if not geographically. More precisely, this was Wellman's hope. After all, he wanted both for himself and for the greater glory of the *Chicago Record-Herald* the honor of being first to the Pole.

9. (Opposite) Exploration generates headlines: Walter Wellman and his airship America *attempt to fly across the Atlantic Ocean in 1910, sponsored by the* New York Times *and reported on the front page, October 19, 1910. (From the author's collection.)*

*I*n 1893, at age thirty-five, Wellman made a pilgrimage to Norway, to consult with sealing skippers. He sought knowledge of the ice conditions around Spitsbergen and, in the process, as had so many others before him, a shortcut to the Pole. There had to be, Wellman convinced himself, a quicker passage than sledging. It went against both his get-the-story-first training and his comfort-loving constitution to spend years on a boat stuck in pack ice like Nansen, or years plodding behind a sledge like Peary. In the years before wireless communication, Arctic expeditions could be out of contact with the civilization to the south for years at a time, something completely abhorrent to a journalist who had started his career as editor of the city desk in Cincinnati.

After his fact-finding tour of Norway, Wellman raised the funding to hire a Norwegian ice-steamer called *Ragnvald Jarl* (*Chief Ragnvald*), and filled its hold with three aluminum boats and several sledges. In the spring of 1894, he sailed on board his charter for Spitsbergen, eventually pitching camp in early May on the shores of Virgo Harbor.

"We spent three days at Danes Id. [Danskøya] arranging our headquarters,"[8] Wellman wrote to a friend in Chicago. This letter, combined with Wellman's annotated chart of "Spitzbergen," shows that his expedition advanced from Sørkapp (South Cape) to the Sjuøyane (Seven Islands) between May 3 and 12, with three days spent on Danes Island beginning on May 7. Wellman made use of the house built at Virgo Harbor by the Britisher Arnold Pike, who overwintered there in 1889.

On May 10, Wellman sailed north and east on the *Jarl* and arrived at the Seven Islands forty-eight hours later, another extremely fast passage. "Capt. Bottolfsen," wrote Wellman, "says we might try for forty years without doing it again."[9]

At the Seven Islands, Wellman's luck ran out. After leaving the *Ragnvald Jarl* and taking to the sledges and aluminum boats, Wellman saw for the first time the ice that guards the North Pole. Like many before and since, the journalist was shocked by its apparent insurmountability. Incidents that would have been dismissed—or accepted—as minor irritations by a Nansen or Amundsen, were reported by Wellman as life-balancing catastrophes. It is impossible now to say whether such descriptions sprang from actual events, or from an almost complete unpreparedness for the environment he had chosen for his exploits, or, as the polar historian Beau Riffenburgh would suggest a century later, from the working necessity that that was what his newspaper and its readers back in Chicago expected of him. Whatever the motivations for his writing, his sledging party had scarcely progressed north at all when a courier overtook them and reported that a northwest storm had pinned the *Jarl* along the western shore of tiny Walden Island.

Wellman retreated to Walden Island to find the *Jarl* "held up only by the ice that had pierced her; when this was withdrawn she was sure to sink to the bottom of the sea."[10] As the ship settled lower in the water, he remembered his steamer trunk with his papers in it. "A hole was cut in the deck of the vessel, and a sailor dove down and brought up the mail . . . and it was dried over the oil stove that they used."[11] Wellman does not record the name of the lucky sailor chosen for this icy assignment.

Apparently undismayed by the disaster, after sending *Ragnvald Jarl*'s crew south in search of rescue, Wellman turned around and again started north. By this time the summer sun had warmed the pack ice into a wet mass of shifting slush. With his sledges useless, Wellman had his sledge dogs needlessly shot. He was now stuck on a melting and splintering ice pack with no other option than to man-haul the boats back to Walden Island. Exhausted and freezing, with their clothes and equipment soaked by slush and falls into open leads of subfreezing water, Wellman's men staggered back to Walden. At top speed, Wellman's sledging never amounted to much more than four miles a day, which, had they persevered that far, would have placed his party at the North Pole, and in their graves, around November 1.

"Pushing and pulling the heavy sledges and boats over the rough ice on this expedition," Wellman later wrote, "the idea first came to me of using an aerial craft in Arctic exploration. Often I looked up into the air and wished we had some means of travelling that royal road where there were no ice hummocks, no leads of open water, no obstacles to rapid progress."[12] "Anyone else," wrote Edward Mabley in his 1969 account of Wellman's adventures, "getting out of such a hell alive might have been expected to confine further exploration, if any, to the tropics."[13]

But Wellman had already found glory near the equator. He had then looked at a map and voted himself into the polar fraternity. After Walden Island, he felt himself a full-fledged member. On Walden Island, he and the survivors of the sinking of the *Ragnvald Jarl* took to the lifeboats that had been salvaged. Soon after, a sealing sloop that had journeyed north to search for them rescued Wellman and his men, and deposited the expedition back at Virgo Harbor. From there Wellman returned to Norway.

Whether or not the thought had actually occurred to him in 1894 of using a balloon to reach the North Pole, Wellman did spend that summer in Paris, witnessing ascents of free balloons. He claimed at the time to have a plan whereby a balloon lifting fifteen thousand pounds of supplies, sledges, dogs, and men would ascend on a favorable wind from Virgo Harbor on Danes Island, travel as far north as possible, and, if not reach the Pole, at least deposit the crew within striking distance of another polar dash.

While professing distrust of free balloons, Wellman nevertheless wrote in his aeronautical memoir, *The Aerial Age* (1911), that only failure to make connections with a potential patron in Paris kept him from making the attempt in 1895. He even selected Pike's house on Danes Island as the jumping-off point for the expedition. With a bit more of his unlucky luck, Wellman might well have been fighting for airspace over Virgo Harbor in 1897 with the Andrée Polar Expedition. Wellman disingenuously remarked that Andrée had "[taken] up the balloon idea; had a balloon built in Paris—not as large and good a one as we had planned . . . and . . . built his balloon house and established his base at the very spot . . . I had picked out."[14]

Even at that, after a summer of watching balloons float over Paris, the idea could not have been especially appealing for Wellman. He never sought potential backers for an attempt by balloon, if indeed any were to be found. Perhaps, too, the memory of the forced retreat over the pack ice a few months earlier had dimmed his enthusiasm.

*W*hatever his motives, Wellman spent the next four years soliciting for not a balloon but another polar dash with ship and sledge. He listed the patrons of his 1898 expedition to Franz Josef Land, an Arctic island group east of Spitsbergen, as men who "assisted" him in raising capital "with," he insisted, "great difficulty."[15] The list is not a modest one and includes President William McKinley, Vice President Garret Hobart, J. Pierpont Morgan, and William K. Vanderbilt.

In the spring of 1898, Wellman chartered another ice-steamer, *Frithjof,* and headed north to Franz Josef Land. Heeding the lessons of Walden Island, Wellman did not sail for Franz Josef Land from the Arctic fishing port of Tromsø in northern Norway until late June. Even so, *Frithjof* hit the pack ice at 77° N, forcing it back to Tromsø to refuel. The expedition ship finally landed in the Franz Josef archipelago in late July of that year and deposited Wellman's polar party and its supplies, which included eighty-three dogs. "To our imaginations," Wellman wrote, "[Franz Josef Land] presented itself as a paradise of opportunity."[16]

Wellman's combined American and Norwegian party had plenty of company in the race to the Pole. Luigi Amadeo de Savoy (the duke of the Abruzzi), an Italian polar explorer and mountaineer, was conducting research in Spitsbergen and would arrive in Franz Josef Land in 1899 for his own polar campaign just as Wellman was retreating. To the west, in the Kennedy Channel off northwest Greenland, Robert E. Peary was preparing for his second assault on the Pole, while the Norwegian explorer Otto Sverdrup, who had captained Nansen's *Fram,* explored the area west of Peary's self-proclaimed "American Route" to the Pole.

At Cape Flora on Hall Island, Wellman's crew searched the abandoned and boarded hut that had served as headquarters for the Jackson-Harmsworth Expedition. It had been this English expedition with whom Fridtjof Nansen and his companion Hjalmar Johansen made their extraordinary rendezvous in 1896 after the dash to 86°13'06" N. Wellman hoped that Andrée, Strindberg, and Fraenkel, knowing there was a cache of supplies at Cape Flora, had headed for this hut after the *Eagle* was forced down.

There can be little doubt Wellman knew that if he succeeded in finding Andrée, he would enter journalism and exploration history on a par with Henry Morton Stanley, who had been sent in 1869 to look for David Livingstone and succeeded in finding him in 1871 at Lake Tanganyika. "Andrée's balloon was drifting in this direction from Spitsbergen," Wellman wrote, "and as he knew of the existence at this point of a good house amply stocked with provisions, it was not impossible he had been able to make his way hither the previous autumn. Great was our disappointment when we saw the doors and windows of Jackson's house all boarded and barred, for we realized that thus ended all reasonable expectation that the brave Swedes were to be seen again among the living."[17] At that moment Wellman was forty years old, an active explorer, and approximately three hundred miles from the island where Andrée had died the previous fall; Wellman would be four thousand miles away, long retired in New York City, and seventy-two years old when he finally learned what became of the Swedish balloonist.

Frithjof pushed on and unloaded its cargo on Hall Island at Cape Tegetthoff, on July 30. They were at 80°05' N, 570 miles from the Pole. Here Wellman's crew built Harmsworth House, the expedition's headquarters. Three days later *Frithjof* steamed for Norway, and Wellman and his men were, he reported, "the only human inhabitants in that vast region, and our nearest neighbors were Russians and Samoyedes in Nova Zembla [Novaya Zemlya], five hundred miles to the southward."[18]

Wellman appointed as the expedition's second-in-command Evelyn Briggs Baldwin, a meteorologist from the U.S. Weather Bureau, and then sent Baldwin off to establish an outpost as far north as possible. Baldwin was to build a hut as far as 82° N and stock it with a ton and a half of dried polar bear and walrus meat and other provisions and supplies. In the following spring, Wellman would make his polar dash after restocking at this advance depot.

After giving this order, Wellman retired to Harmsworth House for the winter. Baldwin, though not as obsessive as Wellman, was himself a man of some ambition. He had been with Peary in Greenland, had fallen out with Peary, and signed on with Wellman's polar expedition. Baldwin kept meticulous notes and a diary, and he saved all of his correspondence. The letters passed by courier between Baldwin and Wellman in the late summer of 1898 are little short of extraordinary. In contrast to Mabley's remark, in his book on Wellman, that "not a single crewman ever was lost on any of Wellman's expeditions"[19]—which was simply not true—and Wellman's own boisterous accounts of his own exploits, Baldwin's letters reveal something of the tragic nature of Wellman's leadership in the field.

On August 5, Baldwin's advance party left Harmsworth House. Almost immediately they sledged into trouble. There was no smooth going over the ice floes, and the ice squeezed and twisted its way over and around the dozens of small islands in the archipelago. To reach 82° N, build a winter hut, and dash back to Harmsworth House before the onset of winter, Baldwin's party would have to cover at least four miles a day. On the days when weather and ice allowed travel, they crawled ahead less than two.

"Your business is to advance as rapidly as possible, and as far as possible this fall, before stopping to establish a winter station," Wellman wrote to Baldwin on the eve of departure of the advance party. "You should stop not later than September 10th, and probably some days earlier." His letter then offers Baldwin no less than fifty-one directions, orders, requests, and authorizations, many of them contradictory. After telling Baldwin, "The details of this hut building I leave to your excellent judgement," Wellman then "suggests" for the winter hut that "a half-cellar should be dug, and then the roof be put over that high enough to enable us to stand erect within. Also, that there should be a vestibule, with an inner and outer door of skins, this vestibule to be large enough for a cook house, that we may avoid scent in the living apartment." In a landscape of glaciers and large ice-corrupted bays, Wellman ordered Baldwin to pass eleven capes, but to do so by "avoid[ing] glacier-crossing . . . [or] . . . attempting to sail far from land in case of open water."[20]

Wellman the next day handed Baldwin an additional dozen orders. Before doing so, he threw a sop to Baldwin's leadership by writing:

"In every detail of the work I trust implicitly in your judgement." He then went on:

> In case through any mischance I should fail to reach your winter camp this autumn, you will, according to your judgement, endeavor to ascertain where we are and if in need of assistance. But you will in no wise endanger your own party on our account.
>
> If I do not join you this fall or early next spring you will not attempt to make the Pole in 1899, but will, after trying to ascertain what has become of us, push out caches as far north as the land extends, preliminary to an attempt to reach the Pole in the spring of 1900. And you are authorized to make that attempt in 1900 if I have not previously joined you or changed these instructions.[21]

These orders not only bound his second-in-command to an unworkable plan, with more than enough contradictions to sap any field commander's self-assurance, but laid the groundwork for Wellman to disclaim responsibility should a debacle occur on the ice. It was Wellman's show, but he could hold Baldwin responsible if something went wrong.

The advance team consisted of Baldwin and the Norwegians Paul Bjoervig, Bernt Bentzen, and Emil Ellefsen. Struggling as best they could, crossing dangerously broken floes and shorelines strewn with the debris of glaciers, the team moved north for fully a month. But the forced march all but broke Baldwin. Two days out, the advance team walked into the teeth of a north wind. "Had hard fight in getting over the ice floe during the last two days," Baldwin wrote back to Wellman. "Surface smooth but *very wet*."[22] The north wind made the party's boats unusable; they were obliged to haul the sledges through the slush.

Encamped on an ice floe in the evening of August 9, Baldwin wrote Wellman that "the ice is in much worse condition than you suppose I fear. We are having a *hard fight* . . . an exceedingly trying time. . . . We have worked at least thirty-six out of every forty-eight hours since leaving Cape Tegetthoff. . . . I shall take no more risks."[23] The sledges, with their soldered silver runners, had all but fallen apart in the slush. Wellman ignored this warning.

By August 25, Baldwin was writing to Wellman, still snug at Harmsworth House: "A hundred times I have wished that I could have made you feel what I *knew absolutely* with regard to use of [our gear and food] at Harmsworth House, before the *Frithjof* left us. But I'm certain that you now have the same *feeling* and so my misery has company."[24] With supplies running low, Baldwin warned Wellman that "no coal other than that for making coffee and cooking be used during September, October and November—leaving every other pound of it, together with spare wood, etc., for use during December, January, February and March. We shall need it most during the bitter cold. . . . I'm bitterly disappointed at the little progress made."[25]

This is the letter of a man in extremis, one who could hardly have been cheered by Wellman's oblivious reply: "I am by no means discouraged as to the general outlook. To the contrary, I feel confident that all things are working out well. . . . Frankly, dear Baldwin . . . you are too prone to look on the dark side of things. . . . I wish you would write more cheerfully."[26] And he added thirty-one more vague requests/orders. But the hope of establishing the advance winter hut at 82° N was gone.

Wellman now asked Baldwin to build the hut "at 81° or beyond," and that "two—possibly three—pass the winter there. . . . The Polar party will expect to get at the outpost next spring. . . . Under no circumstances, short of absolute necessity, will you permit any deviation from these instructions." And, later, to the contrary: "As in my former letter of instructions, you are given authority to vary the programme laid down herein according to circumstances and your own judgement."[27]

While Baldwin worked eighteen hours each day to advance little more than a mile, by the fire at Harmsworth House Wellman planned his polar dash for the following spring. "I am convinced," he wrote Baldwin, "that it is only by *cavalry* speed after leaving the land at 82°30' or thereabouts, that we can [reach the Pole] . . . perhaps an average of twelve miles per day."[28] No dent was made in Wellman's warm calculations by the fact that in twenty days of marching Baldwin's team had averaged just a mile and a half a day. Wellman gave himself just twenty days in the spring to advance from the forward hut at 81° N to the far northern edge of Franz Josef Land at 82°30" N, which meant averaging almost five miles a day. But what troubled Baldwin the most was Wellman's insistence that two or three men winter at the advance hut rather than return for the winter to Harmsworth House. When the advance party stopped in early September at Cape Heller for the winter, short of 81° N, Baldwin did not want to condemn anyone to an Arctic winter alone at that impossibly remote headland.

Wellman "suggested" to Baldwin that he "first explain the circumstances and then ask for volunteers; afterward make your own detail. Whether the number shall be two or three I leave to your judgement and that of the men who are to stay—for their wishes should perhaps be consulted—but two is my preference." He then held out a bribe. "The men who remain will be specially rewarded."[29] Wellman would live to regret these words.

In *The Aerial Age,* Wellman wrote that "late in October . . . [Baldwin] called for two volunteers to remain at the outpost during the winter. . . . All the men offered themselves."[30] But in his letter to Baldwin of August 27, two months earlier, Wellman had already made the decision. "In case you do not want to take responsibility of deciding who is to stay at the Outpost I say Bjorvik [Bjoervig] and Bentzen, and a third if necessary, Emil. But I want you to fix this matter in your own way, for by this time you know the men better than I do. I did say something to Olaf and Daniel about their wintering here [at Harmsworth House], but it was not a promise and you are free to dispose of them."[31] This was another unfortunate choice of words, and, in any case, Wellman's description in his memoir of this winter "volunteering" is somewhat different. "Paul Bjoervig and Bernt Bentzen were chosen," wrote Wellman, "whereat Emil and Olaf Ellefsen and Daniel Johansen were grievously disappointed."[32]

Instead, as Baldwin's diary makes plain, after their experience on the ice, Ellefsen and Johansen had gone so far as to ask Wellman to be allowed to winter at Harmsworth House. Yet Wellman wrote in his Arctic memoirs: "As for Bjoervig and Bentzen, they were delighted. . . . This chance of spending an Arctic winter in a snug little hut, with plenty to eat and smoke, was to them the realization of a dream."[33]

Bjoervig and Bentzen remained at the winter hut while the rest of the advance party retreated to Harmsworth House. The winter solitude gave Wellman the opportunity to engage in his own special brand of writing. He performed heroically, attempting to match the magnificence of his Arctic surroundings to his own frothy style.

> "[I was] . . . under the influence of the Arctic spell. Its glamour was in our eyes, its fever in our blood. . . .
>
> [The glacier at McClintock Island] rose from the ice-strewn, shimmering sea a perfect sheen of purest white, studded with billions upon billions of refracting crystals, to a height of some 2000 feet. At the crest two eminences appeared, side by side; one, bold, rugged, and black, as if by a mighty effort the rocks had shaken themselves loose from the grip of the ice-king, standing forth in sullen independence, a landmark for forty miles around, the other more graceful, submissive, but still proud, lifting its head toward the sky, erect and majestic, though wearing the white robes of its frigid conqueror to the very summit.[34]

So, while before the fire at Harmsworth House Wellman watched "the glaciers debouch into the little valleys . . . and pour musically-gurgling streams down to the sea," out at 81° N, Bentzen and Bjoervig faced a crisis. Bentzen, who'd been with Nansen on *Fram,* had snapped. He became delirious, and there was nothing Bjoervig could do for him. For eight weeks Bjoervig tended to feeding and keeping the two of them warm, while Bentzen hazily passed from one hallucination to the next.

When Wellman and the polar dash team finally trudged to the advance hut on February 27, two weeks late, Bentzen had been dead since January 2. Bentzen's final request was that Bjoervig not allow his body to be scavenged by bears, so Bjoervig had lain at night for two months in a small dark snow cave, in his sleeping bag, next to another sleeping bag containing a frozen corpse.

"I marveled," wrote Wellman, "that Bjoervig was still sane."[35]

Bentzen was buried under a cairn of rocks, and Bjoervig spent an entire day in temperatures of 44° F below zero collecting smaller stones, "patiently chinking up all the little interstices between the rocks which covered the grave."[36] Bjoervig carved a cross and placed it over the grave.

B. Bentzen, Dod 2–1, '99

Wellman's enthusiasm waned again. The polar dash ground to a halt on March 22, 1899, only seventy-five miles north of the advance hut. There, an "ice-quake" broke the surrounding pack ice into thousands of pieces, and Wellman decided to retreat. On the return to Harmsworth House, Wellman slipped into an ice fissure and suffered a compound fracture of his left leg. It turned gangrenous, and Wellman was bedridden for four months at Harmsworth. While his team explored and discovered a few small islands in the archipelago, Wellman from his bed took the honor of naming them for his patrons, like Alexander Graham Bell.

For the privilege of naming a few islands in a remote Arctic archipelago, Wellman had lost one crewman and would himself be left with a permanent limp. Legions of explorers had done worse. He wrote at the time that "it is only by sledging that anyone now proposes to reach the North Pole. . . . [since] Andrée's disastrous attempt to find a royal aeronautical road . . . no one else is likely to try that method."[37] But Wellman himself had had enough of the pack ice. He would never go north again without an airship. He determined to follow Andrée along the "royal" air route to the Pole.

*B*ack in the United States, fully two years passed before Wellman recovered his health. Broke, he lectured and wrote to pay his expedition's debts. Slowly he regained both health and solvency. "I determined," he wrote of his recuperation, "to watch the progress of the arts and mechanics to see if some better means than the primitive sledge could not be found for advancing upon the Pole."[38] Ill and poor, he had few other options left. Luckily, between 1899 and 1905, Wellman witnessed an explosion of developing technology. For, as Andrée's *Eagle* figuratively and literally passed into a long polar night, the nascent technology of *la ballon dirigible* was beginning its long road to refinement.

*W*hile Wellman passed the summer and fall of 1898 at Harmsworth House in Franz Josef Land, in Paris, a diminutive and remarkable Brazilian named Alberto Santos-Dumont on September 20 attached a two-cylinder tricycle engine to the basket of a balloon and made it *dirigible*. Slung far beneath its sausage-shaped air bag, Santos-Dumont in his basket steered this dirigible *No. 1* in any direction he chose.

Little more than two years later, in one of history's greatest flights, Santos-Dumont captured a prize of 100,000 francs by piloting the first flying machine around the Eiffel Tower. His 108-foot-long dirigible *No. 6* turned the round trip of about seven miles in less than thirty minutes. Instead of a basket suspended by cables from the balloon, Santos-Dumont built a long metal keel made of triangular sections. He could remain as navigator-observer at the front of the keel, while the 15-hp engine stayed a comfortable and safe distance to the rear. By 1903, Santos had developed a pat technique, and fascinated Parisians could witness his *No. 9* landing at a *terrace de café* alongside the Bois de Bologne, whereupon Santos leisurely took lunch before lifting off for home.

Wellman of course knew all about these graceful flights. But if Santos-Dumont was an aeronautical artist who operated on a scale too small to suit Wellman's polar ambitions, in Germany the brilliant Count Ferdinand von Zeppelin painted on far too large a canvas.

Construction of von Zeppelin's *Luftschiff Zeppelin 1* began in 1899. The completed 420-foot behemoth was gently maneuvered out of its floating hangar at Lake Constance on July 2, 1900. Radically new in design, it had seventeen drum-shaped cells inside a huge cylindrical tube of metal and fabric, which gave the Zeppelin rigid internal structure and a unique external shape. Although four times as large as Santos-Dumont's *No. 6, LZ-1* was powered by less than twice the horsepower. With virtually no control surfaces, no large fins or rudders, the giant was as uncontrollable as it was underpowered. Its first flight, with the count at the helm, lasted only eighteen minutes. The count attempted only one more flight before he dismantled the

LZ-1. Four years of struggle passed before von Zeppelin, with re-plenished funds and better engines, built his second airship.

For Wellman, a Zeppelin was far too expensive a proposition. He needed some middle ground between the craft of Santos-Dumont and those of von Zeppelin. It had to be a large airship, but perhaps half the size of the *LZ-1,* with an enclosed cabin to protect the crew against polar winds, and with reliable engines.

Wellman's dream came true in the creation of French engineer Henri Juillot and the brothers Paul and Pierre Lebaudy, who completed a nonrigid 190-foot-long dirigible at Moisson in 1902. The *Lebaudy* had a steel tube keel after the style of Santos-Dumont, and a 35-hp engine propelled the airship with more power than *LZ-1's* two engines combined.

The *Lebaudy* flew the thirty-eight miles from Moisson to Paris on November 12, 1903, more than a month before the brothers Wright succeeded in coaxing a biplane eight hundred feet. Little wonder then that Wellman (echoing other lighter-than-air enthusiasts) wrote that the aeroplane would never amount to more than "a limited social ve-hicle . . . [which] does not bid fair in any sort of degree to take the place of the bicycle."[39] Wellman was not alone in this feeling at century's turn. Not until late in the decade could aeronauts write with confi-dence that "the aeroplane will supercede [sic] all other forms of craft in the navigation of the air . . . [because] the aeroplane will weather strong winds in such a way that the dirigible balloon will never do."[40]

*W*hile covering the Russo-Japanese peace conference in Ports-mouth, New Hampshire, in September of 1905, Wellman read fa-vorable notices about a French dirigible built by the Lebaudy brothers. It seemed to Wellman just the machine to reach the Pole without the well-chronicled dangers and miseries of travel by sledge over the polar pack. By the end of the year, Wellman had persuaded Victor Lawson, owner of the *Record-Herald,* to pledge $75,000 toward the construction of an airship similar to the *Lebaudy* that could make an attempt on the pole.

On New Year's Eve the *Record-Herald* announced the airship ex-pedition to the North Pole. By early January Wellman was en route to Paris to consult with Santos-Dumont. The bulk of Wellman's time for the next four years of his life would be divided between aero-nautical concerns in Paris and his advance base on Danes Island, Spits-bergen, and his thoughts would focus on how to best use the vast amount of money Lawson had provided. Unlike Peary, Wellman was all too aware that, nearing age fifty, he would never walk to the North

10. *An unidentified individual stands in the basket of Wellman's 1906 airship car at Virgo Harbor. Once again, the links between the explorer, his sponsoring newspaper, the North Pole, and his nationality are clear. (Courtesy of the Norwegian Polar Institute archives.)*

Pole. His only hope was to buy or develop the technology required to overcome his physical limitations and circumvent the ice that stood between him and his objective. (Much later in the twentieth century, a famous character from science fiction, Captain James T. Kirk, would call it "changing the conditions of the test.") Like Amundsen two decades hence, Wellman would use the airship as a vehicle for extending his career as an explorer by more than a decade.

By March of 1906, Wellman had subscribed the support of the National Geographic Society, the French Academy of Sciences, even the support of President Theodore Roosevelt himself. Combined with Lawson's money, this support enabled the construction in Paris of an airship and, on a remote corner of Spitsbergen, less than seven hundred miles from the North Pole, of a large airship hangar and expedition base camp.

The Spitsbergen site, on Danes Island, occupied the same famous shoreline as the abandoned balloon shed from which Andrée attempted his polar flight in 1897. Though Wellman had some experience in the Arctic by now, through the *Ragnvald Jarl* and Franz Josef Land misadventures, his knowledge and application of what he knew of polar geography and meteorology was if anything more suspect than that of Andrée. Wellman therefore proceeded to spend a lot of Victor Lawson's money vigorously repeating each and every one of Andrée's mistakes.

At the National Geographic Society, Alexander Graham Bell—after whom Wellman had named an island in Franz Josef Land in 1899—made a motion to support Wellman's polar flight, and U.S. Navy Rear Admiral Chester Colby, who would later figure in the society's "endorsement" of Peary's claim to the Pole, seconded it. The society, less than twenty years into its existence, "heartily" approved the plan and appointed Major Henry E. Hersey to lead a scientific party that would add some legitimacy to the whole venture. Like Evelyn Briggs Baldwin, Hersey was a meteorologist for the U.S. Weather Bureau, and by the end of the Spanish-American War he was a ranking major among Teddy Roosevelt's Rough Riders.

In Paris to initiate and observe the construction of his airship, Wellman was his usual irrepressibly optimistic and obliviously preoccupied self. He consulted with Santos-Dumont, dined with Juillot, and introduced himself to those who had some knowledge of dirigibles— maybe not every last Frenchman with a sliver of an idea how a dirigible should be built and operated, but enough of them to lay yet another patina of respectability over the project.

A reporter for the Paris newspaper *L'Univers et Le Monde* caught up with Wellman during this whirlwind. "His straight figure, open forehead, sharp glance, almost scrutinizing, from eyes behind glasses, denote in this Anglo-Saxon a will power and a power of endurance that are uncommon. . . . One sees that Mr. Wellman, like most of his countrymen, is a daring man."[41]

The daring American entrusted the considerable contract to build the medium-size airship to a French aeronaut and balloon and airship builder named Louis Godard. The engineer designed a dirigible

E CHICAGO RECORD-

NO. 284. THURSDAY MORNING, APRIL 5, 1906—SIXTEEN PAGES

NEWS OF THE MORNING.

THURSDAY, APRIL 5, 1906.

Forecast for Chicago and vicinity—Generally fair to-day and to-morrow; not much change in temperature; variable winds. Maximum temperature for the twenty-four hours ended at 9 o'clock last night, 60 degrees at midnight; minimum, 40 at 7 p. m. Sun rises at 5:29, sets at 6:20; moon sets at 3:34 a. m.

CHICAGO ELECTION.

Mayor and his advisers all favor an early test of the validity of Mueller certificates in the court as the necessary stepping stone to municipal ownership. Page 1.

Mayor Dunne is to be given control of the local transportation committee in the reorganization of the new city council. Page 2.

Traction people regard the result of Tuesday's election as highly favorable to their interests and expect a proposition from Mayor Dunne. Page 2.

Stanley H. Kuns expresses satisfaction at his defeat at the polls, while John Schermann, his successor, shows — ——. Page 8.

Former Governor Yates to be open his ten days' senatorial campaign in Chicago this evening, speaking first in Governor Deneen's ward. Congressman Mann will also begin his speaking to-night. Page 9.

DOMESTIC.

Wireless messages from the north pole to THE CHICAGO RECORD-HERALD, in case the Wellman airship expedition reaches the pole, are promised to Mr. Wellman by the American De Forest Wireless Telegraph Com-

WIRELESS TO REACH TO THE NORTH POLE

World to Be Kept in Touch With Wellman Throughout Airship Trip.

TO SEND IN THREE RELAYS

De Forest Company Promises Messages From Most Northerly Point Reached

[SPECIAL TO THE RECORD-HERALD.]
NEW YORK, April 4.—"If you reach the north pole with your great airship we promise to give you the means of sending a wireless message from the pole to THE RECORD-HERALD."

This is what Dr. Abraham White, presi-

PRIEST DIES AT ALTAR DURING FUNERAL MASS

Stricken by Heart Disease, He Falls Across Casket Containing Body of Parishioner, Slips to Floor and Expires.

[SPECIAL TO THE RECORD-HERALD.]
CRAWFORDSVILLE, Ind., April 4.—Stricken with heart failure while chanting the requiem high mass at the funeral of Mrs Catherine Kelley to-day, Rev. John Dempsey, pastor, of St. Bernard's Roman Catholic Church, fell across the casket, writhed a moment in pain, slipped to the floor and died with his head resting on the steps of the altar.

Father Dempsey was seen to hesitate a moment in the service, but regained his voice for a time and was in the midst of the mass when, without warning, he fell. He was dead before any of the parishioners could reach his side.

CHURCH SCENE DRAMATIC.

The mourners thought at first that he had merely fainted, but when the truth became known there was a dramatic scene in the church. Several women fainted, and others ran up and down the aisles wringing their hands and sobbing. Father Dempsey was beloved throughout the parish, and his death, coupled with that of Mrs. Kelley, who, by a singular coincidence, also was a victim of heart disease, caused general sorrow.

The body of the dead priest was carried to the parsonage and the funeral party proceeded with the remains of Mrs. Kelley

BRAVES PERIL OF AIR ONLY TO DIE IN A BOG

Paul Nocquet, Sculptor Aeronaut, Perishes of Exposure on Long Island.

BODY IS FOUND IN MARSH

Terrible Trip Across Icy Creeks and Through Mud Made Amid the Darkness

[SPECIAL TO THE RECORD-HERALD.]
NEW YORK, April 4.—Death from exertion and exposure in the marshes along the south shore of Long Island after escaping the danger of being carried out to sea in his balloon which dashed to pieces in trying to make a landing was the fate of Paul

11. *Wellman's goal was not just to reach the North Pole, but to reach the Pole and send back the first newspaper dispatch from the top of the world. From the front page of the* Chicago Record-Herald, *April 5, 1906. (From the author's collection.)*

with remarkably similar dimensions to the modern GZ-19 Goodyear blimp *Mayflower*. Its obvious differences were in its volume (224,000 cubic ft. of hydrogen, compared with the 147,000 cubic ft. of helium in *Mayflower*), in a conspicuous absence of control surfaces aft, and in power (75 hp for Wellman's ship, 350 hp for *Mayflower*). But the length and diameter of Wellman's craft (164 ft. and 52.5 ft.) were very close to those of *Mayflower* (160 ft. and 51 ft.).

Godard completed the gasbag and accompanying components for the polar airship in Paris in late spring of 1906. Wellman, continuing the upside-down patriotism that had led Andrée to name *his* Paris-built balloon *Sweden* (and would later lead Amundsen to name his Italian airship *Norge*), promptly christened his new French product *America*.

Wellman would eventually oversee the construction or modification of four different versions of the French airship he christened *America*. The airship historian Herman Van Dyk suggests that the 1906 Godard version be termed *America 1*. The complete reworking of the ship done by Melvin Vaniman in 1907 Van Dyk calls *America 2A*, while Vaniman's 1909 modifications, mostly to the rudder arrangement, he calls *America 2B*. Finally, there is Wellman's 1910 transatlantic airship, *America 3*. Historians of these flights would do well to employ this simple and effective system for identifying the four Wellman airships.

Wellman had the engines run up and they seemed to perform better than expected, but he never had the engines attached to the proposed car, nor the completed car attached to the airship and the whole assembly test-flown. Given its low power and little maneuverability, the blimp's chances of reaching the pack ice were slim enough, without further dooming the attempt by leaving the airship untested. Wellman had promised *National Geographic* he would not make the attempt until his gear was in "the best possible order,"[42] but he put off any trial flights until *America* was assembled and test-flown in Spitsbergen.

More than one observer saw failure written all over this procedure. A week after the announcement of the expedition, the *Record-Herald* quoted Ernest Leffingwell, a thirty-one-year-old doctoral candidate in geology at the University of Chicago and scientific leader of the 1901–1902 expedition to Franz Josef Land led by Wellman's old No. 2, Evelyn Briggs Baldwin, as maintaining that the airship, if properly tested, matched the Arctic environment perfectly. More, Leffingwell offered Wellman the only kind of appropriate scientific rationale that could possibly justify such a risky operation. Namely, that the airship served as an ideal platform for visual geographic observation and photographic remote sensing of the Arctic regions, regardless of whether or not it reached the Pole. Wellman ignored this excellent suggestion on four successive airship expeditions and thus lost the opportunity to enter history as a true scientific pioneer.

> Even if Mr. Wellman does not reach the Pole, he will traverse a large unexplored area. That, in itself, will make the expedition worth all the expenditure and risk required . . . Those on the Wellman expedition will be able to get a bird's-eye view of the area traversed. Their view will not be obstructed by piles of snow and ice, as is that of men in sledges. The geographical results alone ought to be enough to make the Wellman expedition truly great. . . .
>
> If [Wellman] first demonstrates, in the temperate zone, that he can travel 700 miles to a definite point by means of a dirigible balloon, then [he] will not be taking large chances. I am not an expert in aeronautics, but I am certain that unless [he] first demonstrates ability to travel a long distance, they will be taking desperate chances. But if they can do this, then they will have the very best possible method of polar travel. If they once get an airship to the Pole, there will be no question about the return trip—the wind will blow them back to civilization.[43]

12. *Camp Wellman under construction in the summer of 1906. The sailing vessel* Frithjof *can be seen at anchor in Virgo Harbor, along with three cruisers carrying Arctic tourists lured by the chance to see Wellman's airship launch toward the Pole. One of the vessels may be Prince Albert of Monaco's research yacht,* Princess Alice, *which visited Virgo Harbor in 1906. (Courtesy of the Norwegian Polar Institute archives.)*

But Wellman conducted no tests in the "temperate zone," for he considered them irrelevant. No glorious headlines awaited him after any kind of "trial" flight from Paris to Berlin, say, or Warsaw, perhaps, or Bamboola, for that matter. The only terminus that mattered to Wellman and his readers was the one at 90° N, the one that he and Peary and Cook and Abruzzi and Nansen had all been seeking for two decades. But unlike all those others, Wellman was attempting to race toward the Pole in a machine that had never been tested in such an environment.

Soon after Godard completed the airship, Wellman sent Major Hersey north in *Frithjof,* the old ship from the Franz Josef Land expedition, to establish a base camp and build a hangar on Danes Island, on the shores of a harbor used by Danish whalers more than two centuries earlier. One mile across a strait that separated Danes Island from Amsterdam Island lay the abandoned whaling station at Smeerenburg, "scattered about among the rocks on the low point of land, only a few Dutch tiles and ruins of stone walls mark the site of the dead and almost forgotten settlement," observed Wellman.[44]

Once on the island, Hersey and his advance team spent most of June waiting for surcease from spring snowstorms. For a week,

Hersey blasted away at the rock and ice along the shore until he had cleared nearly a football-field-size area for the floor of the airship hangar. The hangar when completed would stand 85 feet tall; it would be 82 feet wide and 190 feet long. As it happened, many of the finely hewn Scandinavian timbers from Andrée's balloon shed were lying about, and they were drafted by Hersey for use as the floor of Wellman's hangar. "Thus again," wrote Wellman, "was the site of Andrée's ill-fated enterprise to be the scene of strange activity."[45]

Hersey brought with him not only hundreds of tons of timber and iron for the hangar and ancillary buildings, but over 125 tons of sulfuric acid and 75 tons of scrap iron filings, which when combined with 30 tons of "apparatus and other chemicals" produced hydrogen for the airship.[46] In addition to this enormous load, which required three round trips to Tromsø and back by the ice-steamer *Frithjof,* the base camp was outfitted with "half a ship-load of provisions; the aeronautic machine and all its appurtenances: dog-sledges, motor-sledges, a steam boiler and engine, tons of gasolene, tools, coal, iron rods, bolts, nails, steel boats, and all the paraphernalia of what a London periodical aptly termed 'Mr. Wellman's scientific village in the Arctics.'"[47] There was also a forge for molding the iron rods that would stay the wooden arches of the hangar.

One of the ancillary buildings became Wellman's headquarters, "the best and most scientifically heated and ventilated house in the true Arctics,"[48] as Wellman described it, where forty scientific staff, engineers, aeronauts, mechanics, sailors, and workmen eventually gathered. This building, the ruins of which can still be seen on Danes Island, is called Wellmanhuset (the Wellman House) by the Norwegians. Wellman named it the Chicago Record-Herald House. Other structures included a machine shop and its lathes, drills, and other tools; the boiler house, steam engine, steam pump; and, finally, the shed containing the gas apparatus to inflate the dirigible.

To facilitate the sending of dispatches to the outside world, Wellman had three independent wireless stations constructed. Station No. 1 was built at Hammerfest in Norway and connected there to the station at Tromsø and its connection with the Atlantic cable. Station No. 2 was inside the Chicago Record-Herald House, six hundred miles north of Hammerfest. Station No. 3 was on board the dirigible itself; its wireless, the journalist envisioned, would broadcast the news from nearly seven hundred miles north of his base camp that the airship had reached the Pole. Should he reach the Pole, Wellman was taking no chances that his story would be scooped. In the end, the complicated radio seldom worked, though it hardly mattered since Wellman produced nothing in the way of urgent news.

A dozen sledge dogs arrived, Wellman reported, from "the habitat of the Samoyed tribes on the Arctic shores of the River Ob in Siberia,"[49] in the event *America* was forced down onto the ice pack. The airship was also provided with more modern "appurtenances," such as "barographs, statoscopes, manometers, and other instruments which speak to [the pilot] of the ever-varying moods and conditions of the parts and vitals of his complex machine."[50] It is no wonder, then, with all this extraordinary activity on such a remote shore, that a member of Wellman's 1909 polar expedition would remember many years later: "Tromsø people used to say that they had three main industries: Fishing, coaling trawlers & cargo boats for the White Sea trade, and the Wellman Expedition!!!"[51]

To complete the metaphor of a real-life Verne-like expedition, Wellman borrowed liberally from Verne himself. Like the prophetic fictional voyages authored by the man who died at Amiens, France, in 1905—the year before Wellman constructed his polar airship base on Danes Island—the polar dirigible journey would prove "the superiority of a true airship . . . a cruiser of the air with engines in her hold, a rudder at her stern, and many leagues of steaming in her bunkers."[52]

"The aeronautic experts of France [believe] that . . . Andrée met his fate partly through faulty construction of his balloon," Wellman wrote in Paris.[53] It seemed never to have occurred to him that whatever happened to Andrée—and still, in 1906, almost a decade after Andrée's flight had begun, no one knew for certain—happened because the Swede never tested his balloon before he tried to fly it to the North Pole. No matter how refined Andrée's technology was, he had placed himself and two others in a balloon whose first test flight was also its maiden voyage. Regardless of whatever initial costs served to deter such testing, there could ultimately be no economy so costly, since the failure of untested machinery over the polar pack invariably meant failure at best; at worst, death. But Wellman saw things differently. To him, a successful test of a balloon in Paris would mean little or nothing, since the experimental conditions were so different from those of the Arctic.

"I believe the builder of Andrée's balloon [Henri Lachambre], who is now dead, was a careful and conscientious man," Wellman wrote. "But . . . I was determined to avoid such mistakes if care and prudence and outlay could suffice to do it."[54] They could indeed, if Wellman had bothered to use them. At the earliest he would not arrive at Spitsbergen much before July, and the balloon not be readied until

13. *Walter Wellman in Christiania (later renamed Oslo), Norway, in the late spring of 1906. He is standing on the deck of the 1906 airship car built by Godard. Eighty-seven years later, the remains of this car were identified by the author at Virgo Harbor using this photograph: the eyebolt between the letters R in POLAR and E in EXPEDITION still survives at Virgo Harbor. (Courtesy of the Library of Congress.)*

WELLMAN FLIGHT SOON, IF WEATHER IS GOOD

Big Balloon House Nearing Completion — Head of Record-Herald Expedition Sends Roosevelt Greeting.

BY WALTER WELLMAN.

[SPECIAL CABLE DISPATCH TO THE CHICAGO RECORD-HERALD.]

DANE'S ISLAND, Spitsbergen, July 23 (via DeForest Wireless Telegraph to Hammerfest, Norway, July 23).—The big balloon house, in which the great airship will be sheltered, is now lifting its walls toward the sky.

The result is that we feel greatly encouraged by the rapidity with which the work goes on.

If the weather remains favorable, as at present, we shall have an excellent chance of getting away for the pole this summer.

WELLMAN.

✦ ✦ ✦

[BY THE ASSOCIATED PRESS.]

OYSTER BAY, N. Y., July 23.—A dispatch was received by President Roosevelt to-day from Walter Wellman, who is at the head of the Wellman-Chicago Record-Herald expedition. The dispatch was dated at Hammerfest, July 21, and read as follows:

"Roosevelt, Washington. Greetings, best wishes by first wireless message ever sent from arctic regions.

"WELLMAN."

14. *The first wireless messages ever transmitted from the Arctic. Wellman's messages to the* Chicago Record-Herald *and to President Roosevelt, July 1906, from the front page of the* Chicago Record-Herald, *July 24, 1906. (From the author's collection.)*

15. Wellman visits with Prince Albert of Monaco on board the latter's research yacht, Princess Alice, *which visited Virgo Harbor in 1906. (From* The Aerial Age.*)*

considerably later. Failure to test the airship in Paris meant that, as with Andrée's balloon, the first test flight of Wellman's airship would be on a voyage to the North Pole.

"If upon being carefully tested the dirigible is found to be in fit condition for the voyage, an effort to reach the Pole will be made this year," *National Geographic* assured its readers in the spring of 1906. "If not, the flight over the Arctic Ocean will be deferred till next year."[55] This proviso gave Wellman immunity from having to do any testing in Paris. If nothing worked when he arrived at Spitsbergen, he could write off the expedition as a necessary step in Science's development of the technology, and speed home before the cold set in.

On Danes Island, the pace of the work slowed to a crawl. After the flurry of activity clearing the area for the hangar, Major Hersey and the advance party did little more than rename Andrée's base on the rock-bound shore of Virgo Harbor "Camp Wellman." When Wellman himself arrived, several weeks behind Hersey, he was full of expectation at the thought of steaming into the harbor and seeing a huge airship hangar. But he was greeted instead by only the splintered remains of Andrée's balloon shed.

A German flag fluttered over a small green tent, and inside the tent a journalist-friend of Wellman's named Otto von Gottberg of the *Berlin Lokal Anzeiger* had set up his own camp. "We were . . . indeed old friends," wrote Wellman, "and had sat at the same table at Wentworth Hotel, Portsmouth, during the Russo-Japanese Conference. . . . Herr von Gottberg [had] absorbed from American papers the false notion that we were working this Expedition as an advertising affair."[56] Wellman determined to prove his colleagues wrong.

Wellman asked the Norwegian carpenters to work fourteen-hour shifts laying a foundation and putting down the floor, but the hangar did not scrape the sky until August, and then only because Wellman ordered the carpenters to reduce the number of eighty-five-foot-high arches supporting it from nine to five. The envelope of the dirigible remained on the shore unpacked, much less inflated. The engines, attached to the car and test-fired, promptly self-destructed. "[They] could not be made to work right," Wellman complained. "The driving gear went to pieces, and the propeller could not stand even half the strain which it was designed to put upon them."[57] Of course, Wellman would have known this would happen if he had bothered to check his equipment in Paris. Instead, he waited until the useless car and engines were shipped two thousand miles north.

The excitement of the early summer drifted away on the cold winds of late August. The expedition crew passed much of its time watching a group of Dutch sailors, sent by their government to Spitsbergen to collect the remains of early Dutch sailors laid to rest above the permafrost. They then gave the remains a proper burial, a morose allegory to the 1906 Wellman–*Chicago Record-Herald* North Pole Expedition encamped just across the strait.

As at the advance hut in Franz Josef Land, Wellman left a small detachment from his crew in charge of Camp Wellman for the winter, led by Felix Riesenberg of Columbia University, a former officer in the U.S. Revenue Cutter Service, one of the forerunner agencies of the U.S. Coast Guard. Wellman himself then embarked for more favorable climes. His first thought was not of correcting his deficient gear but of rivals. "The yellow journals [spread the impression] that we were purposely delaying the voyage which we had come up here to make!" Determined to reveal his critics as fakes, Wellman returned to Paris and planned what he called "the campaign of 1907."[58] As *Frithjof* sliced the waters southward toward Norway, Wellman took heart, moreover, that no one, neither on foot nor by air, had yet reached the Pole.

America was as solid a gasbag as the world had seen, but the engines and the car had to go. Wellman met an American engineer by the name of Melvin Vaniman and put him in charge of these modifications. If not an inventive genius, Vaniman was at the least an individual of great cleverness, a violinist, and something of an international aeronautical vagabond. The government at New South

16. *Melvin Vaniman and Walter Wellman (in top hat) stand next to an unidentified individual and beneath Vaniman's redesigned polar airship car, outside Paris in the spring of 1909. (From* The Aerial Age.*)*

Wales had commissioned him to photograph Sydney harbor from the air. With the funds from the commission he bought his first balloon. He then went to Paris in 1904 to improve his aeronautical technique, and it was there that he met Walter Wellman.

*I*n Paris, Vaniman scrapped the original Godard car and designed one of his own. He built the new car with steel tubing and steel-reinforced wood, 115 feet long and 12 feet wide at its open top. The car tapered inward from the top, down to a narrow catwalk, underneath which a long steel 1,200-gallon fuel tank formed the keel. He wrapped the car in oiled silk to protect the crew from wind, and mounted a more powerful engine to the car. For engines, he selected a Lorraine-Dietrich 75 hp, and mounted two propellers, not fore and aft, but side by side, on booms riding out from the sides of the car.

To conserve and make use of hydrogen that might be valved as the gasbag expanded during ascent, Vaniman invented a carburetor for the Lorraine-Dietrich engine that with the flip of a lever changed it from a clanky petrol-powered plant to a smooth-running hydrogen-powered engine. Unfortunately, this invention was too brilliant by half. It is believed that a similar arrangement, mounted by Vaniman in 1912 on another airship, the original *Akron,* led to his death when hydrogen shunted into his unique carburetor mixed with air and created an instantaneous fireball five hundred feet in the air. Vaniman was on board at the time and was the one who threw the switch.

Wellman also insisted that Vaniman saddle what was shaping into a reasonably stout airship with two of his own dubious creations. Before he did so, *America* was cut in half, and a twenty-foot-long section of rubberized fabric was added to the gasbag. This increased *America*'s length to 185 feet and added another ton of lifting power. *America* could now lift over nineteen thousand pounds and would henceforth be identified in photographs by the twenty-foot-long band of off-color cloth amidships. With added power, maneuverability, and lift, with the new solar sextant and drift indicators invented by Vaniman, *America* could now theoretically remain aloft for fifteen days and propel itself on the strength of 1,200 gallons of gas for five of those fifteen days. Wellman then inadvertently ensured it would never get the chance to prove it.

Following Andrée's dubious idea of using guide-ropes, in the mistaken belief that the only way to prevent hydrogen loss at high altitude was to remain tethered in some way to the earth, Wellman invented two long draglines of his own. The first, an extravagant sort of ice anchor, Wellman called a *retardateur,* a long rope covered at its tip with spikes. *America* could not fight strong headwinds, so when adverse winds began to buffet the ship, the retardateur would be thrown down to the pack ice, the spikes would lock in the ice, and backsliding would be prevented. In this way, *America* could grapple-hook its way to the Pole.

The second dragline was inexplicably designed to counteract each of *America*'s forward-moving strengths. Wellman called this line an *equilabrator,* a heavy leather tube 120 feet long and 8 inches in diameter, stuffed with half a ton of reserve provisions. Thousands of overlapping steel scales covered its outer skin, riveted to the leather to give strength when dragged across the ice at the end of a long steel cable running from the car. Wellman believed the equilabrator would act as "recoverable ballast." When photons hit the gasbag, the hydrogen gas inside expanded. Expanded hydrogen increased its lifting power and forced the airship up. But rather than pushing *America* to a height where it would have to valve gas in order to avoid bursting at pressure-height, the sausagelike equilabrator, trailing along behind *America,* would cause so much drag that the dirigible would never rise anywhere close to pressure-height. And when cold temperatures and fog contracted hydrogen and reduced its lift, more and more of the equilabrator would rest on the ice, its weight not directly bearing upon the airship. The craft would stabilize and move forward at a constant height. For someone who had little good to say about Andrée's balloon and its design, Wellman slavishly copied *Eagle*'s most obvious flaw.

Pressure-height should have been the farthest contingency from Wellman's mind. *America* could lift over nine tons, but more than half of this would be taken by the weight of the gasoline, and much of the remaining lift would be used for raising the car, a ton and a half of supplies and provisions, the crew, sledges and sledge dogs, a boat, and instruments. What little sunlight there was in an Arctic summer was more often than not diffused through storms and a nagging, impenetrable fog. It presented little danger of heating *America*'s hydrogen to the extent feared by Wellman—and Andrée before him on board *Eagle*. And even if it did, *America* had sufficient reserve lift to be able to valve off hydrogen if the airship rose too high. If he had set out to invent a ball and chain that would keep him from reaching his goal, Wellman could not have done better than the equilabrator. Both he and Andrée fell prey to the simple, and simpleminded, notion that twenty-four hours of *daylight* in the summer Arctic automatically guaranteed twenty-four hours of *sunlight*.

Wellman, to the contrary, sang the equilibrator's praises. "A steel-scaled serpent," he called it, "half a ton of food in his belly, swimming upon the water or gliding over the surface of the ice in the wake of the big ship overhead."[59] For a man who walked with a permanent limp as a direct result of twisted, irregular ice pack, Wellman had no qualms that a 120-foot-long metal-encrusted leather anchor would not drag but would "glide" over the ice, as if the polar sea were little more than a large hockey rink. But the equilabrator, the retardateur, even the props of Wellman's engines—he called them *propulseurs,* after the French word that was later shortened by English-speaking pilots—all convinced him that he was grandly substituting science and technology for brute force.

With *America* nearing completion, Wellman took several free-balloon flights over the French countryside. And though he extolled the virtues of the successful French dirigibles, such as the Lebaudy brothers' *La Patrie,* he apparently never made any effort to ride in one of them, not even to see how "a real cruiser of the air" handled in the air. The noise seemed to bother him. "[Free] ballooning is a most delightful sport," he wrote of his Paris flights, "being free from the nerve-racking vibration and anxiety which one feels in a motor-driven ship."[60]

It is hard to tell how Wellman could have made this observation, since he'd never ridden in a motor-driven balloon. And he would not do so until he made his attempt on the Pole.

17. *A view of Camp Wellman taken by a German expedition in 1910, showing the hydrogen apparatus and machine shop in the foreground and how the hangar was rebuilt with nine arches in 1907, to replace the five arches that collapsed in the winter of 1906–1907. (From A. Miethe and H. Hergesell,* Mit Zeppelin nach Spitzbergen, *via Dr. Cornelia Lüdecke.)*

"*B*efore anyone permits himself to join the ranks of the ill-informed in imagining that our project is visionary, or reckless, or insincere, or unscientific, he will do well, for his own sake, to learn a little of what . . . we know," Wellman importuned in the spring of 1907 before heading north again. Unabashed as ever, he energetically preempted criticism from every corner. "Some day in July or August, 1907," he continued, "a man standing at the northwestern point of Spitsbergen . . . will behold a strange and wonderful spectacle. He will see, rising from a little pocket of land amidst the snow-capped hills of Danes Island, an enormous airship [with] its nose pointed northward."[61]

Frithjof arrived back at Virgo Harbor in late June 1907, and just as Andrée had found his balloon shed intact when he returned to it in 1897, Wellman's hangar was still standing. The forty guy wires and five slim arches had held through the winds of an Arctic winter. The hangar greeted its creator by promptly and unpatriotically collapsing in a Fourth of July gale. Wellman was now paying the price for cutting corners to rush the construction of the hangar in 1906. Had he built the hangar with the nine arches designed to support it, possibly his luck would have held—luck, as they say, being the residue of hard work. It took four weeks to rebuild the hangar, this time with nine cross-braced arches.

The weather throughout August was atrocious, not at all like the mild summer of 1906. With *America 2A* inflated and the new car attached in mid-August, the expedition crew waited for the winds to quiet. August came and went, and still the airship remained tethered in its shed. The winds did not abate until early September, by which time the expedition should have been on its way home for the winter.

But Walter Wellman already had three ineffectual Arctic summers behind him. He had already boasted in the periodicals that his airship would be seen in the summer of 1907 over the polar sea, and knew that recriminations would be heavy if he returned to Chicago with nothing to show the *Record-Herald* after two years and tens of thousands of dollars spent.

On September 2, 1907, Wellman ordered *America* out of its hangar.

Page one of the newspaper of record for Sunday, September 15, 1907, told what happened next:

WELLMAN'S AIRSHIP TRAVELED 15 MILES

BERLIN, Sept. 14—Walter Wellman has sent the following cablegram to the *Lokal Anzeiger* from Tromsøe:

AFTER THE STEAMER *EXPRESS* CAST OFF THE CABLE, THE BALLOON *AMERICA* DID EXCELLENTLY, BUT AN INCREASING WIND SOON GAVE US A HARD STRUGGLE, AND THE STORM DROVE US TOWARD SOME HIGH, JAGGED MOUNTAINS NEAR THE COAST, WHERE THE AIRSHIP WOULD HAVE BEEN DESTROYED IF SHE STRUCK.

THERE ENSUED A HARD FIGHT BETWEEN THE STORM AND THE MOTOR. THE LATTER TRIUMPHED.[62]

Express, a small German steamer, had been sent north with a complement of German army officers to observe the proceedings at Camp Wellman. *America* and its polar mission had caused a ripple of excitement in Germany, since Wellman's airship ranked second only to Count von Zeppelin's *LZ-2* as the largest dirigible in the world. Zeppelin himself would organize an expedition to Spitsbergen in 1910 to investigate the possibility of establishing lighter-than-air stations there.

After *America* was hauled out of the hangar, a towline attached it to *Express.* The steamer pulled *America* past Smeerenburg Point, past the remains of the seventeenth-century whalers, newly entombed by conscientious descendants, and once clear of land, Wellman gave

18. *Wellman orders the polar airship* America *out of its hangar, September 1907. (From* The Aerial Age.*)*

the order to cut the line. Vaniman started the engine, and the airship motored off under its own power. The equilabrator trailed in the cold waters below.

Only three men were aboard: Wellman, Vaniman, and Felix Riesenberg, upon whom Wellman had devolved responsibility for the winter camp. They loaded *America* with sledges, a boat, ten months' worth of provisions, 25 gallons of oil, 40 gallons of water, and, in the long steel fuel tank, 1,200 gallons of gasoline.

The airship soon outran *Express* and headed north. Vaniman could look out of the stern of the car while he tended the engines and watch as the steamer disappeared to the south. Just as quickly, the prow of *America* was buffeted by a northwest wind that had all the makings of a squall. The heavy weather pushed the airship back to the jagged northwest Spitsbergen coast, across Smeerenburg Fjord from Danes Island, and the ship narrowly avoided the summit of a mountain that lay like a serrated knife across its path. Vaniman increased power to the engines as much as he dared, but even with all his resourcefulness he could not change the fact that the propellers were grossly inefficient, and the Lorraine-Dietrich engine vastly inadequate for a ship the size of *America*. Vaniman would not live to see the day when Goodyear blimps of roughly the approximate size of Wellman's *America* would operate only in the most favorable weather conditions, with huge rudders and elevators, and six times the horsepower of *America*.

It began to snow.

"The wind . . . increased to twelve miles an hour," Wellman cabled to Berlin, "and the snow fell so thickly that we could not see a quarter of a mile. Just then the compass failed to act owing to defective construction."[63] In *The Aerial Age,* Wellman did not write of construction defects but suggested that the compass "had been deranged by an accident," which he did not bother to describe.[64]

Wellman then heightened the drama for his newspaper's readers. "We were completely lost in a snowstorm above the Polar Sea and threatened with destruction." The latter was certainly true, but they were hardly lost. *America* had flown only four or five miles from Camp Wellman and was being hotly trailed by both *Express* and *Frithjof.* Wellman was discovering for the first time how "a real cruiser of the air," especially one with no tail fins or rudders, handled in a squall. "It was impossible," he wrote, "to keep in one direction."[65]

The Pole was quickly forgotten. The crew was now simply trying to land an out-of-control airship on an ice field in a snowstorm. "[*America*] circled three times in the teeth of the wind . . . [and] the only thing possible was to try to land. With this idea we stopped the motor and let *America* drift over a glacier."[66]

America powered up the glacier. Both the equilabrator and the retardateur scratched along the ice, but the retardateur did not perform the function it was designed to do. When it slipped into a crevasse, it simply slid out again; when it wrapped around a boulder in the moraine, it simply unwrapped. The airship was about a half mile inland, hovering over a glacier, when Vaniman pulled the valvecord to let out hydrogen. As *America* began to settle onto the ice, the engineer pulled another rope attached to a ripping knife, which slashed huge rents in the envelope. One hundred thousand dollars' worth of dirigible and gear came down onto the glacier with a thud. The first powered airship voyage to attempt the Pole had lasted little more than three hours.

The three men sat in the snow next to their mortally wounded dinosaur, until *Express* and *Frithjof* caught up with them. It took three days to rope the airship off the glacier and back to Camp Wellman. The squall continued for several days, so it was providential that *America* had not flown farther than it did. Even Wellman admitted that "we were pretty lucky to get out of it as well as we did."[67]

Wellman then proceeded to claim that this "trial of the ship" "[proved] her power and capability of being steered. The ascent was successful in every respect. . . . . We had no idea of giving up the flight. . . . The *America* is from every standpoint the strongest airship and the most durable for a long journey that has ever been built."[68] How Wellman deduced this from a three-hour flight, which was at

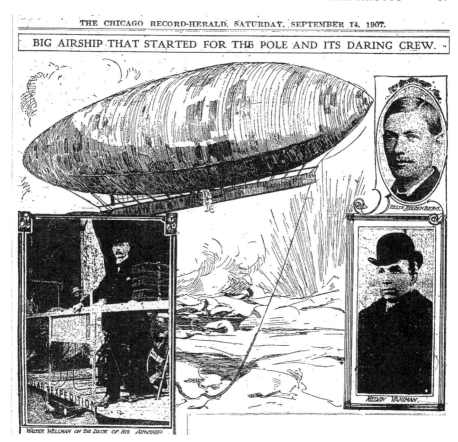

THE CHICAGO RECORD-HERALD. SATURDAY. SEPTEMBER 14. 1907.

BIG AIRSHIP THAT STARTED FOR THE POLE AND ITS DARING CREW.

19. Wellman, Vaniman, and Riesenberg, the first explorers to fly toward the Pole in a motorized airship, September 1907. From the Chicago Record-Herald, *September 14, 1907. (From the author's collection.)*

best an afterthought prior to returning to Paris for the winter, is a mystery. But his motives—to generate headlines and please his sponsor—are clear enough. Camp Wellman was made fast once again, but this time it would have to survive two winters before its inimitable master returned.

"After this successful attempt," wrote Wellman, "we were all convinced that the *America,* in normal Summer weather, can make her way to the Pole."[69] The *Record-Herald,* apparently, was less than impressed. "Mr. Wellman . . . is coming directly to Chicago for consultation," Frank Noyes told the *New York Times.*[70] The *Record-Herald,* after meeting with Wellman, tempered its support for any further adventures and, after sizing the chances of recovering any of its investment—buried under the snows of Spitsbergen, four thousand miles from Chicago—decided that shipping any of Camp Wellman back to the United States was too expensive and ultimately pointless. Before Wellman went north again, the *Record-Herald* gave its reporter the airship and all the trappings of Camp Wellman, free of charge.

From September of 1907 onward, when it came to geographic exploration, Walter Wellman was increasingly on his own.

*T*he *Record-Herald* managed to tether Wellman to its Washington bureau long enough for him to cover the Taft-Bryan election of 1908. Foursquare for the estimable Taft, and therefore satisfied that the outcome ensured the continued survival of the nation for four more years, Wellman after the election planned another flight to the Pole.

*I*n Paris, Vaniman installed another engine in the car of *America* and substituted a triple box rudder system in place of the single rounded rudder of 1907, thus creating, in Van Dyk's system, *America 2B*. Vaniman's brother-in-law, A. L. Loud, joined him in Paris, as did, in April of 1909, a young British airshipman named A. J. Corbitt and a Russian aeronaut named Nicholas Popov. This multinational crew, a forerunner of those assembled later in the century by the ocean raft explorer Thor Heyerdahl, the polar traveler Will Steiger, and others, installed an eight-cylinder E.N.V. engine in the airship and attached it to the propellers by means of swiveling booms invented by Vaniman. These booms allowed the prop wash to be directed up, down, forward, back, "in fact any position of a circle," wrote Corbitt.[71] This simple and ingenious idea escaped other airship designers for nearly thirty years.

In the United States, Wellman distributed a pamphlet that decried his detractors and wrote of the flight to the Pole as if it were already an accomplished fact. Lamenting the predictable dearth of support for another flight—even after his first attempt had gone nowhere and his second barely fifteen miles—Wellman wrote that the results from the "trial trip of 1907" were misunderstood, and he fired off more volleys from the parapets of Science.

> Skepticism was . . . the dominant note among the general public . . . and in this case skepticism found expression in many criticisms and suspicions unworthy of those who voiced them. The prevailing popular belief was that the scheme must be regarded as either foolishly reckless or deliberately dishonest. In other words, this proposal to utilize the progress of the arts and sciences in doing useful work was subject to the same misunderstanding and injustice that ignorance always slings at pioneer endeavors.[72]

And without substantial backing from his newspaper's owner, Victor Lawson, Wellman went fund-raising. As "a believer in the principle that journalism of the best sort is alert and enterprising in trying to do something for progress, I again turned to journalism for financial assistance."[73] He was successful. Popov, a wealthy aristocrat, contributed a large sum to keep the expedition afloat—and secure his place in it. Neither did Wellman's appeals fall on deaf ears in the mahogany offices of J. P. Morgan or Andrew Carnegie. Before long he had the money he needed, and, on June 30, 1909, Wellman, Vaniman, Loud, Popov, Corbitt, and a Russian reporter sailed from Tromsø on another chartered steamer, the *Arctic*. (*Frithjof,* Wellman's faithful ship from the expeditions of 1906 and 1907, had gone down off Iceland the previous year with the loss of all hands.)

*A*rctic arrived in Virgo Harbor the second week in July, and like an old nemesis welcoming the party home, the airship hangar lay collapsed on shore, a tangled piece of wreckage. Having sent his brother Arthur ahead to scout the camp, Wellman was aware of the accident before he embarked. He had brought forty-five Norwegian carpenters and tons of wood north to repair the damage. He paid the Norwegians bonuses to speed their work, and they built a huge derrick with which to raise nine solidly cross-braced arches.

He had also learned that one of the Norwegians left in charge of Camp Wellman during the winter of 1908–1909 had fallen through a hole in the ice, and drowned. Wellman had lost the second man from one of his winter parties.

Corbitt recorded twelve consecutive calm days in July, remarkable for Spitsbergen and more than enough time for a flight to the Pole and back, but the hangar was not finished until early August. *America 2B* was finally inflated and the car in place on the morning of August 15.

"Again we carried dogs, sledges, small boat, and enough provisions and fuel to enable the crew to stay out the whole winter," wrote Wellman, "making a comfortable camp on the ice with the thousands of square yards of cloth of the balloon, and sledging back the following spring, the only season in which travel with sledges is fairly practicable over Arctic sea-ice."[74]

At 10 a.m., August 15, with a slight south wind blowing, *America* was eased out of its hangar. Wellman, Vaniman, Popov, and Loud climbed into the car. At the last moment Wellman ordered Corbitt to stay behind, saying the five would comprise too much weight. The

20. *The polar airship* America *being assembled in the hangar at Virgo Harbor, summer 1909. (Courtesy of the Norwegian Polar Institute archives.)*

fact that Wellman was attempting to drag a 1,200-pound dead weight behind the balloon all the way to the Pole must have done little to temper Corbitt's disappointment.

America's engines were run up. Corbitt took to a small launch, to tow the airship out of Virgo Harbor, but Vaniman's engines soon outran Corbitt. He shouted to Vaniman to cut him loose, and *Amer-*

ica 2B was on its way. Arthur Wellman stood on shore, cranking the handle of a motion picture camera, recording the sight of the dirigible as it moved off past Smeerenburg Point, where its equilabrator dragged slowly over the graves of the Dutch whalers.

"At the wheel I steered her several times around the strait," wrote Wellman. "The engine was running steadily. The equilabrator seemed to be riding well. . . . we were making close to twenty-five knots. . . . At the rate we were going we could reach the Pole in less than thirty hours."[75]

*A*merica responded well at the helm. The Arctic beauty of the Spitsbergen archipelago spread beneath the airship. Vaniman joked with Loud; Popov and Wellman traded grins. Maybe, just maybe, Wellman's hour had struck.

America swung out over Virgo Harbor with Wellman at the helm. He tried first to reach the polar sea through the east passage, Smeerenburg Fjord, but a north breeze through the passage forced *America* too close to shore. Wellman brought the airship around and tried to force it out the west passage with the same result. *America* then dragged its equilabrator across Smeerenburg Point, and after a quarter hour the dirigible was sailing north over open water at a height of 250 feet.

Popov thrilled as he took the helm. "The spectacle was marvelous," he later recalled, "as we looked down upon the tiny islands set in a green sea. . . . Eastward were the great snow-covered mountains and glaciers . . . and northward of us was the limitless sea of ice, just coming into our view. As I stood at the wheel I found that *America* steered well and easily where she had plenty of room. The slightest movement of the wheel was sufficient to turn her up the wind. Our compass course was northwest by north, with the wind from the southwest. . . . We were all happy, believing we had at last overcome all obstacles."[76]

*N*orth of Spitsbergen cruised a Norwegian coast survey steamer named the *Farm* (its name not to be confused, as it so often has been, with Nansen's *Fram*). On board the steamer, Captains Isaksen and Hermansen were on deck around 11 a.m. on August 15, when from the bridge *Farm*'s ice-pilot called out to them. There seemed to be, off to the northwest, a strange flying object.

"What the devil is that?" cried the ice-pilot.

After looking through his field glasses, Isaksen explained that the

21. *Wellman's last chance at the Pole: the polar airship* America *emerging from its Arctic hangar, August 1909. (From* The Aerial Age.*)*

"devil" was Wellman's airship flying to the North Pole. The two captains calculated that the airship was moving north at about twenty-two knots. Suddenly, they observed it shoot upward to a height of six thousand feet and disappear into the clouds. Both captains kept their binoculars trained on the spot where the airship had disappeared into the clouds, and after a time it settled back down underneath them. Isaksen rightly concluded that the airship had suffered some mishap, so he had *Farm's* engines run up and headed his ship northward toward the pack ice.

On board *America* as it reached the pack ice, Wellman gazed over the side of the car at the waters far below, dotted with floes. Vaniman and Loud tended the engines, and Popov was at the helm. Suddenly the airship lurched and began a steady and rapid climb.

"At that instant I saw something drop from the ship into the sea," wrote Wellman. "Could one believe his eyes? Yes—it was the equilabrator."[77]

Wellman did not seem to be affected by the loss; perhaps he never believed in his invention anyway. But as *America* shed over half a ton of ballast and shot into the clouds, Loud panicked. Vaniman's brother-in-law grabbed the release cable, which led to the top gas valve, and refused to let it go. *America 2B* continued its ascent, the temperature dropped, and stronger upper winds began to push the airship farther to the northeast. Wellman could see the entire northern half of the archipelago beneath him.

"Would the Arctics never bring me anything but bad luck?" wrote Wellman. But even with the loss of the trailing snake, he was still thinking about the Pole. "I sat there wondering if I had the right to take the lives of my crew in my hand by holding [*America*] to the north, equilabrator or no equilabrator. My own life, yes; theirs, no."[78]

It is false nobility for Wellman to fall back on this argument when he did, for he himself had made much of how well equipped the airship was in the event it came down on the pack. And Wellman *already* had the lives of his crew in his hands; moreover, they were all volunteers (Popov had even *paid* to be on the flight). More likely, it suddenly dawned on Wellman that if the ship did go down, he had no trained dog driver to keep the sledges moving (an oversight that could have been easily corrected by substituting one of the Norwegians for the timid Loud). Moreover, his crew was ill fitted both physically and psychologically for a winter on the pack (Wellman himself was fifty-one and no Peary). Certainly the prospect of sledging again held little appeal for Wellman.

"We'll have to fight our way back to Spitsbergen!" Vaniman yelled, after at last prying his brother-in-law's hands loose from the gas valve.[79] A much baggier *America* settled down toward the broken pack ice, and Vaniman let out the retardateur to check the dirigible's progress.

"Unfortunately," Wellman wrote, "this improvised equilabrator had a loop of steel cable dragging from its lower end, and every ten or fifteen minutes this loop caught fast upon the sharp edge of an ice floe. Popov and I soon became quite expert in swinging the ship about with her helm, describing full or half circles, till that pesky steel loop would slide off the ice hook in which it had made fast."[80]

At *America*'s helm, Wellman and Popov maneuvered the ship back toward open water. Wellman looked below to see the *Farm* steaming toward the accident. He turned the nose of the ship down and headed it for the steamer. A few hours later, dirigible and steamer met and though *America* could probably have returned to its hangar under its own power, Wellman dropped a towline. After several minutes of jockeying, the towline was fast aboard *Farm,* and the steamer began pulling the airship toward Virgo Harbor.

It was a short trip. The giant airship, drooping in the sky from the loss of hydrogen, presented a misshapen profile to the wind and jerked the towline first to port, then starboard. The car was thrown violently sideways, and Wellman feared it might be ripped from the gasbag altogether. He ordered Vaniman to bring the ship down to the water, and then gave the order to abandon ship.

The car settled into choppy Arctic waters, and lifeboats from *Farm* were dispatched to bring over the dogs, the scientific instruments, and, last, the crew.

"We were reassured," Isaksen later wrote, "when we saw Mr. Wellman take out a big cigar, light it, and sit there calmly smoking while he gave orders to his men, which were as calmly obeyed."[81] It either didn't bother or didn't occur to the Norwegian that Wellman's lighted cigar was only a few feet below several tens of thousands of cubic feet of inflammable hydrogen. But Wellman's unlucky luck held once again.

*A*t about midnight—and still daylight at that latitude—*Farm* towed a battered *America 2B* back to Camp Wellman, where Corbitt joined the crew in trying to wrestle the airship ashore. With that accomplished, Corbitt climbed into the car and began dismounting the engines. At the same moment, toward the bow of the car, Vaniman stove in the front of the fuel tank to let the gasoline run out. As the

22. *The Norwegian survey vessel* Farm *comes to the* America's *rescue amid the ice of the polar pack, August 1909. (Courtesy of the Norwegian Polar Institute archives.)*

airship unburdened this weight, the gasbag began to rise once again. It lifted the car—and Corbitt—into the air. At an altitude of about twenty-five feet, the car and Corbitt both fell away from the gasbag. Corbitt landed heavily but unhurt on the pebbles along the shore, and the car came smashing down next to him.

Corbitt and the rest of the men at Camp Wellman looked skyward to witness the unencumbered gasbag loft to more than a mile, where it reached pressure-height and exploded. Bits of the airship rained down on the *Farm,* where in one account sailors jumped overboard to avoid the shower. "It was the most thrilling thing I'd ever seen," Corbitt later wrote.[82]

Miraculously, the envelope was retrieved largely intact, and Wellman stowed it for future use. The car was a wreck, however, so Wellman ordered it junked; exactly where, he did not record. He directed the Norwegians to begin lengthening the hangar, for he was, he claimed, already planning a fourth airship try for the Pole the following summer. The work on the hangar went on during four consecutive days of fine weather. If Loud had not panicked, if Wellman were not frightened of the ice, if his luck had matched his ego, it is possible *America* could have reached the Pole as a proper dirigible. But the world would have to wait another seventeen years before Roald Amundsen and Umberto Nobile proved the worth of airships at the Pole.

As *Arctic* made its way back along the coast of Norway, Wellman was handed a telegram at the town of Bodø. The journalist looked strained. He tipped the messenger boy who had brought the cable and said simply, "No reply."

"Not very good news, sir?" asked Corbitt.

"No," replied Wellman. "We shall not be going to Spitsbergen again. . . . Dr. Frederick A. Cook has found the North Pole."[83]

Cook, a medical doctor and friend of Amundsen's from an earlier expedition to Antarctica, claimed to have reached the Pole on April 21, 1908, but was soon challenged by Robert E. Peary, who claimed he himself had reached the spot a year later, and that Cook was a fraud. A steaming controversy ensued, one that Wellman joined unequivocally on the side of Peary. Cook was soon discredited as a fraud, albeit a likable one, when his logbooks were examined by Danish scientists, who pronounced him a complete incompetent.

Peary himself lobbied for and received promotion by Congress onto the U.S. Navy's retired list as a rear admiral. His claim to the Pole received the unsurprising imprimatur of his sponsors at the National Geographic Society, whose descendants there continue to carry the admiral's ice water to this day. It would be eighty years before

Peary's logbooks would be grilled as Cook's had been. When they were, by the superlative polar explorer Wally Herbert, he concluded that Peary had missed the mark by perhaps a hundred miles. Partisans for the doctor and the admiral continue to let blood over the controversy, now carried on via dueling Web sites on the Internet. One such locale suggests that any critiques of Peary are in truth veiled racist attacks on his African-American valet, Matthew Hensen, demonstrating that postmodern radical deconstructionism has reached even the North Pole.

As for poor Wellman, enough of a cloud had gathered permanently over the Pole to dampen any enthusiasm for another try by airship. Be it Peary or Cook, their combined egomania had tainted the greatest of geographic prizes, and no one would look upon it the same way again.

*F*or Walter Wellman, the tortuous and vain climb to glory in the "Arctics" was over. Had he flown north with both a skilled airshipman—Santos-Dumont, say, or even Corbitt—as well as a skilled dog driver, in the event of disaster, his chances of success over the Pole would have improved to a virtual certainty. In the very same year that Peary required thirty-seven days from northern Greenland to reach the spot he claimed as the Pole, Wellman possessed the sublime opportunity to prove he could cover the same route in little more than twenty-four *hours,* with none of the grinding agony of sledge travel over the twisted and arcane pack ice.

More important, perhaps, was the missed opportunity to inaugurate a radically new method of scientific and geographic exploration in the Arctic. Wellman had constructed a spectacular infrastructure barely seven hundred miles from the North Pole, one accessible by surface ship throughout the short Arctic summer. From the hangar at Danes Island, Wellman could have charted the whole of northern Spitsbergen, conducted survey flights to Greenland or Franz Josef Land and back (as Nobile would do in *Italia* in 1928), and studied Arctic meteorology and biology. At the very least, he could have turned Camp Wellman over to an American or Norwegian university, or to Isachsen's Norwegian Svalbard Expeditions, as the basis for the kind of permanent scientific research station now in year-round operation at Ny-Ålesund (King's Bay).

But in the end Wellman was as ill equipped to navigate an airship across the Polar Sea or lead a scientific revolution as he was skilled at raising the money to build an airship and hangar in the first place. For all his sincere, I believe, genuflections to the new god of Science,

Wellman devoted too little of his time to mastering the vast array of new technology that Science required he assemble for the flight to the Pole. His obstinate refusal to test the airship prior to assembling it on Danes Island is the most obvious and egregious example of this pattern of behavior, and it constituted an unforgivable failure. In this he was the very opposite of the calm and calculating Amundsen, who in 1926, aboard the *Norge,* would prove the correctness of Walter Wellman's aeronautical vision in 1906.

Wellman, like many explorers before and since, was obsessed with the dramatic, episodic feat, as the mistaken measure of science, not the long-drawn-out time study which was becoming the norm in scientific research, and which held so little appeal for explorers and newspaper readers alike. The public understood Wellman's brand of science, the grand plunge into the main chance. The other side of science, the slow, methodical testing of hypotheses in competition, was as deathly dull to a journalist as it was to his readers.

In this sense, Wellman and his fellow explorers of the late nineteenth and early twentieth centuries opened a chasm of disinterest and, later, distrust, between scientists and the general public, a gap that grows wider as we approach the turn of another century. Just as science has become even more straitlaced and corporate, exploration since Wellman has taken on even more the tincture of showmanship. The words *scientific exploration,* the credo of such institutions as the Explorers Club, have become an almost unreconcilable oxymoron.

Throughout his life, Wellman had two not inconsiderable strengths. Say what you will about his dubious plans, his absence of method, his incompetence as a leader, and his skill at masking that incompetence behind clever writing. But you have to give Wellman credit for getting himself out of one disastrous situation after another. Second, he had an uncanny ability to raise money for extravagant adventures. Other, more qualified explorers endured years of humiliating fund-raising to mount even the most spare expeditions.

Wellman went north five times, advanced toward the Pole a total of about two hundred miles in those five tries, and spent something on the order of a quarter million 1905 dollars. That dollar amount works out to a stunning average of $1,250 for each mile he managed to advance toward the Pole.

Wellman extracted this sort of backing in part because he had something to give: the overinflated articles he wrote, which were devoured by an Edwardian age hungry for humans and their machines to break Nature down to manageable size. The blank areas of geography challenged human supremacy over the natural world. The public wanted its measure of vicarious high adventure, and liked it best when it came wrapped, correctly or not, in the guise of Science.

Wellman appealed to that public, even as he himself was after only the juiciest plums—the first polar dash, first aerial crossing of the Atlantic. These forays into the unknown never made more than the slightest pretext of doing anything other than filling Wellman's notebooks with good stories, and made hardly a dent in the geographic ignorance of the world.

*W*hile Wellman was in Spitsbergen in 1909, Louis Bleriot became the first human to cross the English Channel in an airplane. When Wellman returned to the United States, with the durability of his airship now "proved," he thought, Why not challenge the Atlantic itself?

Wellman turned his back on the Pole, his obsession for almost two decades, and fulminated another, larger obsession. And unlike the Pole, the Atlantic bestowed some brief glory upon Wellman. After lifting off from Atlantic City, New Jersey, in the fall of 1910, his dirigible drifted in a huge arc past Cape Cod and then southeast for over one thousand miles—a far greater distance than that from Virgo Harbor to the Pole—before engine trouble forced Wellman and his crew to abandon ship not far from Bermuda. His unlucky luck held once again, and the ship came down within a mile of another providential steamer, which fished Wellman from the sea and delivered him ashore. *America*—this time *America 3*—and all the inventiveness Melvin Vaniman had adorned it with, drifted away over the Atlantic, never to be seen again.

Almost as much publicity was generated when it was learned that Wellman and crew had taken a cat along on the flight. "Kiddo" even earned his own *New York Times* editorial on October 20. The *Times* wondered why everyone was showing so much concern over a cat, a "creature so self-centered, so imperfectly domesticated, so unmindful of past favors, so ready with sharp claws to punish an unintended affront or injury which the infinitely nobler dog would either ignore altogether or instantly forgive." The newspaper also hinted darkly that as the airship was going down and Wellman and his crew were risking their own lives to save the cat, Kiddo no doubt dug in his claws and resisted rescue to the last. On the other side of the cat question came this haughty catty jibe from Wellman's crosstown rival the *Chicago Tribune:* "We can fully understand why Wellman and his companions embarked on a voyage which for foolhardiness exceeds anything in the history of human recklessness, but what gets us is how a perfectly sane cat ever consented to go."[84]

Wellman's Atlantic adventure set a new record for the longest airship flight. For a brief moment in New York City, Wellman was the center of attention, the biggest story of the day. But one could easily imagine that as *America 3* slid beneath the waves, back on the northern shore of Danes Island, the hangar at Camp Wellman was collapsing noisily in another heap. In fact the hangar waited in vain through three Arctic winters for its master to return, before finally collapsing in a gale in 1912.

After the failure of the Atlantic flight in 1910, Wellman lived on until 1934, but he never got into another airship. He never again left the surface of the earth.

PART TWO

ARCHAEOLOGY:

Exploring the Aerial Polar Base Camps
of Salomon A. Andrée and Walter Wellman
on Danes Island, Spitsbergen, 1993

Certain people do not travel the way most of us travel; not
only do they sometimes choose odd vehicles, they take
dangerous and unusual trips for incomprehensible reasons.

—*Evan Connell, writer*

CHAPTER THREE

Arctic Ghosts: Technology and Memory on the Island of Airships

*I*n June of 1928, several ships and aircraft converged on Virgo Harbor, which became the advance base for several attempts to locate General Umberto Nobile, whose airship *Italia* had crashed on its return from a flight to the Pole. Nobile and part of his *Italia* crew, stranded on the ice northeast of Foyn Island (Foynøya), were eventually rescued. But six crewmen who had drifted away in the wrecked hull of the airship, when it rebounded into the air after hitting the ice, were never to be seen again.

Alexander McKee writes that several newsmen who chartered ships to Virgo Harbor to follow the progress of the search noted that "the remains of the shed used by the Swede Andrée . . . still showed above the snow."[1] As Andrée's hangar had long since been reduced to splinters, it is more likely that the reporters, like many visitors to Virgo Harbor, mistook Wellman's great hangar for the long-vanished shed of Andrée. Even when the world's press descended on Virgo Harbor to cover a story about the crash of an airship, it seemed Walter Wellman was forgotten.

He did reappear, briefly, during the summer-long *Italia* saga, when an enterprising reporter thought to ask the retired polar aeronaut's opinion on where the rescuers might find Nobile. But then Wellman lapsed back into obscurity. When the spectacular news broke two years later that the bodies of Andrée and his companions had been found on White Island (Kvitøya), no one showed up at the door of Wellman's New York City home for a comment. Three and a half years later, on the last day of January, 1934, he was dead of liver cancer, and while his obituaries extolled him as a man of progress, they also strongly hinted that his place in history was within the ranks of eccentric failures.

*E*ven though he wrote a strong defense of Peary's claim to the Pole in the fall of 1909, Peary ignored Wellman in his 1910 book about his still-disputed dash. In his biography of Peary, Wally Herbert quotes from a letter to Peary from his wife, which offers a glimpse of how Peary likely estimated his polar rival. After Wellman's failure at Franz Josef Land in 1899, Josephine Peary wrote to her husband that "Wellman's expedition did *nothing as was expected*."[2]

Fridtjof Nansen, perhaps the greatest polar explorer in history, could barely contain his contempt for Wellman. Visiting Virgo Harbor in 1912, Nansen gazed upon the remains of Camp Wellman and remarked that they are the "ruins of that great humbug. . . . The workshop where they made hydrogen gas was still standing. Most of the things of value, especially those made of metal, had been stolen, but a lot was still left. The trappers and the tourists did not have time to get it all yet."[3] In Nansen's view, Wellman was a calculating journalist who had lived through the international sensation created by Andrée, one who planned to garner publicity for himself on an even greater scale. Except that, in Nansen's view, Wellman never had any intention of risking his life by actually flying north to the pack ice.

> [In 1907], we heard that finally the balloon was filled. Wellman would finally take off. The summer went, but he did not. And boatload after boatload of tourists went home disappointed for not having lived through the historic moment.
>
> When most of the people had returned home in the fall, he really went out one day—I believe it was 9 September [it was in fact September 2]—with a brisk wind from the west, so he could be sure that he wouldn't be carried toward the north. The airship drifted only across Smeerenburg Fjord, where it fell onto a glacier and was completely demolished. . . .
>
> [In 1909] the big thing was really going to happen. The new airship was filled, waiting ready in the balloon house for the first opportunity. The world was shaking with tension.[4]

Other polar explorers likewise dismissed Wellman or else ignored him altogether. Walter Mittelholzer, pilot of a Junkers monoplane that made the first serious aerial reconnaissance flights in Spitsbergen, producing maps of parts of the archipelago in 1923, found himself at one point looking down at Virgo Harbor from an altitude of 4,920 feet. In his book about his flights, he reports: "Here are still to be seen the ruins of the huts of Andrée and Wellman, the balloonists. . . . Wellman was engaged upon his great advertising stunt."[5] Earlier in the same work, a historical account of exploration in Spitsbergen written by Professor Kurt Wegener also describes Wellman's expeditions as "little more than an advertising stunt."[6]

Amundsen does not tilt his cap to his predecessor in his account of the 1926 flight of the *Norge* across the polar sea.[7] Nor does George Wilkins, who writes in his account of his April 1928 flight from Alaska to Spitsbergen that the idea of using an airship or airplane in the Arctic came to him as early as 1913.[8] By 1939, one popular account of aeronautical history describes Wellman as "daring and imaginative" but also "pretentious."[9]

In his account of the *Italia* disaster, Alexander McKee notes that on the flight northward toward the Pole, at an altitude of 1,350 feet, the crew of the *Italia* "had a close view of Danes Island as it went below them, the highest peak there being 1,121 feet. Twenty-nine years before, in 1897, the Swede Andrée and his two companions had set off in their balloon from Danes Island, to drift with the wind over the North Pole."[10]

More recent histories of polar exploration that discuss Andrée, Amundsen, Nobile, and their expeditions in varying degrees have ignored Wellman,[11] as have the occasional popular books on Arctic exploration.[12] Others discuss Wellman's expeditions in a few, usually disparaging, lines: a "ridiculous failure";[13] both attempts "ended ignominiously";[14] such failure was to be expected from a "feeble 70-horsepower dirigible."[15] Nor does Wellman appear in Arlov's *A Short History of Svalbard.*[16]

Among both popular and scholarly airship and polar aviation histories, an almost bewildering number of misstatements occur in descriptions of Wellman and his expeditions. One notes that Wellman, "a former Akron resident . . . undertook polar and transatlantic airship ventures between 1906 and 1909, both of which failed."[17] In fact, Wellman never lived in Akron, and his three polar and one transatlantic expeditions took place between 1906 and 1910. Another recounts that in "a hastily constructed, 165-foot semirigid dirigible, Wellman and his party took off from Andrée's jumping-off place, Smeerenburg, on September 2, 1907."[18] In fact, Wellman's 1907 airship was a patiently constructed 185-foot nonrigid dirigible, and neither Wellman nor Andrée had taken off from Smeerenburg, which lies a mile northeast across Danish Strait (Danskegattet) from the separate launch points on Danes Island used by the two men.

Grierson's account of Wellman is probably the most considered from the point of view of traditional aviation historiography, but even here errors exist: the 1909 crew is placed on board the 1907 airship; Loud is described as Wellman's brother-in-law, when he was in fact Vaniman's; Wellman's birth date is incorrect; and the airship is seen ending its 1909 flight by crashing to the polar pack, something that never happened.[19]

These conflicting and in many ways misguided accounts point strongly to the need for an aerospace archaeology that "gets under the skin" of traditional aviation history, a history that places so much faith in flawed documents. More, they point toward the necessity of new interpretations, generated from the archaeological patterns that are ignored by aviation historians.

I found it difficult to accept the easy—if not downright breezy—dismissals of Wellman. Was he really the fraud most, if not all, made him out to be? And could archaeology provide new insights into these old accounts? Modern historical analysis has largely dismissed the accomplishments of Peary, of Cook, and of Byrd. Could archaeology add anything to Wellman's profile—and to the distressing lineage of American polar fakery—that we don't already know?

And with these words I must add a warning to my readers. Modern archaeological methodology, to say nothing of its theory, can be a hard slog, which is one reason so many historians have no use for it. It took nearly seven years of intense concentration for me to break parts of its code, and I still don't have a handle on much of it. But what I did learn, I can assure you, was worth the effort.

Casting aside the more arcane theoretical considerations, I restrict the discussion here to the nuts and bolts of archaeological analysis. This is a strenuous enough slog, but one which nevertheless includes material details that I believe are of significant interest to aeronautical and polar enthusiasts and general readers alike. For none of the previous histories written on the subject of polar aviation, many of which I have just quoted from, reveal any knowledge of the base camps at Virgo Harbor. The following pages offer for the first time the material details of such undertakings, details recorded at their source.

Archaeologists search for general patterns in artifacts and landscapes, and the archaeological remains at Virgo Harbor contain many prosaic artifactual signatures: residues of the chemical processes involved in the generation of hydrogen and the fueling of internal combustion engines; fuel tanks of long-distance airships; as well as artifacts that comment on the nature of advertising in early polar aerial exploration. If exploring behavior is patterned in any way, studies of the residues of aeronautical exploration at this site might reveal patterns inherent in the failure of Andrée and Wellman as expedition leaders and enable us to assess their roles as pioneers.

For Wellman's own part, as a journalist he was certainly intent on building public excitement in his expeditions in order to retain the interest of his readers (and hence his newspaper). But the key point is that his newspaper dispatches are only one of several parts of his personal record relating to his expeditions. The other two are his contemporary journal articles, in *National Geographic* and *McClure's,* and his later memoir *The Aerial Age,* written five years after his first airship expedition, and seventeen years after his first visit to Danskøya in 1894.

Evaluated one against the other, and then against both the later histories and Nansen's critique, all offer opportunities to use the material record at Virgo Harbor to build screens through which to filter these oftimes conflicting historical accounts, thereby generating a picture that is closer to what actually happened.

After such filtration of the historical record through the screen of the material record, I use the archaeology of, for example, the airship cars, to identify and / or to clarify technological trends in the historical record. Then I suggest ways in which the archaeological remains can be seen as material representations of larger cultural concerns during the great age of technological expansion that began with the introduction of the internal combustion engine in the 1880s, emphasizing the transformations wrought by the aerial age.

*A*t the perimeter of our camp at Virgo Harbor, my guide set a tripwire system armed with contact mines, in the event a polar bear wandered near our camp while we slept. The mines—little better than firecrackers—were designed to awaken us in time to fire warning shots that should scare off a bear. Actually shooting one of the lords of the North is considered a grave quasi-offense in Spitsbergen, a sin of the unprepared or incompetent, complete with official investigation and official frowns. It was to be avoided at all costs short of sacrificing one's own life or limb.

Two conical tents marked our temporary intrusion onto this remote landscape, and, unlike Wellman, we would leave behind no trace of our visit. I set up a map table for my site drawings and field sketches in one tent, where my guide and I also shared sleeping quarters. We cooked and ate in the second tent.

My arrival marked the beginnings of an attempt to relate, and in some ways challenge, the history of aeronautical exploration in the Arctic with the archaeological remains left behind by the aeronauts themselves. I also envisioned a parallel effort to document polar archaeological sites with advanced remote sensing stations and state-of-the-art multimedia computer technology. Ever since zoologist Dr. Robert B. Hill and I developed and taught "Great Expeditions of the Nineteenth Century," an introductory course at the University of Rhode Island in 1989–1990, my goal has been the creation of an undergraduate curriculum on the history of exploration based upon archaeological examinations of important sites from around the globe. Virgo Harbor is my first step toward that goal.

After the zodiacs from the *Polarsyssel* left us, I hiked west toward the small amphitheater of crumbling rock that encloses the American and Swedish airship base camps. I stumbled over a field of broken gray rocks, piebald with lichen. I passed a rock cairn with a guy wire support embedded in it—once a support for Andrée's hangar—built over a Dutch grave dating from the seventeenth century. A few steps farther, down a gentle slope, is the west end of the small Dutch whaler's graveyard. Next to the graves are the foundation stones and the few beams that once supported a small house built in 1889 by a British sportsman named Arnold Pike. Behind Pike's *hus* is a large wooden box with holes cut at each end and filled with a powdery white substance. It is a giant filter that once separated impurities out of hydrogen gas, the last surviving remnant of the elaborate apparatus that once generated the lifting power of Andrée's balloon.

As I approached the remains of Wellman's camp, the near-constant fog lifted to a height of more than three hundred feet, and the sky brightened to highlight the green moss and yellow lichens that survive in patches and carpets between the rocks and boulders. From a distance the camp was dominated by the imposing wreckage of Walter Wellman's airship hangar, but a close reconnaissance revealed several other pockets of interest: the ruins of Wellmanhuset, "the most scientifically ventilated and heated house in the Arctic," as we have seen Wellman himself describe it; the remains of Wellman's hydrogen-generating machinery; a considerable debris field of rusting and coagulating metalwork; a field of thick ceramic shards stamped with the mark of the British manufacturer Doulton; and, like the incarnation of a Verne fantasy, the wreckage of the two gondolas, or nacelles, of the airship *America,* in which Walter Wellman sought to be the first human to explore the North Pole.

*B*efore our small expedition, no one had ever done what I call aerospace archaeology at such a latitude, a result of the facts that few archaeologists conduct research so far north, and even fewer are interested in aircraft or aeronautical history and culture. But by studying at close hand all the physical remains left behind by explorers—and in the Arctic and the Antarctic these remains are preserved better than virtually anywhere else on our planet—we can then begin to match words with deeds, ideas with reality, paper and emulsion with steel and rock, and start to reach well-grounded interpretations about

23. *Walter Wellman at work on a dispatch in his office at the Chicago Record-Herald House on Danes Island. (Courtesy of the Library of Congress.)*

the motives and challenges of explorers who are no longer here to be questioned directly.

Many may think that a field as young as aeronautics cannot possibly possess an archaeology to examine. But archaeology, as forward-thinking anthropologists have recognized for some time, is the study of material culture unbounded by time and space. And journeying to a remote place central to the history of exploration, going with questions developed from the competing hypotheses of today and yesterday, might uncover something vital that is lost, or unresolved, in the written record. Just as important for me on this trip was the chance to stand alone on isolated shores where nearly miraculous events once took place, to see and feel directly what so many writers have described as the mystery of the Arctic landscape, sensations no history book can accurately convey.

Danes Island, I felt, could fill in many of the fine technological details of Wellman's expeditions that had fallen through cracks in the written record. If I could gain some direct connection with Walter Wellman and his world, perhaps I could extend these discoveries from Wellman's time to our own. Danes Island, disturbed over the course of the century by small knots of chill tourists, trappers, tracks of rein-

24. The remains of the Chicago Record-Herald House on the shore of Virgo Harbor, July 1993. (Photo by the author.)

deer and polar bear, by ice and snow and rock slides, was for me the source of such connections. But no aviation historian or archaeologist had ever been motivated to set foot on the island to explore what it might reveal about Wellman, about aviation, or about human exploration generally.

You will note that in my archaeological analysis I am not as tough on Wellman as I was in the earlier, strictly historical account. There are two definite reasons for this. First, there is no question that the archaeology as I recorded it at Virgo Harbor in 1993 supports, at least in part, Wellman's claims as to the purity of his own motives. (Had the hard facts led to a less favorable conclusion, that would have been all right with me, too.)

Second, I realized it had been far too easy during ten years of research for me to offer criticisms of Wellman from the comfort of the library stacks or the study. No matter what my archaeological science concluded, after I had lived for a month on the same Arctic shoreline as Wellman, I appreciated so much more personally the magnitude of the problem he had set for himself.

I had gained, like a good staff officer scouting a potential invasion site in advance of an army, a geographic bridge to the validity of my criticisms. Some day, I hope to gain an even greater sense of what Wellman and the other early air explorers experienced by taking an airship flight over the Arctic regions, as I continue my historical and archaeological chronicle of the airship flights to the Pole.

I was not the first person to investigate the archaeology Wellman left strewn around Spitsbergen. Sir William Martin Conway nearly circumnavigated the archipelago in 1896, along the way visiting tiny Walden Island, a chunk of gnarled rock remote even in this land of remoteness. It was to Walden Island that Wellman retreated after his 1894 expedition ended when the *Ragnvald Jarl* was crushed by ice on May 28 and sunk near Walden's ice-fouled shore. There, on some of the earth's earliest crustal rock, near a bay on the eastern shore, Wellman's crew erected a wood-frame hut, cached some dynamite from the *Ragnvald Jarl,* fended off a polar bear, and, a week later, was plucked off the rock by a sealing sloop. As I walked for the first time among the ruins of Camp Wellman on the shore of Virgo Harbor, I remembered Conway's words about Walden Island: "The shore is eaten away into little coves, intricately bent. The surface of the rock is scored into deep undulations of ridge and gully, and every yard of progress involves a scramble.

"We made our way to the ruined framework of the Wellman hut, drawn by the resistless attraction of a human interest. Footprints in a steep gully piled with sand showed the way to it. They had been preserved beneath a covering of snow."

Conway felt the site of little significance—"a mere framework of beams, the wreck of sleeping-bunks, floors, and doorways, a heap of coal, piles of withered-up potatoes and peas, foul remnants of old clothes, empty cartridges, a packet of photograph developer, and such like rubbish"—save for the stick of dynamite he mistook for a frozen candle and hurled to the ground, fortunately without incident.

Nearly one hundred years later, Conway's disappointed description of the Walden "rubbish" reads like an archaeological nirvana. In forty disparaging words he tells us how and where the survivors from the wreck of the *Ragnvald Jarl* slept, what they ate, that they discarded clothes, how they hunted and heated themselves, and, importantly, that they were taking photographs.[20]

I wanted to go to Walden for a day. Had any of the items in Conway's description survived the intervening century? What were the hut's dimensions, had the bitter elements preserved any of the food or clothes, what kinds of cartridges was Wellman carrying, was the coal mined in Spitsbergen itself? Most important for me, Conway describes the wreck of the *Ragnvald Jarl* as having been "destroyed close to [Walden Island's] shore." With those few words I had a likely shipwreck site, which gave me a reason to test Robert Ballard's remote undersea "telepresence" technology near one of the Arctic's most inaccessible islands. If I managed to locate the shipwreck, it would be the most northern shipwreck ever found.

After that success, the next step would be inevitable: an expedition to nearby Foyn Island to deploy an Autonomous Undersea Vehicle (AUV) probe in search of Nobile's infamous airship *Italia*. I might not be thrilled with the new robotic exploration of our solar system, but I have few reservations about trying to employ it under the polar sea. Besides, I don't have NASA's budget; if I did, an entire fleet of long-range submarines would now be surveying archaeological sites at the bottom of every sea and ocean on the planet. It is to our great national shame that our largely mothballed submarine force, which helped win the Cold War, cannot now be sent out on a grand undersea cultural reconnaissance, a new mission to inaugurate the new millennium. I would go so far as to take old subs named after bottom fish and rechristen them with famous names from the fields of underwater archaeology and maritime history: I could envision the USS *George Bass,* the *Philippe Tailliez,* the *Jacques-Yves Cousteau,* and the *William N. Still, Jr.*

Such intoxicating thoughts, however, had to await another day. I had my hands full with what Walter Wellman had left behind on the shores of Danes Island.

*T*he aeronautical remains at Virgo Harbor and their incorporation into the geography of the harbor and the surrounding Arctic all suggest the kinds of cognitive and cultural landscapes the Danish archaeologist Christer Westerdahl posited for maritime cultural adaptations. In this context, we can refer to Virgo Harbor as an *aeronautical* cultural landscape, one that can be studied comprehensively only with reference to the totality of records, artifacts, structures, ecology, geography, and psychology that contributed to its unique creation.

The site plan revealed the palimpsest nature of Virgo Harbor, with remnants of a large seventeenth-century Dutch whaling station overlaid by considerable aeronautical remains from the late nineteenth and early twentieth centuries. Both Andrée and Wellman built their base camps directly over the ruins and skeletons left behind by Dutch whalers. The unidentified circular structure to the west of Wellman's hut does not appear to be associated with his camp; it is possibly the ruin of a Dutch observation post overlooking the harbor, but this hypothesis needs to be tested archaeologically. While the extensive nature of Wellman's camp is obvious, the plan also reveals that a considerable amount of residual material survives.

Virgo Harbor is a popular destination for tourists in Spitsbergen; I noted more than 250 tourists in my three weeks on the island. Tourists generally landed by zodiac near the monument to Andrée that the Swedes built on the site of his hangar in 1957. Then they walked past the Dutch whaling ovens and graves, and worked their way to the Wellman site and its vast array of remains. They picked up artifacts and cast them down; they trod upon the soft wood of the hangar; and they stepped on the mass of metal debris. After their wanderings, many tourists gathered along the shoreline to share champagne and peanuts, and one part of Wellman's hydrogen-generating apparatus was in reuse as a garbage bin for bottles and plastic wrappers.

The guides working these tours varied in their historical knowledge of the site, with some mistaking Wellman's camp for Andrée's. I gave informal guided lectures about the site to groups that requested them, in part to steer them around the most fragile artifact concentrations. Virgo Harbor does not have an easy shoreline around which to walk; it is strewn with rocks and boulders from the crumbling ridges that surround the site. The ages of the tourists (many were in their sixties and seventies), the significance and fragility of the sites and artifacts, the difficulty of the terrain—all impel the comprehensive cultural resource management plan now being devised by the Norwegians to protect Virgo Harbor.

*F*or the archaeology of aeronautics, the greatest significance of Camp Wellman lies in the remains of the cars, or nacelles, of the first two airships ever brought into the Arctic for exploration. It took three weeks of intense and minute inspection of the shoreline for me to identify and uncover all the remains of Wellman's airships, and to be certain of my identification. As I sat in my tent one rainy afternoon, studying old photographs and comparing them with my sketches and preliminary site plans, it suddenly occurred to me that Virgo Harbor held the remains of not one, but two early airships.

This realization, that here on the very shoreline where I was camped were the artifacts I had searched for during a decade of wandering through library stacks and photographic archives, sent chills through me. The written record of these airship expeditions contained no certain disposition of these historic cars, so determining whether or not they were still at Virgo Harbor was the major goal of my journey to Spitsbergen. I could not have been more excited if I was surveying the site of *Apollo 11* on the moon.

Wellman himself wrote little as to the fate of his two polar airship cars. Both were constructed in Paris, and Wellman expressed some displeasure with the 1906 car, built by the firm of Louis Godard. This 1906 nacelle was apparently abandoned, but Wellman made no record of where or when, or if it was returned to Paris for modification.

As we have seen, in early 1907, Wellman met and hired Melvin Vaniman, a young aeronautical jack-of-all-trades who designed and built a completely new, V-shaped car. This nacelle was used on the short flight of 1907, when *America 2A* flew about thirty-five miles (56 km) from Camp Wellman before a snowstorm forced Wellman to bring the ship down upon a glacier, from where both crew and airship were rescued a few hours later.

Vaniman redesigned the nacelle again before it was reattached to the gasbag in the summer of 1909, to create *America 2B*. On August 15, 1909, on the second of his two Arctic flights, Wellman managed to navigate *America 2B* more than sixty miles (97 km) north, reaching the pack ice and slightly beyond, before he was forced to turn back. The crew and airship were again rescued, and Wellman only noted that the "steel car was partly destroyed."[21] When or where it was disposed of, he did not record.

The remains of these two nacelles at Virgo Harbor represent the oldest American airship cars in existence, and both are in advanced stages of deterioration. The 1906 car is virtually undetectable, so little of it remains, while many of the fittings and large sections of the fuel tank of the 1907–1909 car have rusted into the thin layer of soil.

*E*asily the most imposing structural remains at Virgo Harbor are the ruins of Wellman's airship hangar. This massive hangar was built of wood in 1906 with five arches towering more than eight stories high. The arches were formed around large iron bending frames, several of which can still be seen scattered on the shoreline. When the hangar partially collapsed in a gale on July 4, 1907, Wellman had it rebuilt with nine arches. The structure collapsed again during a storm in the winter of 1908–1909 and was rebuilt again in the summer of 1909.

The hangar dominated the Virgo Harbor landscape during Wellman's campaigns, when it towered over tall ships and steamers nearby.

It is located to the southeast of the machinery spaces and is surrounded by at least forty-eight rock piles and stakes for guy wires that once supported the arches. The final collapse of the wooden hangar in 1912 created a twisted and chaotic assemblage of deck planks and beams, and arch beams and wires. In several places, especially toward the rear of the hangar, sections of the original deck planks can be seen, and small patches of the original flooring remain, which can be stood upon. Small sections of floorboards have been taken up and stacked, suggesting that systematic removal of parts of the hangar may have taken place either before or after its collapse, possibly to be used for firewood. It appears that attempts were made to set other sections on fire, as there is evidence of a limited amount of charring in several places. The beams are in progressively better condition toward the rear of the hangar.

When the hangar collapsed, it apparently fell from back to front, or south to north, since the forwardmost of the nine arches now lies nearly one hundred feet (30 m) from the front of the hangar. From the ridges that surround Virgo Harbor on the east, west, and southwest, the outline of the hangar appears much more clearly than it does on the ground, where the weathered gray wood tends to blend in with the surrounding gray shoreline rock.

Wellman's own measurements of this structure varied. He initially placed it at 82 feet (25 m) wide and 190 feet (58 m) long,[22] and later at 85 feet (26 m) wide and 210 feet (64 m) long.[23] My 1993 measurements differed slightly from both of these: the width of the hangar today is 92 feet (28 m), and the length 187 feet (57 m).

The spring that Wellman diverted around the western side of the hangar to provide fresh water to his hut has resumed its course directly under the hangar. This has caused rotting and disintegration of the support beams, especially at the northeast corner of the hangar, which now rests above the same boggy area where the remains of the 1906 airship car are located.

*W*ellman left no plan of the machinery areas of his camp, other than to say that they consisted of a machine shop with lathes, drills, and other tools; a boiler house, steam engine, and steam pump; and the shed containing the hydrogen-generating apparatus.[24] My survey identified the ruins of the machine shop, which consists of a northern section and a smaller southern section, located a short distance east-southeast of Wellman's hut. The southern section appears to have collapsed in on itself, while the northern section is severely charred and appears to have been burned to the ground.

To the south of the southern section of the machine shop is a scatter of large-diameter ceramics—apparently plumbing pipe—stamped with the mark of "Doulton & Co; London, Lambeth." In contemporary photographs of the site, a few of these pipes are seen being used as supports for the water main leading from behind the hangar to Wellman's hut. The majority, however, appear to have been brought to Danes Island with no specific purpose; they remain in the area where they were originally stacked, although they have all been broken. Underneath a section of this scatter are fragments of broken glassware, preserved only because the much larger ceramic vats shielded them from both weather and tourists. It was in this section where the fragments of a bottle marked "Lambert Pharmacal Company" were found.

At the time of Wellman's flights, Lambert Pharmacal was located in St. Louis, and its only product was Listerine. These remains raise several interesting questions. If these fragments represent items from the Wellman expeditions, did he pack them himself? Or were midwestern corporations donating supplies to Wellman's expeditions, and did they have ties with his newspaper, the *Chicago Record-Herald?* If so, what advertising advantage did Lambert hope to gain by having its mouthwash first at the Pole? (Mack øl, the popular Norwegian beer, uses the phrase "First on the North Pole" on its cans today.)

Wellman acknowledged that many observers characterized his polar exploits as "an advertising scheme."[25] He routinely deflected such criticism by citing his overriding desire to produce not only good journalistic products but, more important, "good work for the country, for humanity, for progress, [and] for the spread of knowledge."[26]

Near the ceramic and bottle debris lies the hydrogen apparatus area. It consists of four distinct floor areas; four ceramic Doulton vats are cemented into the ground adjacent to the southwest corners of the four floor areas. Trailing out to the east is a length of iron filing debris spilling from the wooden casks that once contained them, iron filings that once served as a component in the hydrogen-generating cycle. To the northeast lies a dump of metal barrels, apparently where the fuel for the airship fuel tank was stored.

Adjacent to the southeast corner of the machinery spaces, and overlapping to some extent the iron filings debris, is a large metalwork scatter. The extraordinary variety of metal pieces there supports Wellman's contention that he had his machine shop continually working on improvements to the complicated airships. In addition to the routine pieces of metalwork found on many sites, such as household items (forks, springs, and door lock mechanisms), there are unusual items such as several horseshoes, decorated iron, and what appear to be parts either from the airship engines themselves or from the motor sledges Wellman tested in Norway for use at Virgo Harbor in 1906. This entire mass of ironwork is coagulating into a giant rust heap.

The westernmost structure at Virgo Harbor is Wellman's hut. All that remains are the stone foundation walls, pieces of the stove, and several wood frame members, all scattered toward the west. This debris, along with the fact that there is no record of Wellman's hut having been moved—as was Pike's house, which was moved in 1925 to another location in Spitsbergen—suggests that Wellman's hut was physically blown off its foundations by a gale from the east.[27]

The amount of the debris, however, does not appear to contain enough elements to comprise what was once an impressive structure. Photographic evidence from a German expedition to Virgo Harbor in the mid-1930s shows that the hut was off the foundation by that time. This suggests that at least parts of the hut, like Pike's house but without the accompanying record, were picked up and moved elsewhere in Spitsbergen sometime between the geological congress that was held at Virgo Harbor in 1912 and the arrival of the German expedition in 1938.

Virgo Harbor, then, is a much-transformed landscape, imprinted with the footsteps of many visitors with innumerable motives. Walking around it, picking through its material culture with my eyes, I felt as if I had started to read a book backward. I would have to peel back page after page, until I could read the Wellman chapter with something approaching a clear vision of what the place looked like when this unusual American had built his dream there.

CHAPTER FOUR

The Spam What Am:
Advertising in Search
of a North Pole

*W*alter Wellman lived through and participated in the transition of newspaper journalism from relatively modest operations controlled by a single owner-editor to the era of corporate journalism, when the management and editorial sides of the newspaper business separated and intense competition began for high circulation and the advertising revenue that followed it. One method that ensured high circulation for newspapers was the promotion of geographic exploration, in the knowledge that, as Beau Riffenburgh put it, "the public could be intoxicated by exciting reports about heroic struggles to master nature, particularly in what were perceived as her most dangerous environments, Africa and the Arctic."[1]

During Wellman's newspaper career, the "percentage of newspaper revenue coming from advertising, as compared to circulation income, rose from half in 1880 to 64 percent by 1910."[2] The space newspapers devoted to advertising also rose in the same period, from 25 to 50 percent of the newspaper's content, as manufacturers honed strategies of trademark and brand name identification.

Wellman's expeditions were often evaluated against this backdrop. Fridtjof Nansen claimed that Wellman's airship expeditions were essentially promotional schemes that showed how, "by the great art of advertising, [Wellman could] hold the attention of the world's press year after year without having a single thing of value to report."[3] When his plan to reach the North Pole was announced at the end of 1905, several of his rivals in the press took up this criticism. These comments generally followed those of the *Cleveland Plain Dealer*, which editorialized that "the expedition would seem to promise results more profitable to the advertiser than to the geographer."[4]

But *did* Wellman hold the attention of the world's press year after year? And did his expeditions really offer much to the advertiser? To test these questions archaeologically, I spent a considerable amount of my precious time at Virgo Harbor looking for artifacts that had manufacturers' imprints on them. I felt that I might be able to link the brand names imprinted on artifacts at Camp Wellman with advertising found in Wellman's newspaper, the *Chicago Record-Herald*.

If such advertising was found, I could evaluate its nature and frequency, and match it in a temporal relationship with articles relating to the Wellman airship expeditions. If this relationship proved to be a regular and measurable one, I would have uncovered firm data to support the widely held belief that Wellman had organized his airship expeditions as advertising ventures for the *Record-Herald*.

At Virgo Harbor, there were indeed several artifacts with brand names attached to them. The greatest number of these was a field of ceramics with the mark of "Doulton, London"; underneath a section of this field was a collection of bottles, one of which had the name "Lambert Pharmacal Company" molded into it. A can with a tarlike residue inside and labeled "Chicago, U.S.A." was located and retrieved from a spot twelve feet due east from the end of a trail of iron filings residue left from the apparatus that generated the hydrogen for Wellman's airship. Closer study of this can in the United States located the name "Armour & Company" on it. Its measurements mark it as a rectangular "Spam-type" meat can, possibly one of the earliest in existence.

To add to the advertising data, I also examined photographic records of Wellman's airship expeditions at the archives of the Norwegian Polar Institute in Oslo, Norway. One of these showed supplies on the deck of Wellman's supply vessel *Arctic* being delivered to Virgo Harbor. These supplies included "Mauna Coffee" and "Huntley & Palmers Biscuits." Then I combed Wellman's writings for evidence of what supplies he used and whether these were identified by brand name. This "digging in the documents," which is every bit as important as the field research, allowed me to combine documentary and archaeological data and identify nine distinct brand names associated with Wellman's expeditions.

When I returned to the United States, I journeyed to the Library of Congress and scrolled through microfilm of the *Record-Herald* for the three years of Wellman's airship attempts on the North Pole: 1906, 1907, and 1909. The advertisements for those years provided documentary evidence that I could use in evaluating both photographic records from the expeditions as well as artifacts I located and recorded at Wellman's base camp.

*J*ournalist Walter Wellman described himself as a man who lived "with a desire to achieve something in the way of exploration and scientific progress for the good of mankind and the advancement of knowledge."[5] As such, he wanted to mate some form of aeronautics to exploration in search of geographic "firsts." He quickly realized that journalism could both fund and provide an outlet for accounts of his adventures. His journalist's instincts told him that when it came to geographic exploration, only stories of "difficult and dangerous" expeditions told in a popular style would interest readers and boost his newspaper's circulation—to say nothing of his own career. So, perforce, only expeditions that could "stir the blood . . . [and] warm the heart" would satisfy both his personal and professional ambition "to please, to inform, to help educate, to win the approval of the people."[6]

Yet the same ambitions led Wellman to hurry the planning of his expeditions, to allot little if any time for such niceties as physical training, shakedown cruises, or trial flights. Wellman saw his job of combination explorer-journalist as one wherein he was almost required to plunge directly into the main chance. As he wrote of the failed airship expedition from Danes Island in 1906: "Perhaps it would have been better not to try to go on with the expedition that summer, but we Americans like to do things rapidly."[7] But it was not just as an American but as a American *journalist* that Wellman saw himself uniquely positioned to triumph where so many professionals had failed. One newspaper editorial that appeared after Wellman announced his expedition made the point: "When a newspaper man is given an assignment he gets results."[8]

As we have seen, Wellman spent seventeen years searching for the North Pole, failing as the leader of five separate North Pole expeditions. Fortunately for Wellman, he did not need to attract many corporate sponsors to his flag; he only needed to interest Victor Lawson, multimillionaire owner of the *Chicago Record-Herald.*

*I*f we dig even a bit further into the documents, we find that on December 20, 1904, Wellman received a reply from Lawson regarding his proposal for a renewed attempt on the Pole.

> I have your letter of the 17th inst. I have read and carefully considered all the data you have submitted on the North Pole project and have discussed the matter with Mr. [Frank] Noyes [editor of the *Record-Herald*]. The more I study it the more interested I am. The difficulty, however, is that the propo-

sition comes at a time when neither I nor the *Record-Herald* can wisely act on it. . . . Mr. Noyes tells me that he at once informed you that so far as the *Record-Herald* is concerned he cannot, on his own account, commit it to an outlay of this magnitude at this time. Possibly I ought to have at once recognized these limitations and have saved you the consideration you have been giving the subject since your first talk with me. My failure to do so can only be excused on the ground that the project has made a strong appeal to my imagination and to my newspaper inclination to try to do important things.[9]

Wellman, however, was not so easily put off. Within a year, he had persuaded Lawson to support the polar airship project. "Only incidentally," wrote Wellman, "did he think of advertising his newspaper, and he knew that as a business proposition it would be a losing one— that if it was advertising he wanted he could get much more in other ways at far less cost."[10] But what Lawson couldn't get "at far less cost" was the North Pole, which, as Beau Riffenburgh writes, was rapidly turning into "as much a competition between . . . newspapers as it was a feud between the rival explorers."[11]

And so the Wellman–*Chicago Record-Herald* Polar Exploration Company was formed late in 1905, with Lawson as president and majority stockholder, by one account to the amount of $75,000.[12] Frank B. Noyes, publisher of the *Record-Herald* and president of the Associated Press, became treasurer, while Wellman operated as general manager. In the December 31, 1905, issue of the *Record-Herald,* Wellman announced the formation of the company and its intent to reach the Pole by airship. He also announced that the famous Brazilian airshipman Alberto Santos-Dumont would accompany him to the Pole as pilot of the airship.

The key to the newspaper's ability to bring the news of the expedition's progress to its readers quickly lay in the construction of three wireless telegraph stations, which would link Wellman on Danes Island with the *Record-Herald*'s editorial room in Chicago.[13] In the end, the firm contracted to build the stations, the De Forest Wireless Telegraph Company, managed to install only the one at Hammerfest, and a wireless was also installed on board Wellman's expedition transport vessel *Frithjof.* But only a small number of dispatches were heard from the island. "The number of messages we were able to get through in nowise compensated us for the outlay of money, labor and annoyance," wrote Wellman.[14]

As he had when he journeyed to Franz Josef Land in 1898, Wellman clearly wanted the chance to solve the mystery of Andrée. The Swedish explorer Otto Nordenskïold held out the hope that Wellman's airship might land on some as yet undiscovered island in the unexplored regions around the Pole, where Wellman would be able to "search for relics of the Swedish pioneers of arctic aerial navigation."[15] If he could accomplish no more than that, Wellman would score one of the journalistic coups of the century, as was eventually shown when Andrée's last camp was finally located on White Island in 1930. In the words of one writer decades later: "There are well-informed, sensible people who assert that the find on Vitön [Kvitøya, or White Island] marks a turning point in the history of journalism, [a model for] present-day newspaper reportage—hectic, excitable and with a thirst for illustrations."[16]

Yet despite these laudable attempts to advance exploration technology, the advertising issue continued to dog Wellman, even after he reached Danes Island. There, in 1906, a German journalist told him that it seemed as if he was trying for the pole "as an advertising affair."[17]

By 1909, after Victor Lawson had tired of funding Wellman's polar ambitions and had agreed to give his journalist the use of the airship and facilities at Virgo Harbor free of charge, Wellman was confronted with having to find other financial backers. This brought back the stigma of appealing to advertisers directly for their support. It was a situation Wellman never escaped. Perhaps because he was himself a journalist, he seemed more vulnerable than his contemporaries in exploration to the "advertising scheme" criticism. The more Wellman protested the purity of his motives, the more it seemed to his critics he was covering up for a crude commercial venture.

*W*ithin three days of Wellman's announcement of the polar airship expedition in late 1905, the plan was greeted by newspapers across the country and around the world by a combination of comment that ranged from interested optimism to tolerant bemusement to open ridicule. For almost a month thereafter, the *Record-Herald* published excerpts of these editorial comments, favorable or not, regarding its sponsored expedition. If the *Record-Herald* had sought to bring its name to the attention of the nation, it had succeeded.

The editorials can be divided into three categories. First there were the unfavorable notices that concentrated their criticism on the benefits that would accrue to advertisers in the *Record-Herald* if the expedition succeeded; these notices often took dryly humorous jabs at Wellman's predilection for writing long dispatches.

The second category was a somewhat skeptical although more neutral one, and included references to three men: Stanley, Verne, and Peary. These editorials compared Wellman's "editorial" assignment with that given to Stanley, or invoked the memory of Jules Verne, the father of science fiction who had passed away little more than six months before Wellman's announcement, or offered advice to Wellman if he should meet up with Robert Peary, who himself would be making another of his over-ice sledge assaults on the Pole in 1906. In some cases, two of these names were mentioned in the same editorial. A related theme found in these editorials centers on the Stanley-esque faith reporters had in themselves, a notion that went something like "it's time for the scientists to step aside and let the reporters handle the problem."

The third category comprises serious comment, wherein the newspaper involved made a genuine attempt to evaluate Wellman's chances. In this category, some newspapers even took credit for advancing the idea of a polar airship expedition themselves. Many editorials in this category mentioned the progress of science and technology in the eight years since Andrée's disappearance.

A sampling of the comments in these editorials gives a sense of the national impact of Wellman's plans, as well as his standing among his peers, a standing that ranged from buffoon to a kind of journalistic hero. Let us begin with several comments in the first category, which saw Wellman as a buffoon and puppet of advertisers. These comments were published in the *Record-Herald* between January 3 and January 6, 1906.

From January 3:

> There may be some difference of opinion as to whether the announcement that two men are to start for the north pole in an airship would not have been more in accordance with the fitness of things had it been made on April fool's day instead of Dec. 30. [Wellman] is a Chicago newspaper correspondent who made some years ago a widely heralded "dash" for the pole, whose only notable result was a generous supply of "copy" which threw no light on the polar mystery. . . . On the face of it the expedition would seem to promise results more profitable to the advertiser than to the geographer (*Cleveland Plain Dealer*).

> Walter Wellman may not find the north pole, but if he fails he can tell a longer story about it than any other man could write (*Toledo Blade*).

> Walter Wellman ought to reach the north pole on air if anyone can (*South Bend* [Ind.] *Tribune*).

> A Chicago newspaper has assigned one of its reporters to the task of building an airship and finding the north pole. Might as well make it strong and assign him to bring it back with him (*Indianapolis Star*).

> Walter Wellman's manifestation of confidence in the administration [of Theodore Roosevelt] could go no further than his decision to make a dash

for the north pole, leaving the President and Congress to look after national affairs. It will be their fault if they fail (*Washington Post*).

From January 4:

Walter Wellman is supposed to have spurned the idea of discovering the north pole by means of a submarine boat as entirely too simple and non-spectacular (*Kansas City Star*).

From January 5:

In this [expedition] there evidently is more desire to advertise a newspaper and increase circulation than to achieve a scientific victory (*Denver Republican*).

A more harebrained expedition was never planned by men, with the possible exception of the balloon voyage of the ill-fated Andrée, who paid the penalty with his life. . . . Mr. Wellman is welcome to his experiment. It is a pity, for he was a good newspaperman (*Grand Forks* [N.D.] *Herald*).

It is almost superfluous to add that [Wellman's] newspaper will do all the blowing the airship may require (*Toronto Star*).

Whether Walter Wellman reaches the north pole or not there will be a lot of interesting news connected with the daring venture, and the newspaper that backs him is well aware of this fact (*Cleveland Plain Dealer*).

Probably Walter Wellman will take some of his Washington dispatches along as a form of compressed hot air (*St. Paul Pioneer Press*).

From January 6:

That hardy arctic explorer may be a Wellman when he starts, but considering the hardships, does he expect to be a well man when he returns? (*Des Moines Register and Leader*).

Mr. Wellman wants to be careful the north pole doesn't puncture his airship when he hits it (*Calumet* [Mich.] *Mining-Gazette*).

Comments in the second category, which viewed Wellman as another Stanley, can be judged from the following excerpts, published by the *Record-Herald* from January 3 to January 5, 1906.

From January 3:

Correspondent Walter Wellman's assignment to build an airship, proceed to the north pole and report by wireless is the biggest one yet. It even outdoes Mr. Bennett's memorable order to Mr. Stanley to go to central Africa and find Livingstone (*Boston Herald*).

Walter Wellman's programme for an airship dash to the north pole has all the imagination of Jules Verne's own romances. . . . It is a fascinating possibility, and we hope he will be able to navigate without an air wreck. We shall watch him with closest attention and hope that if he notes Peary anywhere on or in the ice, making slow headway, he will stop and pick him up. It would be a generous chapter to the aeronautic adventure. Then, if all went well, Lieutenant Peary, having studied the route from overhead, could go on and carry it out along the earth's surface if he chose (*Boston Record*).

One newspaper gave Henry M. Stanley an assignment to go to Africa and find Livingstone, and he did it. Now, another has given Walter Wellman an assignment to build an airship and find the north pole, which is a much more difficult task. . . . At last the north pole is going to be discovered. There is no doubt about it this time. Walter Wellman, who tried it once [sic] before, and Santos-Dumont, the young Brazilian who flies airships, are going to do it. There is no trouble about it at all. All that is necessary is to build a proper airship, transport it to Spitzbergen and then sail over to the pole, 550 miles away, plant a flag and sail back again. That's all. Just as easy as rolling off a log. . . . All is arranged—all save the disposition of the pole after it has been captured and properly tagged. Up to date no one interested seems to know just what to do with it (*Philadelphia Inquirer*).

When Stanley found Livingstone in the darkest jungles of Africa he was backed by a newspaper man, James Gordon Bennett. But Stanley had Wellman bested, for he went to a country where the weather was warm and there were people. Mr. Wellman is going to venture into the unknown region of ice and snow, where typewriter oil freezes solid (*Ottumwa* [Iowa] *Courier*).

A Chicago newspaper proprietor has given a staff correspondent an assignment to get an airship and find the north pole. He may be in earnest. Once upon a time a newspaper reporter was told to find Livingstone and the reporter did so. . . . And it is to be remembered that Jules Verne lived to see some of his dreams outstripped by accomplished facts (*New York World*).

From January 4:

How disappointed Walter Wellman and Santos-Dumont will be if when they reach the north pole in their airship they find Peary just carving his initials on it! (*Boston Globe*).

Walter Wellman is arranging to make a trip to the north pole in an airship. He is being provisioned by that enterprising paper, the *Chicago Record-Herald* (*Benton Harbor* [Mich.] *News-Palladium*).

If [the expedition] shall fail, all the newspapers will print the story of the sailing, and, after months of weary waiting, hoping against hope, rumors of strange white men seen by natives in the far North will drift over the borders of civilization, followed . . . by a tardy acknowledgement that more lives have been sacrificed in the interest of science (*Evansville Courier*).

From January 5:

Such a daring conception is possible only in the dingy office of an American daily newspaper. . . . Indeed there is a strong possibility that the organization of the expedition under the practical guidance of a great business enterprise may bring success where the merely scientific attempt failed (*Sioux Falls* [S.D.] *Argus-Leader*).

[Wellman] is one of those newspaper men of whom the late Henry Stanley was a type—energetic, adventurous and full of pluck and determination. Poor Andrée met a sad fate, and the public curiousity [sic] as to what had become of him has never yet been satisfied. But he had no wireless telegraph apparatus, as Wellman will have, and he was not a newspaper man, as Wellman is. When a newspaper man is given an assignment he gets results (*San Antonio Express*).

Now that the newspapers have gotten after the north pole it will have to give up the way Africa did (*Peoria Herald-Transcript*).

Comments in the third category, which viewed Wellman as a scientist and technologist, though far less numerous, were for the most part written in greater detail, and can be judged from the following excerpts. They appeared in the *Record-Herald* between January 3 and January 5, 1906.

From January 3:

The Chicago Record-Herald is a newspaper not given to advertising itself by the employment of claptrap and buncombe. Its Washington correspondent, Walter Wellman, has for years been rightly regarded as representative of the best type of present-day journalism. For these reasons the announcement that *The Record-Herald* has commissioned Mr. Wellman to start from Spitzbergen in June in an airship in search of the north pole is not likely to be followed in a few weeks with a positive denial after the newspaper and its correspondent have received all the benefit possible from the newspaper discussion which the plan is certain to provoke. The scheme is spectacular and its success is problematical. Should it fail, it will have met with no worse fate than has befallen every other attempt to reach the pole. Should it succeed Mr. Wellman and *The Record-Herald* will have performed a service which the world has long asked. Santos-Dumont is to be Mr. Wellman's companion and the airship, which is to be completed in April, will be given thorough tests in trips across the Mediterranean and North seas. After the final start is made daily reports of the events of the voyage are to be sent back by wireless telegraphy. . . . The project is one which five years ago would have been considered worthy of the imagination of Jules Verne. Now, though regarded as a desperate chance, it may, if not successful, point the way to a method by which, when the construction and control or airships has come to be something of an exact science, the pole can be reached (*Louisville Times*).

From January 4:

What Mr. Wellman is now planning to do is to act on the suggestion repeatedly made by the Tribune and rely on an airship for transportation after he has reached Spitsbergen. Andrée's lamentable failure shows the folly of employing an ordinary balloon, and the lesson of the brave Swede's mistake is emphasized by Dr. Otto Nordenskjold, who is now in this country and who says that in summer the prevailing direction of the winds in the vicinity of the pole is northerly. Hense [sic] only an airship which is self-propelled could be of any real use there; and as between an aeroplane and a machine of the Santos-Dumont type, the latter at present seems to give the better promise of performing the desired service (*New York Tribune*).

From January 5:

The aim of the undertaking is not to land at the pole, particularly, but to learn all that is possible of the circumpolar region: its conditions; whether it is made up of land or water; what its climatic conditions are; whether any forms of life exist there; . . . the phenomena of the earth's magnetism in that part of the globe (*Rockford* [Ill.] *Register-Gazette*).

All the latest discoveries of science will be at their disposal, and such an attempt as this compared with that of Andrée would seem to be far from foolhardy (*Providence Journal*).

The project . . . is not novel, for it is but an elaboration of the plan of Andrée. . . . Wellman will have the advantage of being able to communicate by means of wireless telegraphy, which had not been perfected in Andrée's day (*Utica Press*).

The *Record-Herald* kept up this drumbeat of editorial comment throughout the month of January, 1906. The mere announcement of the expedition was in itself enough to drive press coverage for weeks, while keeping the name of the *Record-Herald* before the nation.

In his own writings, Wellman dismissed the first category of criticism as that "which always accompanies pioneering endeavours," and made by small-minded people who would always equate a high aim like trying to reach the Pole with stunts like "going over Niagra [sic] in a barrel."[18] And he made it quite clear that even if advertising *was* involved in polar exploration, it was no more improper there than in any other venture, "as much a part of modern business as bookkeeping or payday. . . . If goods are to be manufactured to meet the demands of modern civilization, they must be sold. Advertising is part of the selling machinery." But Wellman went even further. Indeed, in Wellman's view, "to sneer at advertising is to sneer at civilization itself."

More than anything else in the world, advertising has served to make industrialism, commercialism, the handmaidens of literature, of art, of science, of the diffusion of knowledge and culture among the human mass. So, please do not take advertising out of our modern life. If you do, at a blow you stop all the magazines and newspapers, cut short the careers of thousands of writers and illustrators, send the world backward to the dullness of the *Quarterly Review* read by one man in a hundred thousand, [and] make the almanac and the family bible the principle [sic] literature of the masses.[19]

*F*rom an analysis of all these documentary, photographic, and artifactual records, it appears that the common assumption made about the advertising nature of Wellman's airship expeditions may have been mistaken. In Wellman's aeronautical memoir *The Aerial Age,* he writes of the preparations for supplying his airship expedition. "Tons of provisions were purchased from Armour & Co., Chicago, and Acker, Merrall & Condit, New York, and shipped across the Atlantic. . . . Steel boats I ordered from Mullins, the well-known builder of Salem, Ohio, and a good supply of malted milk from the celebrated Horlick establishment at Racine, Wis."[20]

Of the five brand names found at Virgo Harbor, only one, that of Armour & Company, was found repeated in Wellman's writings. The other four (Mauna, Huntley & Palmers, Doulton, and Lambert) were not represented in Wellman's dispatches, his magazine articles, or his memoirs. Conversely, of the four brand names mentioned in his memoirs (Armour, Acker, Merrall & Condit, Horlick, and Mullins), only Armour & Company was found to be represented by a surviving artifact at Wellman's base camp.

As the only direct material link found to exist between the site and Wellman's writings, the discovery of a can on the site of Wellman's base camp bearing the imprint of "Armour & Company" merited further attention. It led to the notion that perhaps the brand name could be pursued further, into the pages of the *Record-Herald.* If the "tons" of Armour provisions brought to Virgo Harbor by Wellman were represented by a single surviving can, perhaps Armour was promoting itself during the years of Wellman's expeditions as the kind of "official sponsor" so common to contemporary advertising ventures. Certainly if such advertisements could be found, they would lend credence to Wellman's critics.

An examination of the *Record-Herald* microfilm did in fact locate Armour advertisements throughout the months of the 1906 Wellman expedition, but in far different circumstances than those I had anticipated. In the month that the expedition was initially announced, the *Record-Herald* published twenty-one articles relating to it, while Armour & Company placed eighteen advertisements for their packaged hams in the paper. But these advertisements for *"Armour's 'Star,' The Ham What Am,"* were small, two-line, one-column ads, all buried deep in the newspaper. Not only was no mention ever made of the Wellman expedition, but much larger, quarter-page advertisements were routinely purchased in the *Record-Herald* by Armour's main competition in Chicago, the Swift Company.

Comparing the number of Armour advertisements with the number of articles on the Wellman expedition in 1906 during its most significant months (January, July, August), one finds that the level of Armour ads remained fairly constant, while the number of Wellman articles dipped sharply from the end of December 1905, when the initial announcement was made, to August 1906, when the expedition was struggling with the inadequacy of the airship itself at Virgo Harbor.

Even this small direct link between the Virgo Harbor artifacts and the *Record-Herald* advertisers is broken for the expedition years 1907 and 1909. No Armour advertisements are found in the paper in the months of the Wellman expeditions in these years. Furthermore, of the eight other brand names located in the combined documentary, photographic, and artifactual record, none is found advertising in the *Record-Herald* in any of the months of the Wellman airship expeditions. The expeditions, moreover, cannot be linked to the rampant practice of selling useless over-the-counter tonics and cure-alls, which otherwise provided so much revenue to newspapers in the period from 1880 until the First World War.

Perhaps of more significance was an ad placed by the *Record-Herald* itself on January 5, 1906, which described the newspaper as "the best advertising medium in the United States." Wellman denied that his paper had any overarching interest in gaining an advertising advantage from his expeditions ("if it was advertising [the paper wanted, it] could get much more in other ways at far less cost"),[21] but the absence of a substantial link between the brand names associated with the expeditions and the newspaper leads one to set aside the brand names and examine more closely the link between the newspaper and the expeditions themselves. For this examination, I took the number of articles written by Wellman or about his expeditions as an indicator of interest in the expeditions on the part of his newspaper and, by extension, by the public buying the newspaper.

The torrent of articles about the expedition that began with twenty-one in January of 1906 dwindled during the months of preparations leading up to the establishment of Camp Wellman on Virgo Harbor in June of 1906. Four articles appeared in February 1906, one in March, three in April, and one in May. Beginning in June, the summer months can be compared with the coverage that appeared in the *Record-Herald* during the summer months of the expeditions in 1907 and 1909.

In June 1906, three articles on the Wellman expedition appeared. By July, when the wireless station was put into operation at Virgo Harbor, the number of articles climbed to ten. By August, when the mechanical problems of the airship car were becoming apparent and the wireless refused to function with regularity, the number of articles dropped to four. In June 1907, once again three articles appeared, signaling the start of the summer campaign. Possibly because of the failure of 1906, the number of articles in July 1907 remained at three. With the anticipation of the airship finally lifting off in September 1907, the number climbed slightly, to six, in August, but did not approach the number seen at the height of the expedition's popularity in July of 1906. By 1909, only one article appeared in June, and this was followed by complete silence in July. Only when Wellman made his most successful polar flight, in August 1909, does the number of articles increase, and only to three, or the level his publicity *started at* in June of 1906.

The *Record-Herald,* which had covered the expedition of 1906 with such breathless anticipation, and which had cut its coverage slightly—and made that coverage somewhat more subdued—in 1907, was almost ignoring Wellman's expedition altogether by 1909.

If public interest in the expeditions, as reflected in the number of articles published, can be seen to have peaked during the first expedition at the same moment when Wellman had the least to report from Virgo Harbor, this reaction can be attributed to an expectation, or "hype," effect, built up by Wellman himself. This effect was followed by a "let-down" effect in coverage when it became apparent the expedition was going nowhere in 1906.

After the failure of the first expedition, a leveling, or "caution" stage, of public interest can be seen during 1907, followed by slightly renewed interest when Wellman actually made a flight in 1907, but this renewed interest did not match the level of the "hype" effect in the summer of 1906. After the failure of the second expedition, there was an almost total lack of interest, or "dismissal," effect, during the start of the third expedition, just at the moment when Wellman's chances of actually attaining the Pole were the greatest. When Wellman made his most successful flight, in 1909, public interest did not even rise to the point of the lowest number of articles in the summer of 1906.

To gauge whether this disinterest in Wellman could be attributed to the failure of the expedition or to a lack of public interest in aviation generally, I compared the number of articles on aeronautical progress in the summer of 1909 with those concerning Wellman.

This comparison shows that public interest in aviation climbed steadily in the summer of 1909, even as interest in the Wellman polar expeditions waned.

The one article on Wellman appearing in June 1909 was one more than general aviation received. By July, when interest in Wellman dropped to nothing, four articles appeared on aviation generally. This was the month of Hubert Latham's unsuccessful attempt to cross the English Channel, which was followed by Louis Bleriot's successful crossing on July 25. Combined with Count Ferdinand von Zeppelin's announcement of his own planned airship expedition to the North Pole, this month signaled the end of the geographic isolation that some countries—like Britain—had enjoyed for centuries.

In August, interest in aviation was heightened still further by the great air meet held in Rheims, France, where world records were set one day only to be broken the next, and by Count von Zeppelin's flight of 450 miles from Friedrichshafen to Berlin, a feat which set off near-riots of enthusiasm in the German capital. Eight articles on these aeronautical advances were published in this month, compared with only three from Wellman on Danes Island.

Clearly, there was no lack of interest in aviation on the part of the *Record-Herald* or the general public in August of 1909. But the newspaper, like the public, had patience with progress that could be quantified in readily digested geographic metaphors: the cross-channel breach, the city-to-city Zeppelin service, the sexy "sound bites" of exploration. Abbreviated flights across anonymous pack ice held little public appeal, unless they could be "sold" as new geographic accomplishments.

For Wellman, his Arctic airship odyssey ended with a somewhat ignominious flight of sixty miles, which seemed insignificant next to Bleriot's channel flight, even though it traversed three times the distance. Contrary to the general perception of him as an advertising shill, archaeological analysis suggests that Wellman was ignored even by his own newspaper just as the possibilities for aviation seemed brightest.

CHAPTER FIVE

Broken Dreams:
The Airship Wrecks
of Danes Island

*T*he polar historian Dr. Beau Riffenburgh suggests that newspaper accounts can be used as primary sources for accounts of expeditions, because they offer an idea of "what the 'common man' actually knew about explorers . . . more clearly than would a study of expedition accounts, society publications, or private journals or letters."[1] The case of Walter Wellman and his attempts to reach the North Pole in an airship is rare in that he was at once both explorer *and* newspaperman. It was not a secondhand reporter offering the public an account of some far-off expedition, but the expedition leader himself.

For an archaeologist following the lead of Richard Gould's work, this leads to the notion that both factual and conceptual aspects of Wellman's contemporary newspaper and magazine accounts of his expeditions might lend themselves to being evaluated against the backdrop of his later memoirs, with the archaeology of Camp Wellman serving as a mediator for any discrepancies arising between the written accounts. Articles written for daily newspapers are written on the emotion of the moment, while memoirs are considered at length, many times with a view toward painting the past in a particular shade of truth. Where differences in wording, interpretation, or emphasis are found between the immediate and the secondary accounts, they can be posed as questions to be asked of the archaeological record.

This is an especially valuable exercise since Wellman's personal correspondence and personal diaries, if they exist for his airship expeditions, have not so far been located. This immediate correspondence is what one would normally attempt to match against later memoirs and expedition accounts. Yet in this case, they almost wouldn't matter. Part of the rationale for Wellman's polar airship initiatives was to increase the speed by which newspapers received news of polar expeditions, in part by setting up a wireless station in his expedition headquarters at Virgo Harbor, headquarters he called the Chicago Record-Herald House, but in the main by installing a wireless transmitter on board the airship itself and sending the message directly to the *Record-Herald* when the airship reached the Pole.

Up to that time, accounts of polar expeditions had often arrived months or even years after the event. But after Marconi's development of wireless telegraphy between 1895 and 1900, and in particular after Marconi's transmission of an electromagnetic signal from England to Newfoundland in December 1901, newspapers realized the competitive advantage to be gained by such rapid communication with correspondents in the field.[2] By the summer of 1907, the *New York Times* established regular transatlantic wireless communications. Priority for the first wireless message ever sent from the Arctic, however, goes to Wellman, who on July 22, 1906, sent a wireless dispatch from the Chicago Record-Herald House at Virgo Harbor to his newly built station at Hammerfest in northern Norway, which passed it to the station at Tromsø, which in turn sent it by cable across the Atlantic to President Theodore Roosevelt in Washington, where it was redirected to the president at his summer home at Oyster Bay, Long Island, New York. The message read: "Roosevelt, Washington. Greetings, best wishes by first wireless message ever sent from arctic regions. Wellman." He immediately sent another message to Chicago, which was printed in the morning edition of the *Record-Herald* on July 23, 1906.

Wellman's dispatches by wireless are notable not only for their speed and priority, but because they offer his almost instantaneous assessments of his expedition's activities, without recourse to more than a few moments of deliberation over particular events. Such descriptions for other expeditions of the era were months or years in coming, and then only after filtration through hindsight, or better judgment, and often with a view toward book sales, or reputation-building, or face-saving. The key point is that these dispatches form one of three facets of the documentary record relating to the construction of the different versions of Wellman's airship *America*. The other two are his contemporary journal articles, in *National Geographic* and *McClure's,* and his later memoir *The Aerial Age,* written five years after his first airship expedition, and seventeen years after his first visit to Danes Island in 1894.

The limitation of these documentary texts is that they present sometimes conflicting accounts. But if we turn to the archaeological record, we can use it as a screen through which to filter the texts and reach a closer approximation of what actually happened. In this chapter, I constructed my archaeological screen from data gathered from the remains of Wellman's airships, which I found and mapped at his base camp at Virgo Harbor.

The filtered history of these wrecks is then used to search for technological trends in the historical record,[3] and to suggest ways in which the archaeological remains can be seen as material representations of larger cultural concerns.

*T*hough the first flights of Santos-Dumont and Zeppelin lasted but minutes, they announced the opening of the airship age and, with it, the reorientation of human thought and ambitions from the horizontal to the vertical. Not only were these giant aeronautical technologies the most obvious heralds of a time of radical progress in transportation and communication; they also signaled the start of the era of insecurity. The psychological comforts of European borders, which had changed little since the defeat of Napoleon, began to crumble before the specter of aerial armadas capable, quite literally, of extending warfare to new heights.

More progressive voices were also heard, suggesting that aeronautics would lead to the scientific removal of warfare as an option for the resolution of human conflict, demolish the barriers between East and West, and extend the reach of science.[4] Wellman himself felt this way, remarking that if the "airship was good enough for the purposes of war, it ought to be good enough for geographic exploration, as an instrument with which to extend man's knowledge of the earth."[5]

As a witness to this momentous technological and psychological change, while enduring both the humiliation and pain suffered as a result of his first two attempts to reach the North Pole across the tortuous pack ice, Wellman began to formulate his own plans to extend the new aerial age to the shores of the Arctic Ocean.

*I*n late 1905, Wellman was drawn to favorable notices on the new French *Lebaudy* dirigible because it had made a large number of short voyages.[6] It seemed to him just the machine to employ in an attempt to reach the Pole while avoiding the miseries he had suffered at Walden Island in 1894 and in Franz Josef Land in 1899. After he persuaded Victor Lawson to finance an attempt by air, Wellman's first polar airship expedition was announced in the *Chicago Record-Herald* on December 31, 1905. It was noted prominently in this story that Santos-Dumont would accompany Wellman as pilot of the airship.

Less than a week later, a notice in the *Record-Herald* related that Wellman was on his way to Paris to meet with Santos-Dumont, and that the two of them would "immediately confer with the celebrated aeronautic constructor, Louis Godard, who is to devote all his time until the task is completed to building the largest airship that has ever been launched. M. Santos-Dumont will supervise the growth of the colossus."[7] Thus, though stating in his memoirs that he went to Paris in January 1906, consulted with the leading French aeronautical designers of the day, and concluded that the airship as then developed offered "at least a promising means of reaching the Pole,"[8] it would seem that this, as well as contracting with Godard to build the airship, was something he had decided before he left Chicago. Perhaps Wellman did not wish to seem, at least in his memoirs, as hasty in his estimation of the possibilities of the airship as he had been with his sponsor.

Wellman signed a contract with Godard for the construction of the polar airship on January 30, 1906. In his dispatch to the *Record-Herald,* Wellman made clear that "the machine will be the most solid and enduring, and will be regardless of expense," and, as example of such construction, Wellman stressed that "the car frame [of the airship] will be of steel tubes." He further noted that his plans "will be closely adhered to, generally following the methods of the Lebaudy airship, without unnecessary experimentation."[9] And in *National Geographic* he wrote, "M. Godard is a conservative, careful man, and I have much faith in him."[10]

Godard himself remarked that he had long considered the possibilities of aerostatic polar exploration, even going so far as to claim credit for the idea. "But this time my projects take form," Godard was quoted as telling a reporter. "My dream is realized, or soon will be."[11]

Despite these shows of faith both in and from Godard, little more than a week later Wellman seemed to be hedging his bets, cabling Chicago to say that should trials of Godard's airship be unsuccessful, he would return from Spitsbergen to Paris in the autumn of 1906 and "construct an entire new airship for the attempt in 1907."[12]

In future dispatches from Paris, Wellman repeated that a steel car for the airship was a necessity. In May, the wireless engineer who was to accompany the airship to the Pole and transmit messages back to the Chicago Record-Herald House, Maxwell J. Smith, explained why the wireless experiment would be such an interesting one: "We will have to use the steel frame of the airship as an artificial ground. . . . Instead of having a solid mast or anything of that sort, we will have to drop our wires from the frame of the ship. Four long wires will be suspended, each 230 feet long. I am taking an alternating generator along and this will be connected with the fifty-five horse power motor, the larger of the two motors on the airship. All of these appliances I shall attach to the frame of the ship in Paris."[13]

If we compare Wellman's April 1906 article in *National Geographic,* describing the airship, and the same article when it appeared five years later as a chapter in *The Aerial Age,* the differences are interesting. The 1906 version, from *National Geographic,* contains praise for Godard and notes that the car of this airship will be built of steel, compared to contemporary efforts built of "a light framework of bamboo or wood."

> The dirigible which M. Godard and his corps of experts have in hand is an entirely different sort of affair. Its great size enables it to lift not only the balloon, but the car of steel, the three motors, comprising a total of eighty horsepower, two screws or propulseurs, a steel boat, moto-sledges, five men, food for them for seventy-five days, instruments, tools, repair materials, lubricating oils, and 5,500 pounds of gasoline for the motors.[14]

In *The Aerial Age,* this passage is modified, significantly, in light of Wellman's experiences with Godard in the spring of 1906 and with the airship car on Danes Island in July and August 1906:

> Our polar dirigible is an entirely different sort of affair. Its great size enables it to lift not only the balloon, but the car of wood and steel, the three motors, comprising a total of eighty horsepower, two screws or propulseurs, a steel boat, five men, food for them for seventy-five days, instruments, tools, repair materials, lubricating oils, and 5,500 pounds of gasoline for the motors.[15]

Immediately apparent in the later passage is Wellman's dropping of any mention of Godard, as well as the subtraction of the motor sledges he had projected in 1906. But, more significantly, for the first time he mentions that the car of the 1906 airship was constructed not of steel but of "wood and steel." A few pages later, Wellman modifies this description yet again, writing that the car "was of wood reinforced with steel. . . . Upon it were placed the motors and machinery. Each motor was to drive a propeller of wood with canvas facings placed at either end of the car. A tent-like roof gave protection to the crew from wind and weather, and a huge basket was to be swung underneath the car for carrying supplies of gasoline and provisions."[16]

The "huge basket" was originally designed to be a steel boat.[17] In the event the airship was forced onto the pack, such a boat would be necessary for crossing leads of open water on the return march. But, as Wellman writes in 1911, and as can be seen in a photograph from the archives of the Norsk Polarinstitutt, this car, when it arrived at Virgo Harbor, was instead made of wicker.

There is also a discrepancy in the written record regarding the length of the car. In the *National Geographic* article, Wellman writes, and a design drawing confirms, that the car is to be "16 meters, or 52.5 feet [long]; width, outside, 1m. .80, or 71 inches; width, inside, 1m. .70, or 67 inches."[18] In *The Aerial Age*, Wellman writes of the car as "a platform about thirty feet in length and five feet wide."[19]

The Godard airship was completed in pieces in Paris in late May 1906, and then only after a strike by engineers at Godard's aeronautical works had delayed Wellman's program and forced the journalist to find the engines for the airship himself when Godard proved unable to do so. A public demonstration of the motors—attended by, among others, Prince Albert of Monaco—was labeled "eminently successful" when the 70-hp main engine developed 100 hp instead of the 75 hp contracted for.[20] The airship was provided a barograph for an altimeter, a statoscope that measured whether the airship was rising or falling, and manometers that gauged the pressure of gas in the balloon and air in the ballonet.[21]

Returning to his *Record-Herald* dispatches, we find one cabled to Chicago from Tromsø, dated July 1, 1906, wherein Wellman writes that he has no intention of delaying the expedition to 1907 ("I will make a determined effort to reach the north pole this summer, if possible") and, ignoring Zeppelin's *LZ-1*, repeats the claim that his is the "largest and most scientific aerial craft ever constructed. . . . Attached to the balloon will be a steel car, made entirely of steel tubing. This car is 52 and one-third feet long."[22] It is inconceivable, at this point, that Wellman did not know that the car of his airship was not "entirely of steel tubing," yet this is what he states.

Wellman raced his expedition to Virgo Harbor, and once there, as he cabled to the *Record-Herald* on August 14, several "minor defects [were] discovered in the mechanical parts of the airship, but these are remediable, time permitting. The motors work excellently."[23]

In his memoirs, Wellman told a different story. Once on the island, he wrote, the weakness of the Godard design became immediately apparent, as it would seem it should have been in Paris, had Wellman bothered to run tests on the entire airship there. The envelope of the dirigible was never unpacked, much less inflated. The engines, attached to the car and test-fired, promptly self-destructed. "[They] could not be made to work right," Wellman complained. "The driving gear went to pieces, and the propeller could not stand even half the strain which it was designed to put upon them."[24] Wellman realized the error of shipping untested technology into the Arctic. "It was well we [tested the car at Danes Island]," Wellman wrote, somewhat late in the day. "As it turned out it would have been impossible to make an airship voyage that year even if the buildings had been finished in time, because the mechanical part of the *America* was a failure."[25] Wellman sailed south, ready to spend the winter in Paris completely reconfiguring his airship.

*W*ellman returned to Paris in search of someone to redesign his airship. Major Hersey, who had superintended construction at Camp Wellman, returned as well, and with Lieutenant Frank Lahm of the U.S. Army made a flight from Paris to Scotland that won the 1907 James Gordon Bennett balloon race. Through Lahm's father, Wellman met Melvin Vaniman, a creative spirit who occupied a place somewhere between skilled mechanic and full-fledged aeronautical engineer.

Vaniman completely redesigned and then built a new airship for Wellman, then became *America*'s flight engineer once the expedition reached Danes Island. The *Record-Herald,* which went to such lengths in 1906 to promote the work of Godard, is strangely subdued about Vaniman's work, perhaps because he was an unknown designer who did not have Godard's reputation. Vaniman scrapped Godard's conception of a polar airship and replaced it with his own. The airship was lengthened from 164.04 feet to 185 feet, with its capacity increased from 224,244 cubic feet to 258,500 cubic feet.

Vaniman built a new car 115 feet long, 8 feet high, 18 inches wide at the bottom, and 3 feet wide at the top. The bottom of the car consisted of a hollow steel tube 18 inches in diameter, separated into 14 sections, and serving at once as the keel, fuel reservoir, main deck, and engine mount. Once again, Wellman stressed the strength of the "steel nacelle";[26] "a car . . . all in steel tubing, with joints of steel castings, and cords and binders of the strongest steel wire."[27] In *The Aerial Age,* he wrote of the "steel car suspended by steel suspension cables,"[28] and the "steel car, 115 feet long, and containing a steel gasoline reservoir of like length, 18 inches in diameter, [with a] capacity of 1,200 gallons."[29] Gone even in these comparative descriptions is any mention of any part of the car being constructed of wood, or in fact any other material than steel.

Wellman arrived back at Virgo Harbor on June 8, 1907. His dispatches to Chicago spoke of Vaniman's "cleverness" but did not carry the same voice of authority they had when describing Godard.

25. *Melvin Vaniman at Virgo Harbor. (From* The Aerial Age.*)*

After his rescue by the Norwegian survey ship *Farm* in August of 1909, Wellman claimed that he immediately set his crew to work lengthening the airship hangar at Virgo Harbor for another try at the Pole in 1910, while seeming to suggest just the opposite with the car: "The steel car was partly destroyed; but that was small loss, as we should not have used it again in any event."[30]

As we have seen, Wellman offered three varying accounts of Godard's construction of the airship car: from "steel" to "wood and steel" to "wood reinforced with steel." Wellman wrote that he was "far from . . . satisfied with many of the details of this installation,"[31] but decided to bring the airship to Danes Island anyway. The focus on steel construction, especially in the *National Geographic* article, led me during much of my survey of Virgo Harbor to dismiss the wooden frame structure I passed several times a day while surveying other parts of the Wellman base camp. It was farther to the east than any other Wellman structure on the shoreline, and I thought it at first to be possibly no more than the partial remains of a ramp used to transfer supplies from the shoreline to the base camp and hangar. Not until I had lived on the site for two weeks, continuously comparing structures with documentary and photographic sources, did I identify this plain wooden frame as the surviving remains of Godard's airship: surviving eyebolts on the framework coincided with similar fittings shown in a photograph taken of Wellman posing inside the car in a hangar at Christiana (Oslo) in 1906.

Godard's general three-view design drawings, published by Wellman in *National Geographic,* show that the base of the frame was intended to stretch to fifty-two feet (15.8 m) long.[32] Only a rough half of this, about twenty-six feet (7.9 m), has survived. This would tend to support the description in *The Aerial Age,* that the car delivered to Virgo Harbor was only "a platform about thirty feet in length and five feet wide."[33] Yet a photograph I found in the Norwegian Polar Institute archives after my field survey shows the Godard car abandoned in the position it now occupies, with the basketwork gondola just to its south with the name "Wellman Chicago Record Herald Polar Expedition" painted across it. This car appears to be closer to the design specification of fifty-two feet than the twenty-six feet I found in 1993. Wellman in *The Aerial Age* is apparently referring to the area of the main engine deck, and not the tapering sections of the car that supported the drive shafts.

The ruin of the Godard car is located in a bog about one hundred yards from the shore of Virgo Harbor, lying in a north-south direc-

26. *The remains of the wooden Godard 1906 airship car, on the shore at Virgo Harbor in July 1993. (Photo by the author.)*

tion. It consists of two, two-by-four-inch pieces of wood separated by three metal tubes two inches in diameter. The eastern section of wood is thirteen feet one inch long; the western section is twenty-two feet long, with an additional piece at its southern end, collapsed into the bog, forty-five inches long. The width of the car is five feet seven inches along the inner edge of the frame, and five feet eleven inches measured along the outer edge of the frame. Notches are cut every twenty inches into the inner side of the wooden frame.

The metal separating tubes are surmounted by short lengths of wood, four inches wide, that form the basis of the main deck, and these are attached to the metal tubes with screws set sixteen inches apart. Two of the three metal tubes have rusted to such an extent, they have collapsed into the bog. The spacing between these three remaining separating tubes is not uniform. The middle tube is twenty inches from the southern tube, fifteen inches from the northern.

The tubes end in metal casings, which are in turn attached to the wooden side frame by two bolts bolted through the wood. These through-bolts attach on the outer edge of the wooden frame to what was once metal sheathing that ran from one end of the outer edge to the other. Along this outer sheathing are the eyebolts that led to the identification of the car as Godard's. One eyebolt remains on the outer edge of the eastern frame, and five on the outer edge of the western frame. One of these eyebolts on the western frame still retains a small length of wire, showing that these eyebolts were used as wire stays.

What is immediately clear from this description is how much it varies from Wellman's. This has important implications for how we view Wellman's thought process after the turn of century, and what he believed his readers would accept as "progress" in the search for the North Pole. Clearly, an airship with a wooden car was seen as primitive and unworthy of the great challenge, so Wellman chose to cover this wooden construction, literally and in his dispatches, with steel.

*M*elvin Vaniman's drawings of his redesign of the Wellman polar airship have never been located. Therefore the only way to gain an appreciation of this design, and to compare it against the Godard design and other contemporary airships, was to travel to Virgo Harbor, discover if any of the airship had survived on the site, and record the details hidden from the historical record.

The remains from the redesigned car built by Vaniman for the 1907 and 1909 flights consist mostly of a long tubelike construction discarded at the southwestern end of the site. From pieces of wire and fabric still attached to it, I soon identified it as the remains of the 115-foot-long fuel tank.

The fuel tank's four sections consist of three large tubes lying more or less east to west (the southern, middle, and northern sections), with a shorter tube lying north to south across two of the longer sections. These tubes are 18 inches in diameter as measured across an inner side of the flange at the end of the tube, and 19.5 inches measured across the outer edge of the flange. This flange was bolted to the end of the fuel tank with rivets spaced 1.25 inches apart. Where the flange was used to connect the long sections to each other, it contained boltholes spaced 2.5 inches apart.

The long tube sections were formed by riveting together two sheets of steel, with the rivets spaced an inch apart and at right angles to each other. The southern section is 22 feet 6 inches long; the middle section 24 feet 8 inches long; and the northern section 23 feet 5 inches long. The smaller north-to-south section is approximately 6 feet long. Taken together, this amounts to 76 feet 7 inches, from a fuel tank that originally stretched to 115 feet. The differences in the length of these recorded sections is attributed to crushing, bending,

27. *The bow of Wellman's 1909 airship, found at Virgo Harbor in 1993. The rotting wooden planks, sheathed on the inner surface by metal, are clearly visible. (Photo by the author.)*

and decay of the steel in the tubes. These sections are formed from smaller sections that measure 8 feet 2.5 inches long, which overlap the following section by approximately 2 inches. At the point of these overlaps, the tubes are riveted together with a ring of rivets traveling all the way around the diameter of the two joined tubes, the rivets spaced 1.25 inches apart and at right angles to each other.

I recorded tabs on an average of 16 inches apart. These tabs were bolted to the tank with a .25-inch bolt, and a small triangle of solder placed above and behind the tank to separate the top of the tab from the tank. A hole .125 inch in diameter at the top of the tab served as an attachment point for the main deck of the airship, where the crew walked and where the machinery was attached.

The southern section is evidently the engine deck of the airship, and the middle part of this tube contains two square, boxlike arrangements, 19 inches long by 18 inches wide, where the engines were connected to the main deck. A semicircular depression 9.75 inches long and 16.5 inches wide appears between these two boxlike sections.

Across the top of the smaller north-to-south section of fuel tank, the remains of the wooden frame have fallen. These wooden members are clad in a sheet metal skin, 2.5 inches wide, that is attached along the inner edge of the wooden frames with rivets spaced 3 inches apart and diagonally from each other. These wooden framework sections, 1.75 inches wide and 2 inches high, were, to my surprise, fluted down their length, and the sheet steel covers this fluting.

Of the remains of this upper framework I observed at Virgo Harbor, the wooden sections have all parted at the point where a steel casing joint meets the wood, while the metal sheeting, even in the absence of the wooden spar, has remained intact. One cross beam steel tube 1 inch in diameter remains attached to two side frame members, spacing them apart by a width of 30 inches along the inner edge of the frame and 34.25 inches along the outer edge. These 1-inch steel tubes are spaced every 99 inches along the wooden frame. This 99-inch measurement is in sync with the 8-foot-2.5-inch length of the steel fuel tank sections. Between these 1-inch cross beams, smaller guy stays were placed that also acted as holders for smaller, .5-inch, steel cross beams. These were spaced every 33 inches between the larger cross beams, down the length of the metal cladding of the wooden frame.

The steel casings, 2.125 inches wide, form a multiple attachment point, joining lengths of wooden spar together, serving as the attachment point for the steel tubes joining the fuel cell to the upper frame, connecting the steel tubes joining two sides of the wooden frame together, and serving as attachment points for the bracing wires stretched diagonally to form the box truss that stiffened the upper framework.

All of these details have a direct connection with Vaniman, and how he sought to modify Godard's original conception of an airship that could travel very long distances, to the point where he eventually replaced it with one of his own. (I should point out that none of this is clear when you are in the field measuring these small rivets and long fuel tanks. As with those funny glass birds that eventually topple over onto their beaks when the water in them reaches a certain level, these details gather in your brain until they reach a kind of critical mass. If you are lucky, they then spill over into some new insight.)

*E*ven with the evidence of a small wooden frame lying in ruins upon an Arctic shore, it is still hard to imagine an open wooden car being employed for a polar airship flight, even in 1906. Yet Wellman's airship was infinitely superior to Andrée's free-floating hydrogen balloon.

When the same fates that had cursed Andrée fell upon Wellman, he had the option of turning his ship around and retreating to Virgo Harbor, an option that was never open to Andrée. In twelve years of technological development between 1897 and 1909, aerial polar exploration had progressed to the point where failure of the technology did not automatically mean certain death. The explorer had new options, and Wellman used them to save his life.

Wellman had another option as well, one he never mentions and does not seem to have considered. Even with the loss of the ballast from the trailing guide-rope, he still had the option of using Vaniman's swiveling propellers, with their wash directed upward, to bring the airship closer to the pack. In fact, Vaniman himself intended to use this very method for his planned transatlantic flight in 1912. Had Wellman adopted this solution, the *America* could have continued the journey northward with the forward propellers pulling and the rear swiveling props keeping the airship in equilibrium.

The question then becomes, Was this construction typical of other airships of the day? And if such construction was standard on other French dirigibles of that era—*La Patrie,* for example—what was the basis for believing it could survive conditions in the Arctic? I examined these questions after searching the archives of the National Air & Space Museum in Washington, D.C., for aeronautical engineering records relating to airship design at the turn of the century.

The files related to Louis Godard contain published résumés for the French balloon and airship designer. The first of these contained a design drawing for Godard's 1902 airship, a craft with two gasoline engines generating 100 hp and driving two propellers mounted fore and aft.[34] The twin engines are listed as generating speeds of fifty kilometers an hour. The Godard car of this 1902 airship design exhibits the basic features, in this elevation view, of the polar airship designed for Wellman in 1906, without the basketwork gondola that was to have been slung underneath the engine deck and serve as a hold for gasoline and other supplies.

In this same year of 1902, Paul and Pierre Lebaudy, under the supervision of engineer Henri Julliot, designed and built the first large-scale practical dirigible in France. Beneath the envelope of their *Lebaudy I* was a car made of steel tubing, and slung beneath this steel structure was a gondola of basketwork that contained the powerplant and crew.[35] This airship on November 12, 1903, flew thirty-eight miles (61 km) from Moisson to the Champs-de-Mars, Paris, gaining recognition as the first controlled voyage by a practical dirigible.[36] It was this somewhat proven design—a basketwork gondola slung beneath a steel frame—that Wellman apparently believed he was getting when he contracted with Godard in the spring of 1906. And it seems clear that Godard was influenced in his designs by the success of *Lebaudy I,* at least to the extent of imitating certain of its design characteristics in the polar airship.

Godard's 1906 design for the framework of the Wellman polar airship is little changed from his 1902 conception. However, two prominent changes have been made. First, Godard has, incredibly, *reduced* the horsepower from 100 hp in his 1902 design to 75 hp for the polar airship. Second, Godard has apparently borrowed the slung basket concept from the successful Lebaudy design, but for the polar airship it is announced that the basketwork gondola will be replaced by a steel boat, which will not only carry fuel and supplies, but enable the explorers to return to land should the airship crash or run out of fuel. The Lebaudy brothers had by 1906 built additional models of their basic 1902 design, and these were used by the French military. Other copies were purchased by Britain, Russia, and Austria. The Lebaudy military version, named *La Patrie,* incorporated the significant modification of replacing the basketwork gondola with one of steel.

Historian Stephen Kern writes that in "the complex interaction between need and technological invention, it is difficult to identify one or the other exclusively as causal."[37] Wellman's announcement of a steel boat on his airship, set against my discovery in the photographic archives of a gondola constructed not of steel but of wood and basketwork, comprises an important discrepancy. Wellman repeatedly disparaged Andrée's balloon and wicker basket as a "mere toy of the winds."[38] His own polar airship, he repeatedly assured readers of the *Record-Herald* and *National Geographic* in the spring of 1906, would confront those winds with internal combustion and steel, not wood and basketwork.

Both the archaeological and photographic data indicate just the opposite. Wellman brought to Danes Island in the summer of 1906 not a boat of steel attached to a car of steel tubing, but rather a wooden airship car carrying a wicker basket underneath. Worse, this polar airship was supplied with less horsepower than an airship designed four years earlier for pleasant excursions over the warm summer fields of France. The propellers, mounted at each end of the car, were built of fabric stretched over radius sticks. Clearly, Wellman's writings that the airship had become a practical reality by the spring of 1906 were vastly overstated in light of the archaeological findings.

Wellman's decisions to make up for deficiencies in design and range of the Godard polar airship through the adoption of motor sledges, and when that proved unsatisfactory, to go ahead and attempt the

28. *The wrecked car of* America *is returned to Virgo Harbor in August 1909. The buckled wood of the upper framework is evident. Smoke rises from the chimney of the Chicago Record-Herald House in the background. (Courtesy of the Norwegian Polar Institute archives.)*

flight to the North Pole in an airship he must have known could not take him close to his goal, reflect a notion of technological determinism prevalent at the turn of the century. If the technology became available, it would be used, and used everywhere, and therefore it was to an individual's, or a nation's, advantage to use it first. Hence the notions that the airplane, by its very existence, would break down national barriers immediately and uniformly, that humankind's rise into the third dimension was at once immediate and complete, and that warfare in the third dimension would automatically become so destructive and "scientific" that it would lead to the abolition of war.[39] Between 1896 and 1909, aeronautical technology advanced at such a quickening pace that what seemed so fantastic when Andrée proposed his balloon expedition was considered almost routine by the time of Wellman's third airship expedition.

The pivotal air meet held at Rheims in August 1909—as Wellman at Virgo Harbor readied *America 2B* for its last polar attempt—focused on endurance and range, the twin aeronautical markers of success that had come into such sharp focus with Bleriot's crossing of the English Channel on July 25. In 1906, Wellman was also concerned with range; he was, after all, trying to fly seven hundred miles to the

North Pole. But the archaeological data show no such concern in the remains of his 1906 polar airship (*America 1*). It is a meager thing, ill constructed and hopelessly ill suited to the polar environment. The problem of range and endurance, however, led directly to the re-design *America* underwent in the fall of 1906.

The archaeological remains of the Vaniman car are of a radically different character from those of the Godard car. Where the Godard car lacks an obvious fuel tank or any other indication of the kinds of inherent design endurance needed for an attempt on the Pole, the Vaniman fuel tank, or cell, commands immediate attention for its appearance of being almost overbuilt for the job. The quest for the enduring extension of the human body into space is immediately obvious. The fuel cell dominates the surrounding framework debris, debris which is of interest in itself for the light it sheds on the announced durability of the 1907 polar airship (*America 2A*). It signals a concern for range over speed, unlike contemporary European airship models.

When Vaniman's own airship, *Akron*, was destroyed just at the start of a planned transatlantic attempt on July 2, 1912, killing Vaniman and his crew of four, an editorial in *Scientific American* criticized Vaniman's design for "not follow[ing] any European model."[40] But such criticism was misplaced. No European airship designer had grappled with the problems attending long-distance airship flight as had Vaniman, and the speed-versus-range question was almost always ignored. No one pointed out, moreover, that Wellman had "followed the European model" in 1906, and it had failed utterly in Arctic conditions.

The fluting of the wood I recorded at Virgo Harbor may have been done to save weight in 1909, especially after Vaniman attached the car by block and tackle to a weighing machine at Virgo Harbor in 1907 and found it to be 660 pounds (300 kilos) over its design weight.[41] Yet it also seems like a false economy when compared with the weight Wellman proposed to drag behind the airship in the form of his provisions-filled guide-rope.

Photographs taken after the last flight show the frame buckled at several points, and these weak points can be pinpointed to the vital steel casing joints around which the wooden frame members were joined. Here again the wood-versus-steel question comes back to haunt Wellman. Once again he believes in and announces a new airship based on steel construction, and once again the archaeological data show an airship whose weaknesses can be traced, in part, to wooden construction.

It seems evident, as well, that Wellman believed that his newspa-

29. *Workers in a Paris aeronautical factory assemble the airship car for Wellman's 1910 attempt to fly across the Atlantic Ocean. Note that the wooden spars of the upper framework from 1909 have now been replaced by a framework all of steel. (From* The Aerial Age.*)*

per readers would not think highly of an airship car made of wood. His dispatches always reflected the notion that machines could dominate the environment, and steel was a better metaphor for such dominance than wood. He repeats the theme so often that he almost seems to be willing the airship to metamorphose into that which he believes it should be.

We will never know for certain whether Wellman considered this wooden-and-steel construction substantial enough for polar travel, or noticed how badly it had fared during the journey from the pack ice back to the base camp at Virgo Harbor. But we can infer his answer. A year later, when Vaniman again built an airship for Wellman, this time for an attempt to cross the Atlantic, photographic evidence finally points to the complete replacement of wooden spars with steel tubing.

CHAPTER SIX

Gasbag or Windbag: Was Wellman a Liar?

As we have seen, newspaper accounts of expeditions, official records published by explorers or their sponsoring societies, memoirs of the explorers themselves, and photographic records are all different, and sometimes conflicting. When this material is filtered through the screen of the archaeological record, a fuller, more complete history of exploration is generated. In the previous instances, of advertising and airship cars, the archaeology at Virgo Harbor triggered the consideration of new perspectives on large questions: Were polar expeditions merely extravagant forms of corporate promotion? How did entire cultures react to the increasing and intimidating range of aircraft?

But can archaeology tell us about things much smaller, or even minute? Can the material we leave behind testify to the truthfulness, or lack thereof, of our individual statements? I believe it sometimes can, and the archaeology of hydrogen production at Virgo Harbor is one such area that allows us to evaluate such questions.

Walter Wellman left behind a series of newspaper dispatches that chronicle his experiences at his base camp at Virgo Harbor. A few dispatches filed by wireless from Camp Wellman describe the generation of hydrogen gas to lift his airships toward the Pole in 1907 and 1909. These dispatches can be examined, placed against the backdrop of the history of hydrogen production for exploratory flights, and then further tested against archaeological residues recovered from Wellman's base camp in the summer of 1993. Similar comparisons as they relate to hydrogen production can be found in the documentary record related to Andrée's 1897 polar balloon flight, and tested against similar residues recovered during the same survey.

For more than a century after its discovery by the physicist Henry Cavendish in the eighteenth century, hydrogen was produced by a chemical reaction of strong caustic solutions acting upon certain metals and alloys.[1] But published histories of Arctic exploration,[2] as well as both general histories and specific technological histories of airship development,[3] have ignored the exact processes by which the hydrogen was produced that enabled early exploratory flights. Aviation historian Dr. Tom Crouch provides elegant descriptions of the production of hydrogen for an ascent by Jeffries on November 29, 1784, and of methods developed by the American Civil War balloonist Thaddeus Lowe, but these paragraphs stand virtually alone in the historiography of ballooning.[4] By 1928, less than two decades after Wellman's last polar flight, an aviation ground school textbook described the acid-on-metal process for generating hydrogen only as something that was done back in "the early days."[5]

Technical descriptions of gas-generating devices are included in contemporary texts that explain how such machines were used to fuel gas and petroleum engines,[6] but even these detailed technical manuals do not, and probably could not, quantify the exact nature of the chemical constituents used in the generation of hydrogen for such unique and episodic occurrences as polar exploratory flights.

It is necessary, therefore, to place the expeditions at Virgo Harbor against the history of hydrogen generation for balloon and airship flight. In this way, particular questions that appear in the documentary record can be examined against the backdrop of the archaeological residues recovered from around the hydrogen-generating areas at each base camp. And with at least one question—that of the quality of supplies Wellman procured for his airship—they also form the basis for a direct evaluation of the veracity of Wellman's statements, veracity which, as we have seen, was challenged often by his rival newspaper reporters and by fellow explorers like Nansen.

During my survey of the aeronautical remains at Virgo Harbor in 1993, I retrieved seven samples from in and around the hydrogen-generating areas of the Andrée and Wellman base camps. The nature of these residues was identified by subjecting them to a process called Inductively Coupled Plasma Atomic Emission Spectrometry (ICP-AES, or simply ICP). These tests revealed that the chemical composition of the iron residues resulting from the manufacture of hydrogen gas on both sites can offer fresh data with which to test very specific statements embedded deep within the documentary accounts.

*H*ydrogen, which Cavendish in 1766 had shown to be at least seven times lighter than air (it is in fact more than fourteen times lighter), was first used as the ascensional force for a balloon on August 27, 1783, in Paris, by the physicist J.A.C. Charles, who sought to improve upon the performance of the Montgolfier brothers' hot-air balloons of 1782 and early 1783. The flight of Charles's unmanned balloon lasted forty-five minutes, reached a height of three thousand feet, and covered some fifteen miles before the balloon was torn to shreds by frightened peasants in a field near Gonesse. Little more than three weeks later, the Montgolfiers' famous flight carrying a sheep, a rooster, and a duck took place in a hydrogen-filled balloon. On December 1 of the same year, Charles became the first person to ascend in a hydrogen balloon, carried in a car slung beneath a ring surrounding the middle of the balloon and fastened to a net draped over the top of the balloon. Charles's basic design of a gas balloon has gone unchanged for more than two centuries.

*T*he hydrogen balloon's uses for scientific observations were likewise not ignored. Experiments were conducted by the St. Petersburg Academy of Sciences in the years 1803–1804 to test whether temperature, pressure, magnetic force, gravity, and composition of air changed with altitude (the first two did, the latter three did not). Further scientific research in hydrogen balloons was not taken up until the 1850s. Charles Green from Kew Observatory made four high-altitude ascents—one of which reached 22,370 feet—and observed a regular decline in temperature with altitude. These observations were confirmed in the 1860s in similar high-altitude ascents in England by James Glaisher and in France by Camille Flammarion. The inherent dangers attending manned high-altitude flight led in 1892 to the use of unmanned balloons (*ballons sondes*) fitted with automatic recording instruments, devices which are used to this day for meteorological observations.

*T*he hydrogen balloon was almost immediately put to use in geographic exploration, voyages consisting principally of a successful east-to-west flight across the English Channel by Jean-Pierre Blanchard and Dr. John Jeffries on January 7, 1785, and an unsuccessful and fatal attempt in the opposite direction by J. F. Pilatre de Rozier and

P. A. Romain on June 15 of the same year. As we have seen, more than half a century passed until a balloon constructed in 1836 by Charles Green and filled with about 85,000 cubic feet of hydrogen lifted off from London carrying three passengers and came down eighteen hours later in the duchy of Nassau some five hundred miles away. In 1863, the largest gas balloon to date, *Le Géant,* containing over 200,000 cubic feet of hydrogen, lifted off from Paris for a four-hour flight with thirteen passengers—including the two aeronauts Jules and Louis Godard, who four decades later accepted the contract to build Wellman's polar airship in 1906.

In 1873, the *New York Daily Graphic* sponsored a transatlantic attempt by the American balloonist John Wise, who in 1859 had piloted a balloon 1,120 miles from St. Louis to Henderson, New York. Wise's balloon was filled with over 325,000 cubic feet of hydrogen before a rent was discovered in the envelope and the balloon and the project collapsed together. Just three years later, during the Centennial celebrations in Philadelphia, Wise would offer aeronautical instruction to a visiting nineteen-year-old Swede named S. A. Andrée.

*A*ndrée realized that for his polar balloon to have any chance of success, it would be necessary to construct an advance base camp in the Arctic where the balloon could be assembled, inflated, and sheltered until such time as favorable winds could push it toward the Pole. Therefore, one of Andrée's four preconditions for the success of his polar flight was that the production of hydrogen "must take place in the polar tracts."[7]

"The filling of the balloon with gas could very well take place in the polar regions, as the requirements of military balloons had led to the construction of transportable hydrogen-gas apparatus, by means of which a balloon of the size of Andrée's could be filled with gas in the space of thirty to forty hours. And, moreover, hydrogen could very well be conveyed to the starting point in a compressed form in steel cylinders."[8]

The latter course, however, was rejected on account of cost,[9] and so, according to the official account of the expedition published after the remains of the expedition party and its documentary record were discovered on White Island in 1930, Andrée arranged for an apparatus to be delivered to Virgo Harbor that would combine zinc and sulfuric acid to produce hydrogen gas. The costs (in kroner) were estimated as follows:[10]

Hydrogen apparatus for 5,300 cubic feet per hour	1,950
Raw material, zinc, and sulfuric acid	
(with calculated loss of 20 percent)	3,000
	4,950
Technical expert for gas production and filling	1,600

Sven Lundström, in his 1988 account of the Andrée expedition, provides a somewhat different account of the hydrogen-generating process:

> One of the most difficult problems to solve for the expedition was the production of hydrogen on Spitsbergen. There was no doubt that hydrogen should be used, but the best method had to be found to produce it in such large quantities as was needed. The safest method would, without doubt, have been to buy the finished gas in pressurized containers, but that turned out to be far too expensive. It was calculated to cost c. 100 000 kroner. Andrée had, therefore, studied several other alternatives for production of the hydrogen. The method carrying least risk had to be found, since they did not have workers who were used to such work. Andrée chose the so-called wet method, where one works with water, sulphuric acid and zinc or iron. Andrée had charged engineer Ernst Ek with the task of working out a suggestion for a hydrogen apparatus. As supervisor for producing the gas, an engineer [named] Stake was appointed. He was also the one who was on Danes Island in 1897 and had the responsibility for filling the balloon.
>
> Ek did a number of experiments to decide which metal was best, iron or zinc. Finally he decided that wrought iron and sulphuric acid functioned best.
>
> For 5000 cubic metres of hydrogen, 23 000 kg of iron filings and 40 800 kg sulphuric acid were used, and during production 76 000 kg water (in addition to 450 000 kg washing water). Luckily sea water at the starting site could be used for the gas production.[11]

Charles, in his first hydrogen balloon ascent in 1783, had created the required hydrogen by passing dilute sulfuric acid over iron filings,[12] although the exact concentration is not recorded. Zinc could be substituted for iron, although more zinc is necessary to produce the same result, which may explain Andrée's choice of iron over zinc, assuming the costs of each were relatively similar. According to C. D. Chandler, to produce one thousand cubic feet of hydrogen gas, 157 pounds of iron must be reacted with 275 pounds of sulfuric acid (57 percent of the amount of acid in iron filings); with zinc, the ratio is 182.5 pounds of zinc to 275 pounds of sulfuric acid, and in actuality one must add 10 percent to all amounts to reach the desired amount. When iron is used, the process is represented by the following reaction equation (where Fe = iron, H_2SO_4 = sulfuric acid, and H_2 = hydrogen):[13]

$$Fe + H_2SO_4 = FeSO_4 + H_2$$

With the generating apparatus in place, all that was required was to connect a hose from the neck of the balloon to the hydrogen plant. Ten years later, Napoleon created two companies of *aerostiers* for military reconnaissance from the air, and these were employed at the seige of Mainz in 1795. Hydrogen was produced in the field according to the same process used by Charles, although with a more sophisticated apparatus known as the *Système Renard*. This method, called the *Vitriol,* or *acid-metal, process,* had remained essentially unchanged for more than a century when Andrée adopted it for the inflation of his balloon at Virgo Harbor in 1896. It was used almost exclusively for the generation of hydrogen until the First World War, when cheaper and more direct electrolytic and steam contact processes became the norm.

In August of 1896, anchoring at what was then called Dane Hole and would soon be renamed Virgo Harbor, William Martin Conway related that on approaching the shoreline of the harbor where he was to meet Andrée, "we were struck by the intense greenness of the water, rendered all the more emphatic by contrast with a brilliant yellow stain on the rocks by the shore, the result of recent gas-manufacture for the balloon."[14] Exactly what chemical residue caused this yellow stain is unknown, and although the ground around the hydrogen gas filter is discolored to this day by iron residue and, closer to Pike's house, the soil is a pale tan color, I observed no traces of such a "brilliant yellow stain" in 1993.

The Swedes were occupying Arnold Pike's house, and had set up "their strangely civilized-looking gas apparatus close alongside," wrote Conway. "Herr Andrée and the two intended companions of his proposed aerial flight joined us. We were shown how the gas was made, and the long silk pipe meandering amongst the stones to convey it to the balloon."[15]

Henri Lachambre, the French aeronautical designer who built Andrée's balloon and accompanied the expedition to Virgo Harbor in 1896, described how the "inflating pipes, passing through an opening made in the middle of the floor [of the balloon house], are joined to the gas apparatus, situated 80 metres away and below the shed, behind Pike House."[16]

Andrée himself wrote: "The ground is firm, free from snow, and dry. The place intended for the balloon-house lies close by the shore so that there will be hardly any transporting of timber necessary. Farther along the beach, the land lies lower. If the hydrogen-gas apparatus is erected there the gas will at once flow easily into the balloon."[17] A photograph from my 1993 survey shows the remaining hydrogen filter on the Andrée site, more or less level with Pike's house, and down the hill from the horizon where the Andrée monument (at the level of the ruin of the balloon house) can be seen.

From June 25 to 28, 1896, the hydrogen gas apparatus was ferried ashore, followed on June 30 by the balloon itself.

During the first week of July 1896, "the chief parts of the gas apparatus were placed in position,"[18] and by the middle of the month the machinery was nearly ready to be put to work. "At two o'clock on the twenty-third, they began to inflate the balloon. The gas apparatus worked perfectly. . . . At four o'clock on the twenty-seventh, the balloon was completely inflated, one of the most difficult and important parts of the work."[19]

When the required winds from the south did not materialize, Andrée was forced to cancel the polar attempt in 1896, and to return to Sweden to await another chance the following year. The gas apparatus was apparently returned to Sweden with Andrée in the fall of 1896, since the official history of the expedition remarks that in May of 1897 the Swedish gunboat *Svenskund* "carried the balloon, the balloon-net, the car, the drag-lines, and the hydrogen-gas apparatus" back to Virgo Harbor.[20] On June 19, 1897, inflation of the balloon with hydrogen gas commenced once again, and it was completed on June 22. The balloon departed Virgo Harbor on July 11 in the early afternoon, sailing north-northeast, and was never seen again.

These details generated several questions which the archaeology at Virgo Harbor might shed some light on. How exactly did Andrée generate his hydrogen, and was the process identical to Wellman's? What materials did he use? Did Wellman use the same materials, even though the years between their expeditions were marked by such rapid technological change?

*F*or his 1906 expedition, Walter Wellman asked French gas engineer Gaston Hervieu to accompany the expedition to Danes Island and set up and operate his gas apparatus there. Consequently, a "hydrogen gas apparatus of large capacity was built in Paris to be transported to Spitzbergen," wrote Wellman. "One hundred and ten tons of sulphuric acid . . . were ordered from Reher and Ramsden, Hamburg, [Germany], and seventy tons of iron turnings were secured in Norway."[21] The 1906 expedition never made use of its hydrogen apparatus when it became apparent that the airship car and machinery were not up to the task at hand. Wellman returned to the Arctic in

1907, and during that summer his airship was inflated for the first time at Virgo Harbor.

Andrée, the scientist and patent engineer, would generally be considered far the superior to Wellman, the journalist and generalist, in his level of scientific knowledge and achievement, and his preparations for the polar flight are meticulously documented in engineering drawings and photographs. Wellman, however, while not leaving behind to any degree a detailed iconography, also went to great pains to describe the technology he was using at Virgo Harbor, as evidenced by the following dispatch published in his newspaper in late August 1907.

BY WALTER WELLMAN

(SPECIAL CORRESPONDENCE [sic] OF THE CHICAGO RECORD-HERALD) RECORD-HERALD HOUSE, Spitzbergen, Aug. 2 [1907]— By to-morrow morning the balloon or gas reservoir of the *America* should be filled with hydrogen. . . . Manufacture of the gas, began last Monday. It has continued day and night. Six men work the day shift and the same number the night, one under the direction of M. [Gaston] Hervieu, our gas engineer, and the other under Major [Henry] Hersey. Every day they have had to handle about ten tons of sulphuric acid, eight tons of iron shavings and scrap, pump forty tons of water, besides other chemicals for drying and purifying the gas. And this goes on for nearly six days in order to produce the 280,000 cubic feet of hydrogen which the *America* holds.

The gas is thoroughly washed with water, piped 750 feet from a melting glacier, fresh water being better for this purpose, and also for mixing with the sulphuric acid, than sea water. The ice water runs through wooden piping to the gas apparatus, and is then hoisted to the tanks by a steam pump. Before it leaves the producing apparatus on its way to the balloon the hydrogen is thoroughly washed and cooled by being forced to ascend through cascades of hundreds of streams of falling water. It is dried by being forced through a cylinder filled with coke, and the acid (which might damage the envelope of the balloon) is taken out during the passage of the gas through another vertical cylinder filled with caustic soda.

Finally it is tested for its temperature by a thermometer; for its humidity by a hygrometer; for its acidity by litmus paper; and for its density by a Schilling test tube.

At the very last it is perfumed, by being passed over sponges filled with muronine, which has a powerful but not unpleasant odor. The perfuming is a precaution. Nearly pure hydrogen is well-nigh odorless. If such gas were to escape into our car and come into contact with the motors a fatal explosion might ensue, as hydrogen mixed with air is highly inflammable and explosive. But with perfumed gas our olfactories will tell us of the slightest escape in time to take precautionary measures.

The gas which has been put into the *America* is nearly pure. It is cool, very dry and free from acid. Its weight is very small, approximating 1.180 kilos per cubic meter. The exact figures we shall not know till certain data have been worked out, which will require a few days work. Had we thought it wise to do so, we could have produced gas much more rapidly, but then it would not have been of such good quality. It was deemed more important to get gas of high lifting power than to save a day in the making of it.[22]

Wellman offered further detailed comments once the airship had been filled with hydrogen, remarking that he was less than satisfied with the quality of the supplies his expedition had to contend with.

AUG 6 [1907]—This afternoon the *America* was declared fully inflated with hydrogen, though she could have been filled much earlier had there been anything to gain by haste. Tested by the Schilling apparatus, which depends upon the principle that the rate of flow of gases through like orifices is inversely as to the square root of their densities, barometric pressure and temperature of course being equal, our hydrogen appears to have a weight of 115 grams per cubic meter, which is equivalent to an ascensional force (with temperature of air at 32 degrees Fahr, and barometric pressure 760 mm. of mercury, or 29.93 inches—the standard for this region and season) of 1,178 kilos per meter, cube, which equals 1.17664 ounces per cubic foot. This does not look like much, but multiply it by the volume of the *America,* which is 258,000 cubic feet, and it will be seen [that the] grand total is almost exactly 19,000 pounds. If the Schilling apparatus has been correctly worked—and we have been very careful—this should be the lifting power of the airship at the sea level at 32 Fahr, with the normal barometric pressure. Of course we shall know this still more accurately by the practical test of how much she actually lifts, as we know the weight of the balloon itself and of everything put upon it. Taking this value for the ascensional force per meter cube, the result is very satisfactory. In short, we have made gas of as good quality as the very best made for aeronautic purposes in France, and better than is produced by the vast majority of engineers. Major Hersey and Gas Engineer Hervieu, who have worked night and day for more than a week producing the hydrogen and filling and manipulating the balloon, have received the congratulations of all members of the staff upon their success, of which they have a right to be proud, considering the conditions under which they have worked, and the fact that a great deal of the iron was not what it was represented to be by the dealers who sold it.[23]

The drying cylinders filled with coke, and the acid filter—another vertical cylinder filled with caustic soda—are similar to the ones that, according to Wellman, he had specially built in Paris in 1910 for use in the preparations for his attempted transatlantic flight (from Atlantic City, New Jersey, in October of that year). He wrote that after being washed with water, the gas was dried and filtered through cylinders containing "coke, permanganate of potash and calcium of lime."[24]

30. Workers in Paris assemble the hydrogen-generating apparatus to be used for Wellman's 1910 attempt to fly across the Atlantic Ocean. (From The Aerial Age.)

31. The remains of Wellman's hydrogen-generating apparatus, on the shore at Virgo Harbor, in July 1993. (Photo by the author.)

Clearly, these are more than the usual details one would expect the readers of the *Chicago Record-Herald* to care about while picking over their breakfasts four thousand miles away. Yet for this very reason they are a mine of information for an archaeologist. These two remarkable dispatches contained several hints as to what I might find among the ruins of the machinery at Virgo Harbor: cylinders for drying and washing the gas, piping to carry it to the airship, residues of the materials used to make the gas in the first place.

But what immediately caught my eye was Wellman's almost off-hand remark that the iron he bought to make his hydrogen gas was tainted. Here at last was a statement that I could test directly. There could be no escaping this one, no wiggle room for interpretation or emphasis. Either Wellman was right about this, or he was not. And the ICP scanning, a process invented almost a half century after Wellman was in his grave, would tell me which.

*A*t Virgo Harbor, I collected five samples of what appeared to be iron filings residue from in and around the surface areas of the shoreline where the Wellman and Andrée hydrogen gas apparatuses were located. I retrieved an additional sample from the sole remaining structure on the Andrée site, apparently a gas filter box, along with a sample of apparent coal or charcoal from the spaces between the Wellman hydrogen apparatus and the four ceramic vats immediately to the south of it. The shoreline at Virgo Harbor as I surveyed it in 1993 shows the positions of the two hydrogen-generating areas in relation to each other.

I gathered a sample of the soil from the ground beneath the fuel dump on the Wellman site, which produced evidence of petroleum hydrocarbons still lingering in the soil in measurable quantities. No such fuel dump exists on the Andrée site, and the presence of such petroleum hydrocarbons on the Wellman site testifies to the introduction of the internal combustion engine in air travel between 1897 and 1907.

The Andrée hydrogen-generating area, near the ruins of Pike's house, including the remaining filter box, is surrounded by an area where the apparent iron filings residue has stained the ground, and a sample (A-2) was removed from this area, while another (A-1) was taken from the white powdery substance inside the Andrée hydrogen filter itself. Four samples of iron filings were removed from the much larger hydrogen-generating area of the Wellman site, where a snakelike trail of iron filings residue in disintegrating wooden barrels begins at the "porch" of the ruins of the apparatus and meanders off to the east. The planimetric map of the area makes this residue area seem more or less regular, but it is anything but. It is a chaotic jumble of metal residue mounds that have broken out of the wooden casks that once encased them.

Qualitatively, the samples differed. The residue from underneath the porch of the Wellman hydrogen apparatus (W-1) appeared to be slightly fused clumps of metal about three to five millimeters long, which had the appearance of having been worked on by acid, while the sample from the midpoint of the residue trail (W-2) consisted of metal curlicues about two millimeters in diameter, and looked to be more oxidized than reacted with acid. The sample retrieved from the easternmost barrel of the metal residue trail (W-3), or, in other words, the sample farthest from the hydrogen-generating apparatus ruins, appeared to be clumps of metal about three millimeters in length and completely fused by reaction with acid. The sample collected from the start of the metal residue trail (W-4) consisted of tubular pieces between one-half and one millimeter in diameter and between one and two millimeters in length. The sample removed from the area around the Andrée filter (A-2) was in clumps of metal about four to five millimeters in length and apparently strongly fused by the acid reaction.

The six samples were subjected to ICP testing. This analytical technique is widely used for identifying trace elements in many types of samples.[25] The samples are diluted and sprayed as an aerosol into a flowing stream of argon gas, and subjected to temperatures of 6,000° to 8,000° K. As the constituent elements of the samples are ionized, they produce an ionic emission spectra. By measuring the intensity of the light emitted at specific wavelengths, it is possible to determine the concentrations of the elements.[26] In this case I asked the laboratory to run as full as scan on the hydrogen-generating residues as possible, paying particular attention to trace elements of sulfur and calcium. The laboratory also ran a mass spectrometer scan on the organic coal or charcoal sample.

The ICP scan indicated that both Andrée and Wellman adopted the Vitriol, or iron-acid, process for generating hydrogen, a process that had already been in use for over a century. This was somewhat surprising, as one might have expected this process to evolve over such a length of time, and more especially in the span between the times Andrée and Wellman occupied Virgo Harbor, the exceedingly dynamic years of technological progress bracketed by the expeditions of 1897 and 1907. In this regard, however, as much as either man might be considered an innovator in other areas, neither was able to improve upon a process for generating hydrogen in the field developed originally for Napoleon's aeronautical corps.

The quantitative results of the ICP analysis show the overwhelming preponderance of iron in the four samples from the Wellman site (W-1 to W-4) and the sample from the stain area around the Andrée hydrogen-generating area (A-2), and the concentration of calcium from the sample taken from inside the Andrée hydrogen filter (A-1). The iron concentration is above 500,000 mg/kg for each sample, well above this mark for the Wellman samples.

The amount of iron filings brought north by Wellman amounted to 63.6 percent of the amount of his sulfuric acid,[27] as compared with a ratio in Andrée's formula of 56.3 percent; Chandler's theoretical ideal is 57 percent.[28] Wellman's higher ratio of iron to sulfuric acid might explain the somewhat higher levels of iron isolated in the Wellman samples compared to that from the Andrée site.

As a point of interest, Jules Verne's fictional Dr. Fergusson, for his hydrogen balloon journey across Africa, used 1,866 gallons of sulfuric acid on 16,050 pounds of iron, a ratio of 107 percent.[29] If he used all his recorded 966 gallons of water to dilute the acid, it would have had a concentration of 66 percent. Per Sundman, in his fictional account of the Andrée expedition, writes that "eighty tons of sulphuric acid and twenty-three tons of iron filings . . . were needed for the production of the gas," a ratio of 28.7 percent.[30] It would seem that, in this case, at least, the real-life technologists were closer to the theoretical ideal than the characters of science fiction.

Sven Lundström's account of Andrée's hydrogen-generating process differs from the official expedition account published in 1930.[31] The ICP data corroborate Lundström's account, which in the event was fortuitous. Besides being a superlative polar historian, Dr. Lundström is director of the Andrée Museum in Andrée's hometown of Gränna, Sweden, and I initially presented these results at an international conference where he was in the audience.

And then I came to Mr. Wellman. As we know, he contended in his 1907 dispatch that "a great deal" of the scrap iron supplied for his hydrogen-generating apparatus was of inferior quality.[32] Was this simply more excuse-making by someone who had made so many excuses for the failure of his expeditions from Walden Island to Franz Josef Land to Danes Island?

The ICP data say no. They indicate clearly that Wellman's gas engineer Hervieu indeed had to cope with a significant percentage of an iron filings supply that was measurably below the standard used by Andrée. In this case, at least, Walter Wellman was telling the truth.

And that leads to another interesting, and unresolved, issue. Of the two cylinders found inside the ruins of the hydrogen-generating apparatus, the larger of the two could have been a coke filter similar to those described as acting as scrubbers for gas generators for gas engines by Robinson.[33] Water was sprayed down through the coke inside this cylinder, cooling and washing dust from the gas, which was then directed into a holding tank. In Wellman's case, the holding tank would have been the gasbag of the airship itself. The smaller of the two cylinders in the hydrogen ruins contained no residue, while the larger contained iron residue visually similar to that recovered from under the "porch." But should these cylinders have been at Virgo Harbor at all? Although it is much more likely that the remains of the hydrogen apparatus that survive today at Virgo Harbor were picked apart over time through the combined actions of other expeditions, souvenir hunters, local trappers, and weather, there is at least one source that claims that the bulk of Wellman's hydrogen apparatus was removed from the site by Wellman himself, to be used in his 1910 attempt to cross the Atlantic. Nansen, as we know, visited Virgo Harbor in 1912, and claimed that the apparatus was intact then. If Wellman had removed it earlier, what was Nansen looking at? And if he hadn't—and the remains that exist today suggest this to be the case—then Wellman apparently managed to raise enough money to build an entirely new generator in Atlantic City in the fall of 1910, as a photograph in *The Aerial Age* implies. In either case, the written record, as in so many other instances we have examined, leaves us far from satisfied.

As for those overarching "big picture" questions archaeology is famous for examining, ICP scans provide little joy. There is not enough variation in the chemical composition to suppose that one could use such data for a cross-cultural comparison between the Swedish and American sites, or indeed even a useful comparison between two separate aeronautical eras at Virgo Harbor.

Even so, we can offer some predictions based on the Virgo Harbor data. For example, at Camp Ziegler, the site on Alger Island in Franz Josef Land where the Baldwin-Ziegler Expedition released fifteen balloons for the purpose of carrying dispatches in June 1902, ICP scanning will almost certainly identify similar iron filings residues and, if Baldwin employed a similar filtration system, calcium residues. A team of Soviet archaeologists from Moscow University studied Camp Ziegler in the summer of 1990,[34] but it is not known if the balloon launch point was located or surveyed during this or an earlier Soviet archaeological expedition to the site in 1965.

There is further the question located in the Louis Godard file at the National Air & Space Museum in Washington, D.C. Godard, the aeronautical engineer who constructed Wellman's 1906 airship, notes in his résumé that he constructed "observation and transport balloons for the polar expedition of the Duke of Abruzzi, 1899" ("ballons observatoires et transports de l'Expédition polaire de S.A.R. le duc des Abruzzes, 1899").[35] If this is so, we can predict that iron residues similar in composition to those at Virgo Harbor will be found at the duke's advance expeditionary base at Teplitz Bay on Rudolf Island, which would also mark the farthest north that hydrogen gas was ever generated for a polar expedition.

The duke of the Abruzzi briefly mentions that he had the firm of Godard & Surcouf in Paris build trial hydrogen balloons, two of which were to have been employed in lifting his sledges off the ground so that they would be easier for the sledge dogs to pull. Altogether the duke spent 5.6 percent of his expedition's budget in developing this "aeronautic outfit."[36] When his ship, *Stella Polaris,* was stove in by ice at Teplitz Bay, the duke wrote that the boiler and pump from the aeronautic outfit were diverted to pump water out of the hold, "another part (the iron filings) had been left in the water at the bottom of the hold, and could not be got out," and as to the hydrogen apparatus itself, "it was useless to waste our time in getting ready apparatus from which we were certain that we could not derive any real advantage."[37]

This leaves the impression that, in the emergency with the ship, the expedition brought none of the hydrogen apparatus on shore, and Abruzzi himself mentions nothing more about it. However, Anthony Fiala, whose own ship, *America,* vanished in Teplitz Bay in January 1904, has a photographic plate in his expedition account that shows a hydrogen apparatus set up at Teplitz Bay with the caption: "The Duke's Steel Gas Generator."[38]

In 1931, the Teplitz Bay site was visited by a melancholy Umberto Nobile, then living a kind of aeronautical exile in the Soviet Union after the crash of the *Italia* northeast of Spitsbergen in 1928. Searching for traces of his lost airship and crew, he instead discovered remains of the expedition of his fellow countryman the duke of the Abruzzi:

> In front of the [overwintering] building I noticed the plant for producing the hydrogen that was to be used for filling the two small balloons (each of 14,000 cu. ft. volume), with which the Duke intended to raise into the air one of the sledges that he meant to take to the Pole. A curious idea, which turned out a complete failure. The two balloons, made of varnished cloth, were still there, neatly folded. I tried to tear the cloth with my hands, but did not succeed. The storms and the terrible climate of that latitude had, of course, damaged the varnish, but the resistance of the material was almost undiminished.[39]

As remarkable as it seems, Nobile had located two 1899 Godard-factory balloons from Paris, surviving on the shore of Teplitz Bay, in the summer of 1931. And the incomparable scene of the disgraced polar airship captain returning to the Arctic and trying to tear apart balloon fabric from an earlier Italian expedition—it's almost too much to believe. Yet here is another case where four historical sources provide four different aspects of a single aeronautical event, differing aspects that will only be resolved through a survey of any remains of the gas-generating plant and its associated material artifacts that survive at Teplitz Bay.

*A*s for Walter Wellman, can we go so far as to say that archaeology has demonstrated beyond a reasonable doubt that he was not a liar or a fraud? Probably not. Archaeology seems to resolve the general question of his proximity to corporate advertising in his favor, but this could just be because visitors to archaeological sites like Virgo Harbor like to pick up and take with them anything with a brand name on it.

I can't really complain about that, because such artifacts are the ones I search for most assiduously myself. Bottles and plates and cans with corporate logos and slogans on them virtually scream at the archaeologist to go back to the library and archive to discover their connection to American civilization at the turn of the century.

In the two instances where I was able to match his words directly against his archaeology—the construction of his airship cars and the generation of hydrogen—Wellman came out badly on the former, just fine on the latter. That puts him just about in the mean of the rest of us human beings, except that Walter Wellman's dream was quite a bit bigger than most, and he got five tries at it. That's four tries more than most of us.

Conclusion:
Virgo Harbor and
the Archaeology of Failure

> The first great thing is to find yourself, and for that you
> need solitude and contemplation: at least sometimes. I tell
> you, deliverance will not come from the rushing, noisy
> centres of civilization. It will come from the lonely places.
>
> —*Fridtjof Nansen*

*T*he airship efforts of Walter Wellman are nearly forgotten prototypes for many twentieth-century expeditions, including the aerial
polar expeditions of Amundsen, Nobile, Byrd, and Mittelholzer, and
their pioneering use of motorized aircraft in the Arctic and Antarctic. Yet despite criticism from competing newspapers and from
Nansen, Wellman does not appear to have taken undue liberties in the
promotion of products used on his expeditions, excesses that can be
noted in the expeditions of Peary and Byrd.[1]

The documentary archaeology suggests that Wellman's polar airship expeditions were hardly the advance guard of corporate advertising of geographic exploration. While Wellman often expressed his
impatience with "this plodding commercial age, this day of hum-
drum money grubbing,"[2] this is the first time the veracity of this feeling has been tested by comparing such written statements with the
archaeological record left behind at Wellman's Arctic base camp, and
using that data to evaluate the level of related advertising in his newspaper during his expeditions.

Moreover, instead of appearing to capitalize on the advertising
possibilities offered by such a high-profile expedition, as successive
efforts failed to reach their objective, the data suggest that the *Chicago
Record-Herald* increasingly distanced itself from its reporter and his

polar ambitions. This distancing reached the point where the expeditions were virtually ignored at the very moment of their greatest success, at the same point in history when the public "craze" for aeronautical exploits began. The data point to an apparent trend, or "hype" effect, in the newspaper recording of major expeditions that may lend itself as a comparative model for similar analysis of other expeditions.

*T*he first time I stepped ashore at Virgo Harbor to study the remains of the Andrée and Wellman expeditions there, I felt that sorting through those archaeological remains on that one shoreline would occupy much of my lifetime. Several years later, I can report that my first impression was essentially correct; we've only begun to explore the archaeological possibilities left to us by Andrée and Wellman.

Traditional American archaeology, practiced for the most part within departments of anthropology, prefers to search for general patterns and themes. Answering very specific questions—what was the composition of an early aeronaut's hydrogen-generating residue? was C. F. Hall poisoned by Emil Bessels?—is for the most part disdained by American anthropologists. Yet it has long been a staple of historical archaeology, and most certainly of the kind of historical archaeology practiced in Scandinavia, where it is called ethnology.

At Virgo Harbor, there were two different accounts in the Andrée record of how he generated his hydrogen; and in the Wellman record was the very specific remark that the iron used in the hydrogen reaction process was tainted. Because so much of the criticism of Wellman centered on the claim, advanced by Nansen and others, that he was an outright fraud, a man who looked for any excuse on which to blame the failure of his expeditions, it seemed important to find some way to gather empirical evidence to test his claims for veracity. Put simply, I expected that, if Wellman were a liar or a fraud, I would find nothing wrong with the iron he used.

At the same time, as an archaeologist who was trained in an anthropology department, I did want to gather data to examine the kinds of general questions relating to technological adaptation and change that in fact are the staple of modern anthropological archaeology. My general hypothesis centered on the notion that the years from 1896 to 1909—the years bracketed by the Andrée and Wellman expeditions—were ones of great and far-reaching technological change, and that I would be able to directly measure this change in differences in the hydrogen-generating techniques of the two explorers.

Again, put simply: if indeed technological evolution was proceeding at an extremely rapid rate between 1896 and 1909, I would find that Wellman's technique for generating hydrogen would differ so markedly from that of Andrée that I would be able to produce a chemical signature of technological progress on this one site, or rather on these two sites on this one shoreline, for comparison with other early aeronautical sites around the world.

In the end, everything worked out exactly backward.

Tests run on the surviving residues of this turn-of-the-century process for generating hydrogen indicated that both Andrée and Wellman adopted the so-called Vitriol, or iron-acid, process for generating hydrogen, both used iron and sulfuric acid, and both employed a process that had already been in use for over a century by the time Andrée arrived at Virgo Harbor in 1896.

More interesting are the general cultural statements this hydrogen-generating process and these balloons and airships can make. For the more I walked around Virgo Harbor, the quicker I found myself in Paris. And in this we can see a trend that occurs throughout airship exploration of the polar regions. Andrée used French balloons and a French process for manufacturing hydrogen in 1896 and 1897. In 1899, the Italian duke of the Abruzzi used French balloons in an attempt to lift his heavy sledges off the ground in Franz Josef Land. And Wellman in 1906 used a French-designed and -built airship.

Even though these early balloon and airship expeditions were conceived and executed as intensely nationalistic expeditions, manned by Swedish or Italian or American crews, their aeronautical technology derived from France. Like Andrée's first balloon, built in Paris but called *Sweden* (*Svea*), Wellman's airship, though built in France, was called *America*. The one truly American piece of technology Wellman attempted to use on his polar flights was his motor sledges, and these failed so badly that he barely mentioned them in his account of the expedition.

Twenty years later, the first explorers to reach the North Pole would arrive in an airship named *Norge,* even though it had been built in Italy. In fact, it is not until one gets to General Nobile in 1928, and his airship *Italia,* that we find a nationalistic explorer who actually uses a balloon or airship designed and built in his own country, named after that same country, and—with the exceptions of the Swede, Dr. Malmgren, and the Czech, Dr. Behounek—manned entirely from that country.

What this seems to suggest is that, for all their nationalistic rhetoric, these expeditions were, from a technological point of view, wholly international. (By constrast, the U.S. space program is just now emerging from its long nationalism and becoming a truly international technological enterprise.) Although designed and in most cases executed as nationalistic scientific adventures with a view toward priority at the Pole, the Andrée and Wellman campaigns were, in fact, and in the main, French-supplied expeditions whose technology derived in most cases directly from the French aeronautical factories and designs of the turn of the century. And the result of this adoption in the Arctic of technology designed primarily for the French countryside was in each instance unqualified failure.

Now, if this is so, we can use this combined historical and chemical delineation of this process as a baseline against which future testing of the residues of polar balloon hydrogen production can be measured at such sites, for example, at the duke of the Abruzzi's 1899–1900 camp at Teplitz Bay in Franz Josef Land, and Evelyn Briggs Baldwin's 1902 base at Cape Ziegler. In either case, we should find French technology and French processes.

These connections point to the historical construction of a multicultural aeronautical landscape at Virgo Harbor, one where Westerdahl's conception of the maritime cultural landscape can be applied to the material remains of aerospace history. This aeronautical cultural landscape, created as a base for explorers, seemingly carries the archaeological signatures of a shipwreck, an isolated and inclusive cargo of technological artifacts and psychological symbols. Yet these symbols were deposited at Virgo Harbor not through accident, as with a shipwreck, but deliberately, in order to effect, I believe, a fundamental redirection of the path of human civilization.

Eventually, this concept—of an exploring landscape—may serve as an archaeological basis by which to examine University of Hawaii anthropologist Ben Finney's thesis that humankind "evolved as an exploratory, migratory animal."[3] In the 1980s, in a tangential relation to his work on the technology of Polynesian seafaring and its bearing on human migration and exploration, Finney began to study an "expansionary phase that was not only of potentially greater import than any terrestrial example, but one that could be studied directly without having to reconstruct and test the vehicles involved or interpret ambiguous texts."[4] Finney is referring to human expansion into space, of course, but his thesis of a human species as an essentially exploratory one is, I believe, of primary relevance to archaeological inquiries into the beginnings of scientific aeronautical exploration.

Though at first it may appear that Finney's notion of *Homo sapiens* as an explorer is ultimately too large and vague to test archaeologically, it contains several archaeological implications that can be applied to the remains at Virgo Harbor. Technological exploration is a uniquely human behavior and produces, in many ways and places, a novel material component. As such, it falls within the hard boundaries of credible archaeological analysis.

The conflicting and in many ways incorrect accounts concerning Walter Wellman point directly to the need for an aerospace archaeology that "gets under the skin" of traditional aviation history, and which not only reveals the error in overreliance on documents but points the direction toward new interpretations and uncovers heretofore unimagined patterns and meanings ignored by aviation historians. Conversely, archaeologists need to understand that field research, in the sense of examining, or mining, the historical record, is as much an intellectual as it is a physical activity.

Future studies of exploring bases must first attempt to link expeditionary goals with the nature of the wreck or base camp structures, in order to take advantage of the insights to be gained with a multiscaler view of the entire aeronautical cultural landscape. In this sense, the North Pole becomes as much a part of the site at Virgo Harbor as Wellman's hangar itself. Specific artifacts can then be employed as triggers to generate links between the historical record and the behaviors encoded at the site, and the combined force of that analysis used to evaluate the methods if not the mind of the aerospace explorer.

I have argued elsewhere that aerospace archaeology can one day be used to examine the impulse in humans to explore. If this is so, we should one day be able to establish links between cultural responses read in the archaeological record and the suggestion that *Homo sapiens* has evolved as an inherently exploring species, one, as Finney writes, "that spread from [a] tropical homeland through developing technology to travel to and survive in a multitude of environments for which they were not biologically adapted."[5]

Testing such a large notion archaeologically on sites from the history of aeronautical and aerospace exploration is at present an impossible task. It will be years before enough sites have been examined to provide the kinds of comparative data that will lead to the productive evaluation of such a thesis. However, by beginning to examine particular expeditions within the context of this notion, we can begin to generate the kinds of data required to evaluate the exploring instinct archaeologically.

As a conceptual model for the examination of sites from the history of aerospace and polar exploration, we can imagine several implications of Finney's idea. If in fact humankind evolved as, and/or into, an exploring animal, then it must be because there exist adaptive advantages to an individual, a culture, or a nation in the production of capable efficient explorers. Obvious examples would be the location of new islands for colonization by Polynesians, new arenas of international importance for small nations, as in Norwegian explorations of the polar regions, or new sources of raw materials on the American frontiers, on the Moon or Mars, for Americans.

Archaeologically, such success might manifest itself in material differences between successful (e.g., Norwegian: Amundsen) base camp sites and unsuccessful (e.g., American: Wellman/Byrd/Cook) base camp sites. Amundsen was the quintessential methodical expedition leader, patient when patience was required, adaptable to local conditions, and bold when he needed to be bold. Wellman, by contrast, was incautious, hurried, without method. We can posit that differences in the archaeological residues of such different camps should show evidence of meticulous craftsmanship (Amundsen model) or of rushed or shoddy workmanship, or else the application of technology inappropriately matched to the geographic objective (Wellman model)—a kind of haste-makes-waste hypothesis.

For when an individual or a group is operating in an environment that exists at the extreme limits of human adaptation, evidence of rushed/shoddy or patient/skilled material culture can be viewed as indicators of planning and competence, the twin hallmarks of successful/unsuccessful expeditions and, by implication, of the expedition leader, if not his or her originating culture or nation. These markers can in turn be used to assess the degree to which the explorer has met the challenge of adaptability to the extreme environment. It would then be appropriate to determine if this patterning reflected individual choices or formed the basis of a determination of group or even national selection.

Differences might appear as well in the archaeological residues contained in camps of those who fall somewhere between these two extremes, who turned back short of their goal (e.g., Shackleton, Nansen, Abruzzi, Peary), or those who reached their goal but suffered fatalities on the return (e.g., Andrée, Nobile, Scott). Are the causes of success or failure due to cultural differences or the application (or misapplication) of national models regarding remote geographic objectives, or are they based in the success or failure of episodic calculations of individual explorers, which in their turn grow out of national mental models of, for example, conditions in the Arctic.

Another hypothesis that could be tested revolves around aerospace technology itself. The archaeological residues should mirror, in some form, what we could term the "cocooning effect" implicit in the idea of humankind exploring farther and farther from its "tropical home-land." One would assume that the explorer adapts aerospace tech-nology in such a way as to maximize the chances for survival in the extreme environment he or she has chosen to explore. For why would an explorer consciously choose to employ a method of adaptation that would cause him or her to fail to reach the geographic objective?

And yet this is precisely what explorers and aeronauts have done throughout the history of exploration and aeronautics. Misapplica-tion of technology and/or inappropriate methods are almost the rule rather than the exception, which is, to my way of thinking, why there have been so few explorers and aeronauts of the first rank, so few Amundsens and Nansens. From Scott's choice of ponies over dogs in Antarctica, to Wellman's idea of carrying impossibly heavy motor sledges on a polar airship, to the British Admiralty's decision to al-low John Franklin to search for the Northwest Passage with two grossly overmatched ships and over one hundred men untrained in the Arctic, to Andrée's attempt to float to the North Pole in a bal-loon—all of these suggest that appropriate exploratory technology and methods are almost *never* matched in a rough one-to-one rela-tionship to the alien environment they are tasked with carrying the human body into and delivering it safely from.

If such deterministic models (individual, cultural, national) hold, we should expect to be able to record the results in the material record. If a nation/group/individual favors technological solutions over cultural/biological adaptation to the environment, archaeo-logical sites created by such entities should reveal a preponderance of evidence from without that environment (everything from man-ufactured goods to canned food to non-human-powered means of transport). Conversely, the camps of exploring parties that try to adapt to local conditions should show evidence that testifies to the modification and reuse of items whose source originates from *within* that environment, be it animal hides, worked bone, reworked drift-wood, or features from the natural landscape.

Yet by logical extension this brings us into a dicey area of inquiry, if for no more reason than its seemingly obvious implication that tools of human ingenuity are increasingly less our servant and more our master. As Lord Kenneth Clark wrote more than a quarter of a century ago: "[Machines] have ceased to be tools and have begun to give us directions."[6] Aerospace exploration increasingly is conducted remotely, marking a turning point in our theoretical considerations of biocultural adaptation. Do machines collect data more efficiently than humans, or do machines ultimately make humans irrelevant?

Andrée and Wellman took the first steps in removing the burden of expedition transport from the backs of men and elevating the human senses over the polar sea. Now the human senses have been removed from the equation altogether and replaced by the pure intellect of an individual in front of a telemetric monitoring station, and of the potential archaeological record created by the actions of machines that in some cases operate on the other side of the solar system from the hand and mind that presumably controls them.

This has implications for biological anthropologists, but probably not ones they will at first be comfortable in considering at great length. By effectively removing the environment as a calculation in the adaptive value of technology, we have taken the first step in developing a theoretical basis for the study, not of human behavior, but of the—for want of a better term—*behavior* of the machines that have begun to explore for us, and how that behavior reflects an originating culture that in future years may exist many light years distant. Are the scratchings made in the sands of Mars by the *Viking* probes in 1976 evidence of human culture or machine culture? And when does the former become the latter?

These are considerations that go far beyond one individual or one expedition, and lead into general considerations of the courses of technological development and human expansion, and the kinds of imaginative notions that contribute either to success or to failure in all explorations of hostile environments.

*E*ach aeronautical landscape possesses its own archive, its own store of memories, of ghosts, and of shadows and light. To explore these scenes properly, one must explore even more deeply the archives. These landscapes gain meaning from those who trod them in the past, sailed by them or landed on their shores, or flew from them or over them in balloons and airships, aircraft and satellites, or dove under their waters in submarines or with aqualungs.

Andrée's hangar ruins, after one stares at them for many days, take on all the appearance of a twentieth-century Stonehenge, a sort of shrine to the new religion of technology. The many visitors to its memorial have been like faithful Druids worshiping not so much a man as his idea—that technology could and would elevate the human senses above and beyond the human body, and would lead, as it inevitably has, to the complete severance of the human senses from the landscape, to be replaced by machines that explore Mars for us, for example, or voyage to the bottom of the sea for us. Whatever their occasional mechanical failings, these machines have no accursed limitations like lungs, bowels, or kidneys. The technological balance between human and machine that Andrée almost perfected has tipped far in favor of the machine, and continues on its way.

The ruins at Virgo Harbor, then, attract us specifically because they represent a time and a place—a very brief time and a very small place—for humans to dream, with some justice, that they would be the ultimate masters of technology, and not its inevitable servants. Like the long-dormant coal-mining tram towers high above the capital of Spitsbergen at Longyearbyen—towers that lean downhill and seem almost to gaze at visitors like the hillside statues of Easter Island—the Andrée and Wellman ruins show how we once believed we could conquer nature with technology, when in fact the real war, that between humans and technology, had just entered its most crucial, twentieth-century phase.

As perverse as it now seems, less than fifty years after S. A. Andrée lifted off from Virgo Harbor in his fragile balloon made of Chinese silk, an aircraft dropped a single weapon on a city and vaporized nearly 100,000 humans. Like us, Andrée and Wellman would have been appalled at this, but, perhaps unlike us, they would have understood it in their way. For they would have been convinced that it was a case of humans using technology to its ultimate effect, rather than technology shaping, limiting, even determining, the actions of humans.

In this there is again a suggestion of balance, that as human problems grow larger, so will their technological solutions. Like Victor Frankenstein, Andrée and Wellman were playing, more or less skillfully, with biotechnological fire. Unlike the doctor, and to their credit, they conducted their experiments in the glare of international publicity, in the full knowledge that failure would be judged harshly.

In this sense, although he did not live to see it, Andrée represented one of the first twentieth-century humans. He and Wellman were among the last such humans to feel they could control their own technology, while at the same moment possessing a realistic chance of actually doing so. In this way, Virgo Harbor and its archaeological remains earn an importance in our biocultural evolution that is little suspected or appreciated today, a place where tool-using humans were fast becoming tool-dominated humans.

*A*s for Walter Wellman, even in failure he understood the need to explore. Without exploration, without lonely, and now forgotten, outposts like Virgo Harbor, without base camps to project our imaginations into unknown regions, humans lose their optimistic drive and begin to drift aimlessly. And drifting with a purpose is another way of describing civilization, and a definition of who are we as Western technological people. I think this was one thing Wellman understood very well, perhaps in a way not understood by any other polar explorers of his day save Andrée and certainly Nansen.

By the time Wellman sought the Pole in his airship, it had long been clear that no great unknown lands lay at 90° N. At best, a lucky explorer might stumble upon a useless skerry or overgrown seamount protruding above the ice, but hardly the great northern continent that would bring the world into the geographic balance the Greeks were sure it possessed. Whoever first reached the Pole—be it Andrée, Nansen, Peary, Cook, Abruzzi, or Wellman—would merely be capping a frightfully expensive geographic reconnaissance begun three centuries earlier.

Even today, scholars and partisans alike argue over which human was the first to reach the North Pole. After nearly two decades of reading and studying archaeological remains, I believe that Roald Amundsen was the first to fly over the Pole, on board the airship *Norge* in 1926. The other claimants, Cook, Peary, Byrd, are all intensely flawed expedition leaders.

A single explorer, a small group of explorers, even the pilot and copilot of an airplane, all could hide their failures through altered logbooks, deliberate deception, and the protection of powerful allies and geographic societies. As Wellman learned—and Nobile would learn in even greater measure in 1928—you can't hide the failure of an airship in the Arctic. For Amundsen, this same notion was reversed: his success was immediately known to all, since the *New York Times* reporter on board sent a wireless message announcing the arrival at the Pole the moment it happened.

After the explorers, the scientists arrived: first the physical oceanographers (although it must be said that Nansen was already among the best—if not *the* best—of these) and then the biologists and meteorologists. Once anything of value was found, the politicians and lawyers and businessmen bartered over it. Once anything of great value was discovered there—such as the mines of Spitsbergen during the Second World War—the admirals and generals, with their sailors and soldiers, would be called upon to fight over that.

Geographic, economic, military considerations, however, all had long since ceased to be the prime reasons for reaching for the Pole. What Wellman also understood—in fact much better than Peary and certainly more than Cook—was the nature of the twentieth century. He sensed correctly that in the new century, the combination of technological exploration and mass media would explode the limits of the meandering sledge and steam vehicles and the ponderous two-volume expedition reports of the nineteenth century.

Wellman's transatlantic attempt came sixty-six years after Poe had, in a sense, already announced its accomplishment, in the fictionalized person of Mr. Monck Mason. As Poe's elaborate hoax suggested, this triumph would be not mere news but:

ASTOUNDING NEWS BY EXPRESS, VIA NORFOLK!—The Atlantic Crossed in Three Days!—Signal Triumph of Mr. Monck Mason's Flying Machine!—Arrival at Sullivan's Island, near Charlestown, S.C., of Mr. Mason, Mr. Robert Holland, Mr. Henson, Mr. Harrison Ainsworth, and four others, in the Steering Balloon, *Victoria,* after a Passage of Seventy-five Hours from Land to Land!

THE GREAT problem is at length solved! The air, as well as the earth and the ocean, has been subdued by science, and will become a common and convenient highway for mankind. The Atlantic has been actually crossed in a Balloon! and this too without difficulty—without any great apparent danger—with thorough control of the machine—and in the inconceivably brief period of seventy-five hours from shore to shore![7]

As Poe's "Balloon Hoax" made clear, the public, as early as 1850, had come to expect that the "great problems" would be solved by science, and "without difficulty" at that. After five failed polar expeditions, Wellman had to know that this was not the case. But what he knew, and what he believed, seemed, as with most humans, to be two very different things. Even the notion that the development of aircraft would bring with it the kind of universal peace envisioned by Victor Hugo and others was not entirely naive. If aircraft have rained death upon us—and they have done so supremely—so have they brought the world tightly together, perhaps too tightly.

The public that bought the newspapers that indirectly supported Wellman's expeditions was hardly different from the newspaper-buying public that cheered Neil Armstrong and Buzz Aldrin on their way to the lunar surface six decades later. And NASA, like the polar explorers at the turn of the century, discovered that it might as well have been playing Soviet Russia in some great sporting contest. Once the trophy was won, the season was over. Never again would funding pour forth for the reacquisition of a place already gained. In an irony that the archaeology of Walter Wellman seems to demonstrate, NASA was penalized for its success.

The explorer who reached the North Pole first would never again find sponsors to lay out good money for a return visit, merely to mop up what would be considered some marginal scientific loose ends. Nor could any explorer ever convince a patron that it was at those loose ends where all the good science was really done.

The discoverer of the North Pole had no logical next goal. NASA, to the contrary, did. Yet when the next goal line was drawn in the red sands of Mars, and the American public came to realize the distance between the new goalposts and the capabilities of their home team, the enthusiasm that cascaded from the stands at the start of the new exploring season was a mere ripple. NASA searched for another mission to satisfy a broad base of taxpayers, but the recent "Mission to Planet Earth" demonstrated just how wan and uninspiring the space program had become.

Now, we send robots to slink furtively around the solar system in a vain attempt to simulate the imaginative capabilities of the neural network of *H. sapiens sapiens,* a species rapidly approaching a techno-genetic crossroads: either physically link with the computer, or alter the genome to keep pace with the increasingly rapid requirements of biocultural evolution. It should be noted that such horrific alternatives turned up a century and a half ago, in the laboratory notebooks of Victor Frankenstein. Yet they seem hardly far-fetched now. And who's to say that without Shelley's literary mad scientist lingering in the collective human imagination, these alternatives would not have forced themselves upon us long ago. The seemingly simple acceleration of exploration technology begun by Andrée and Wellman at Virgo Harbor is spinning out in crazy directions indeed.

*F*rom the shore at Virgo Harbor in 1906 to the *Voyager 2* deep-space probe traversing the limit of our solar system in 2006, these one hundred years would cap the story of humans as technological explorers. The story begun more than two million years ago with a few rough stone tools, in what would become Africa's Olduvai Gorge, would culminate in *Apollo 11.* Now, with probes like *Voyager 2* and the remotely operated deep-ocean probes developed by Dr. Robert Ballard and his colleagues at the Woods Hole Oceanographic Institution on Cape Cod, we have inaugurated the era of robotic exploration. As Bob Ballard has remarked many times, the eyes are wonderful explorers; it's just too bad that they have to drag the kidneys and bowels along with them.

By the time a human finally claimed to have stood at the North Pole, that icy coordinate had come to signify—and continues to represent—the human search for something larger in our culture and ourselves: the sense and the knowledge that our journey is a continuous one, and that the geographic "firsts" we credit to ourselves are merely waypoints on a continuum begun two million years ago. If our culture and our bodies (and, increasingly, our robots) allow it, this path may continue for millions of years more. We have set human feet upon only one North Pole; in space, there are millions of North Poles waiting to be discovered.

For now, we can say that Walter Wellman never made it to the one North Pole that his time and his technology allowed him to reach for. But by studying the artifacts he and Salomon Andrée and so many others left behind on Danes Island and elsewhere in the Arctic, we approach a truer understanding of the means they required and the tools they sought to perfect in attaining that great prize. And by standing among the eerie remains at Virgo Harbor and feeling the winds when they blow toward the pole less than six hundred miles away, we can begin to comprehend what drove Wellman and Andrée and explorers like them to reach for such places.

Acknowledgments

I would like especially to thank Lisen Roll, who at the time of the 1993 survey was cultural officer in the Office of the Governor (*Sysselmann*) of Svalbard, in Longyearbyen. I am also indebted to archaeologist John Bockstoce for providing photographs of Virgo Harbor from his 1992 visit. Captain Tor-Arne Jakobsen, chief steward Ole Knudsen, and crew of the *Polarsyssel* went out of their way to provide logistics assistance during five days aboard that vessel. A visitor to Danskøya, Wilhelm Munthe-Kaas, generously loaned his camera to me after mine was lost off Smeerenburg. Andreas Umbreit of Terra Polaris in Kiel, Germany, was very helpful, and his book, *A Guide to Spitsbergen,* made me believe that an expedition to Danes Island might just be possible. Bjarne Petterson, the baker from Bigdøy, who started me on my education in Bokmål, kindly translated sections of Nansen's *En ferd til Spitsbergen.*

I relied heavily on the expertise, advice, and experience of several historians and archaeologists, including Robert Browning, Tom Crouch, Lars Vig Fensen, Bjørn Hebba Helberg, Tora Hultgreen, Roger Jørgensen, Christian Keller, Anne Millbrooke, Dag Nævestad, William N. Still, Jr., William Turnbaugh, and Bjørn Vidar. I would also like to acknowledge the invaluable insights provided through the written works of and correspondence and conversations with several anthropologists, especially Richard A. Gould, Ben R. Finney, Jack W. K. Harris, Robert Blumenschine, and Scott L. H. Madry, and my close colleague Bill Thomas.

And of course I must acknowledge the inspiration provided by the works and expeditions of the polar explorers mentioned herein, especially Wally Herbert and John Bockstoce, and also those of world explorers Thor Heyerdahl, Jacques-Yves Cousteau, Tim Severin, and Robert D. Ballard.

Herman Van Dyk rendered superb engineering drawings of the airships of Godard and Vaniman, as well as Wellman's misbegotten motor sledge, and constructed a beautiful scale model of Amundsen's *Norge,* which were all invaluable in my research. For these and for his constant encouragement and scholarly discussions of countless issues related to airship design and development, as well as his seemingly limitless knowledge of airship history, I am extremely grateful. Dr. and Mrs. Huettner of the archives of the Marine Biological Laboratory at Woods Hole, Massachusetts, provided access to and cheerful assistance with the polar collection there.

To Michael Aaron Rockland, chairman of the American Studies Department at Rutgers University and genius of generosity, I owe a debt of allegiance for his consistent encouragement, advice, gentle and wise criticism, and good fellowship. So too polar historian Beau Riffenburgh of the Scott Polar Research Institute in Cambridge, England. Cornelia Lüdecke, whom I met at the Andrée Centennial Conference in Longyearbyen in 1997, tracked down some remarkable photographs taken during von Zeppelin's 1910 expedition to Spitsbergen, one of which is reproduced herein. I would also like to thank Urban Wråkberg and Hein Bjerk, who combined with seamless efficiency to make my participation in that memorable conference a reality.

I am also grateful to Sven Lundström, director of the Andrée Museum in Gränna, Sweden, and another participant at the Longyearbyen conference, for permission to reproduce materials from that museum's archives. Many of the photographs of the site as it appeared in 1993 are published here for the first time; others are historic images stored at the Norwegian Polar Institute in Oslo, and largely unknown to North American audiences. I am grateful to the Polar Institute, and especially to Dr. Susan Barr, head of the Section on Polar History and Documentation, for permission to use these photographs from the archives in Norway. Susan is a constant source of ideas, history, and good fellowship. To log on to my computer at sunrise, with my first cup of coffee on the table, and see an e-mail from her office in Oslo, gets my workday off to a perfect start.

Leslie Mitchner at Rutgers University Press is a marvelous editor. Vast sections of the manuscript climbed to new heights on the strength of her suggestions. C. L., Jeremy, and Jenny are the fixed stars on my journey, and distracted me from the computer enough to keep me within the loose boundaries of rationality.

Finally, to my friend and colleague Professor Wynne Caldwell, for twenty years of inspiration and conversation, for bread and butter and tea, for surviving the German Blitz as a girl in Liverpool, this volume is gratefully dedicated. Rule, Britannia!

Notes

Introduction

1. Clive Holland, ed., *Farthest North: A History of North Polar Exploration in Eye-Witness Accounts* (New York: Carroll & Graf, 1994), 29–30.
2. Beau Riffenburgh, "James Gordon Bennett, the *New York Herald,* and the Arctic," *Polar Record* 27, no. 160 (1991): 9–16.
3. Beau Riffenburgh, "Jules Verne and the Conquest of the Polar Regions," *Polar Record* 27, no. 162 (1991): 237–240.
4. Jules Verne, *20,000 Leagues under the Sea* (Annapolis: Naval Institute Press, 1993), 316.

Chapter One. Saint of the Swedes

1. S. A. Andrée, Nils Strindberg, and K. Fraenkel, *Andrée's Story; The Complete Record of His Polar Flight, 1897* (from the diaries and journals of Andrée, Strindberg, and Fraenkel, found on White Island in the summer of 1930), ed. Swedish Society for Anthropology and Geography, trans. Edward Adams-Ray (New York: Blue Ribbon Books, 1930), 56. Hereafter cited as *Andrée's Story.*
2. Ibid., 3.
3. Ibid., 6.
4. Ibid., 8.
5. Ibid., 10.
6. Ibid., 22.
7. Ibid.
8. Quoted in Robert Paxton, *Europe in the Twentieth Century* (San Diego: Harcourt Brace Jovanovich, 1975), 36.
9. *Andrée's Story,* 28.
10. Ibid., 38.
11. Henri Lachambre and Alexis Machuron, *Andrée's Balloon Expedition in Search of the North Pole* (New York: Frederick A. Stokes, 1898), 57. Hereafter cited as *Andrée's Balloon Expedition.*

12. Ibid., 58–59.

13. *Andrée's Story,* 33.

14. Ibid.

15. *Andrée's Balloon Expedition,* 167.

16. Ibid., 159.

17. Per Olaf Sundman, *The Flight of the Eagle* (New York: Pantheon, 1970), 100.

18. *Andrée's Story,* 56.

19. *Andrée's Balloon Expedition,* 272–273.

20. Ibid., 273.

21. Sundman, *The Flight of the Eagle,* 161.

22. *Andrée's Balloon Expedition,* 288.

23. Ibid., 290–291; *Andrée's Story,* 56.

24. *Andrée's Balloon Expedition,* 292.

25. Quoted in ibid., 292.

26. *Andrée's Story,* 56.

27. *Andrée's Balloon Expedition,* 296–297.

28. Ibid., 298.

29. Ibid., 301–302.

30. Ibid., 304.

31. *Andrée's Story,* 76.

32. Andrée file, National Air & Space Museum Archives, Washington, D.C.

33. Ibid.

34. *Andrée's Story,* 64.

Chapter Two. The Greatest Show in the Arctic

1. Quoted in Walter Wellman, "By Airship to the North Pole," *McClure's* 29, no. 2 (1907): 191.

2. Ibid., 193.

3. Walter Wellman, *The Aerial Age; A Thousand Miles by Airship over the Atlantic Ocean; Airship Voyages over the Polar Sea; The Past, the Present, and the Future of Aerial Navigation* (New York: A. R. Keller, 1911), 119. Hereafter cited as *Aerial Age.*

4. Edward H. Mabley, *The Motor Balloon "America"* (Brattleboro, Vt.: Stephen Greene Press, 1969), 64–65. Hereafter cited as *Balloon "America."*

5. H. Jerome Champin to Edward Mabley, May 30, 1970, from the "Walter Wellman" file at the National Air & Space Museum Archives (hereafter cited as "Wellman-NASM").

6. Paul Garber, interview with the author, May 1986, at Garber's office at the National Air & Space Museum, Washington, D.C.

7. *Aerial Age,* 39.

8. Walter Wellman to H. W. Leman, May 15, 1894, Chicago Historical Society.

9. Ibid.

10. *Aerial Age,* 24.

11. H. W. Leman to Edward G. Mason, February 8, 1898, Chicago Historical Society.

12. *Aerial Age,* 35.
13. *Balloon "America,"* 19.
14. *Aerial Age,* 38.
15. Ibid., 40.
16. Ibid., 42.
17. Ibid., 43.
18. Ibid.
19. *Balloon "America,"* 18.
20. Walter Wellman to Evelyn Briggs Baldwin. August 4, 1898, from the Papers of Evelyn Briggs Baldwin, box 7, folder 2, Manuscript Division, Library of Congress, Washington. Hereafter cited as "Baldwin Papers."
21. Wellman to Baldwin, August 5, 1898, Baldwin Papers.
22. Baldwin to Wellman, August 7, 1898, Baldwin Papers.
23. Baldwin to Wellman, August 9, 1898, Baldwin Papers.
24. Baldwin to Wellman, August 25, 1898, Baldwin Papers.
25. Ibid.
26. Wellman to Baldwin, August 27, 1898, Baldwin Papers.
27. Ibid.
28. Ibid.
29. Ibid.
30. *Aerial Age,* 48.
31. Wellman to Baldwin, August 27, 1898, Baldwin Papers.
32. *Aerial Age,* 48.
33. Ibid.
34. Ibid., 50.
35. Ibid., 80.
36. Ibid., 83.
37. Ibid., 85.
38. Ibid., 119.
39. Quoted in *Balloon "America,"* 15.
40. H. Hunter Chadwick, "Balloons vs. Aeroplanes," *Fly,* vol. 1, 1909.
41. Quoted in the *Chicago Record-Herald,* February 14, 1906.
42. Walter Wellman, "The Polar Airship," *National Geographic* 17, no. 4 (1906): 205–228.
43. "Expert Sees Value in Wellman Voyage," *Chicago Record-Herald,* January 7, 1906.
44. Wellman, "By Airship to the North Pole."
45. Ibid.
46. Ibid.
47. Ibid.
48. Ibid.
49. Ibid.
50. Ibid.
51. A. J. Corbitt to Edward Mabley, 1961, Wellman-NASM.
52. Wellman, "By Airship to the North Pole."
53. Wellman, "The Polar Airship."

54. Ibid.
55. Ibid.
56. *Aerial Age,* 150–151.
57. Ibid., 155.
58. Ibid., 154.
59. Wellman, "By Airship to the North Pole."
60. *Aerial Age,* 169.
61. Wellman, "By Airship to the North Pole."
62. *New York Times,* September 15, 1907.
63. Quoted in ibid.
64. *Aerial Age,* 175–176.
65. Quoted in the *New York Times,* September 15, 1907.
66. Quoted in ibid. An "About the Author" note accompanying an article on his experiences overwintering on Danes Island written by Riesenburg in 1931 says that the airship crash-landed on "Foul Glacier in northwest Spitsbergen," and since Riesenburg was on board the airship at the time we can assume this is an accurate statement. By "Foul Glacier" he most likely refers to Fuglepyntbreen at 79°40' N 11° E, about ten miles (15 km) northeast of Virgohamna on the northwest Spitsbergen mainland, which, in the ever-changing nomenclature of Svalbard, was known then as "Fowl Point Glacier."
67. *Aerial Age,* 178.
68. Quoted in the *New York Times,* September 15, 1907.
69. Quoted in ibid.
70. Quoted in ibid.
71. A. J. Corbitt to Edward Mabley, 1961, Wellman-NASM.
72. Quoted in *Balloon "America,"* 33–34.
73. *Aerial Age,* 220.
74. Ibid., 184.
75. Ibid., 185–187.
76. Quoted in the *New York Times,* September 12, 1909.
77. *Aerial Age,* 187.
78. Ibid., 189.
79. Quoted in ibid., 188.
80. Ibid., 190.
81. Quoted in ibid., 193.
82. Quoted in John Grierson, *Challenge to the Poles* (Hamden, Conn.: Archon Books, 1964), 46.
83. Quoted in *Balloon "America,"* 42.
84. *New York Times,* October 20, 1910.

Chapter Three. Arctic Ghosts

1. Alexander McKee, *Ice Crash: Disaster in the Arctic, 1928* (London: Souvenir Press, 1979), 247–248.
2. Wally Herbert, *The Noose of Laurels* (New York: Atheneum, 1989), 137. Italics are mine.

3. Translated from Fridtjof Nansen, *En ferd til Spitsbergen* (Christiania: Jacob Dybwads Forlag, 1920), 145. Nansen also gives the best description in the literature of the Chicago Record-Herald House at Virgohamna, Wellman's Arctic headquarters. The house was still standing when Nansen visited. "The living quarters itself was a large and roomy house, but not cozy. One hallway led to different rooms, and it went all around the house, encircling on all sides a room in the middle of the house where the occupants lived. But there were no windows at all and one could not see out. The light came from a small tower erected in the roof. The house was in good shape. By that I mean the walls, the roof, and the floor. But from the doors all locks and everything of metal had been stolen. So now it was standing open to wind and weather. Unfortuately, such deeds were done by the trappers, and give us an insight into European greed, which should give us something to think about. What a contrast to the moral codes of the Eskimo peoples" (145). Nansen then relates a fable of an Eskimo who finds a piece of driftwood on the shore and drags it up above the tide mark, where he will still be able to find it even if he leaves it there for years. No one will disturb it.

4. Ibid., 143.

5. Walter Mittelholzer, *By Airplane towards the North Pole* (Boston: Houghton Mifflin, 1925), 164.

6. Ibid., 33.

7. Roald Amundsen and Lincoln Ellsworth, *The First Flight across the Polar Sea* (London: Hutchinson, 1927).

8. George Wilkins, *Flying the Arctic* (New York: Grosset & Dunlap, 1928), 3.

9. C. B. Allen and Lauren D. Lyman, *The Wonder Book of the Air* (Chicago: John C. Winston, 1939), 134–135.

10. McKee, *Ice Crash,* 63.

11. See, for example: Pierre Berton, *The Arctic Grail* (New York: Viking, 1988); Wilbur Cross, *Ghost Ship of the Pole* (New York: William Sloane, 1960); Daniel Francis, *Discovery of the North* (Edmonton: Hurtig, 1986).

12. See, for example: David E. Fisher, *Across the Top of the World* (New York: Random House, 1992); Barry Lopez, *Arctic Dreams* (New York: Scribner's, 1986).

13. Beau Riffenburgh, *The Myth of the Explorer* (London: Belhaven Press, 1993), 157.

14. John Toland, *The Great Dirigibles* (New York: Dover, 1972), 49.

15. Richard Montague, *Oceans, Poles, and Airmen* (New York: Random House, 1971), 3.

16. Thor B. Arlov, *A Short History of Svalbard* (Oslo: Norsk Polarinstitutt, 1989).

17. H. C. Meyer, *Airshipmen, Businessmen, and Politics, 1890–1940* (Washington, D.C.: Smithsonian Institution Press, 1991), 84.

18. Toland, *The Great Dirigibles,* 149.

19. Grierson, *Challenge to the Poles,* 41–47.

20. Sir William Martin Conway, *The First Crossing of Spitsbergen* (London: J. M. Dent, 1897).

21. *Aerial Age,* 193.

22. Wellman, "The Polar Airship."
23. *Aerial Age,* 153.
24. Wellman, "The Polar Airship"; also *Aerial Age,* 154.
25. *Aerial Age,* 203.
26. Ibid.
27. Pike's house was moved to Barentsburg, a Russian mining community in Spitsbergen, where it burned down during World War II.

Chapter Four. The Spam What Am

1. Riffenburgh, *The Myth of the Explorer,* 196.
2. M. Emery and E. Emery, *The Press and America: An Interpretive History of the Mass Media,* 6th ed. (Englewood Cliffs, N.J.: Prentice-Hall, 1988), 220.
3. Translated from Nansen, *En ferd til Spitsbergen,* 145.
4. Quoted in the *Chicago Record-Herald,* June 3, 1906.
5. *Aerial Age,* 9.
6. Ibid., 10–11.
7. Ibid., 130.
8. Quoted in the *Chicago Record-Herald,* January 5, 1906.
9. Quoted in C. H. Dennis, *Victor Lawson: His Time and His Work* (Chicago: University of Chicago Press, 1935), 302–303.
10. *Aerial Age,* 128.
11. Riffenburgh, *The Myth of the Explorer,* 1.
12. *Balloon "America,"* 21.
13. "Walter Wellman's Expedition to the North Pole," *National Geographic* 17, no. 4 (1906): 205–207.
14. *Aerial Age,* 138.
15. Quoted in the *Chicago Record-Herald,* June 2, 1906.
16. Sundman, *The Flight of the Eagle,* 3.
17. *Aerial Age,* 150–151.
18. Ibid., 210.
19. Ibid., 212–213.
20. Ibid., 131.
21. Ibid., 128.

Chapter Five. Broken Dreams

1. Riffenburgh, *The Myth of the Explorer,* 3.
2. Emery and Emery, *The Press and America,* 278.
3. The father of aviation archaeology is Richard Gould, who has taught for many years in the anthropology department at Brown University. Introductions to his anthropological approach to historical remains can be found in: Richard A. Gould, *Shipwreck Anthropology* (Albuquerque: University of New Mexico Press, 1983); and in his *Recovering the Past* (Albuquerque: University of New Mexico Press, 1990), a brilliant volume that provides the theoretical basis for historical archaeology for decades to come, and which is the most important theoretical volume to be written on the subject since the work of Stanley South in the 1970s.

4. Stephen Kern, *The Culture of Time and Space, 1880–1918* (Cambridge, Mass.: Harvard University Press, 1983), 246.

5. *Aerial Age,* 125.

6. Ibid.

7. *Chicago Record-Herald,* January 5, 1906. It is unknown what transpired between Wellman and Santos-Dumont in Paris, but after the initial announcements mentioning his participation, Santos-Dumont disappears as a member of the expedition. In a dispatch from Paris in late January, Wellman says that Santos-Dumont is offering endless advice and assistance, but that "the question of his personal participation in the effort to attain the pole is as yet in abeyance and does not need to be decided for some time" (*Chicago Record-Herald* January 29, 1906). He is again mentioned in the 1906 *National Geographic* article "Walter Wellman's Expedition to the North Pole," giving Wellman advice in the manner of attachment of the guide-rope and drag anchor to the airship, advice Wellman apparently heeded, and in advising Wellman to use four 25-hp motors rather than one 50-hp and one 25-hp engine, advice Wellman did not take. In fact, this *National Geographic* article is one example of Wellman offering two different design specifications in the *same* documentary source. The design drawing in this article says that the guide-rope and ice anchor are to be suspended from a steel boat (206), while, later in the article, Wellman says that Santos-Dumont has persuaded him to hang the ice anchor from the prow of the airship envelope itself (217).

In *The Aerial Age,* Wellman remarks only that Santos-Dumont "thought so well of our project that at one time he seriously considered joining me in the effort"(126–127), a rather different thing. One of the reasons the expedition was taken seriously—by the limited percentage of editorial writers who did in fact take it seriously—was the announcement of Santos-Dumont as pilot of the polar airship.

8. *Aerial Age,* 127.

9. *Chicago Record-Herald,* January 31, 1906.

10. Wellman, "The Polar Airship," 214.

11. Quoted in the *Chicago Record-Herald,* February 14, 1906.

12. Quoted in ibid., February 10, 1906.

13. Quoted in ibid., May 7, 1906.

14. Wellman, "The Polar Airship." Wellman announced his intention to use motor sledges in his expedition in a speech to the New York Motor Club on March 23, 1906. In this speech he admitted that the Godard airship would not carry enough fuel to allow him to make a return trip after reaching the Pole. Wellman said that he had solved this problem by the expedient of commissioning the construction of two motor sledges, one in Europe and one in the United States, that would weigh between 210 and 215 pounds. They would be equipped with small engines and carry the two persons operating them. If his tests were successful, Wellman expected to take three motor sledges on board the airship with him. No one at the Motor Club apparently called Wellman on this obvious backward logic, which

we could refer to as a sort of conundrum of technological overkill. In simple terms, if his rationale for carrying motor sledges was that he could not carry enough fuel on board the airship to power its engines back to land from the North Pole, why on earth would he carry over six hundred pounds of motor sledges and the fuel to power them? Surely he could simply abandon the idea of motor sledges entirely and use the saved weight to add more fuel to the airship itself. Nansen, in his 1920 book *En ferd til Spitsbergen,* sarcastically criticized both the idea of a provisions-filled guide-rope, or "sausage," and the motor sledges. "The lower part of the sausage should be dragged along the ice. It was possible pieces of them would fall off. Especially when some of them got jammed into the pack ice. But these pieces would then be left where they fell and would serve to mark the way where they had travelled. If the airship, for one or another reason, should go down, then those daring travellers, when they came driving back on the motor sledges they did not have yet, easily could find their way back by following these sausage-like pieces. And besides, they could live off of their contents. One important thing was missing though. They didn't have any gasoline to keep their engines going" (144–145). In *The Aerial Age,* Wellman wrote of an effort "to build motor-sledges, in accordance with the plans I had previously prepared. But it was not successful. I was compelled to go to America and to leave the details in the hands of assistants. They built the sledges far too heavy—good for work on smooth ice, as they proved when tested out on the lakes of Norway, but useless upon the rough ice of the polar ocean" (133).

15. *Aerial Age,* 139.
16. Ibid., 147–148.
17. Wellman, "The Polar Airship," 206.
18. Ibid., 212.
19. *Aerial Age,* 147.
20. *Chicago Record-Herald,* June 12, 1906. On board his research yacht *Princess Alice,* His Royal Highness Albert of Monaco had conducted oceanographic research for two decades. In 1906, he journeyed to Spitsbergen and was accompanied by the German meteorologist Hergozel, who conducted atmospheric research in the archipelago with the aid of *ballons sondes.* Hergozel showed that the air temperature 1,000 meters above Virgo Harbor was 20° C lower than that at harbor level. Wellman used this data to support his argument that his airship must maintain an altitude of about 200 to 250 meters above the earth (through the use of a guide-rope he called an *equilabrator*), because he feared that traveling at a higher altitude would cause the airship's motors to freeze (*Chicago Record-Herald,* September 1, 1906).
21. Wellman, "By Airship to the North Pole," 190.
22. Quoted in the *Chicago Record-Herald,* July 2, 1906.
23. Quoted in ibid., August 25, 1906.
24. *Aerial Age,* 155.
25. *Ibid.*

26. *Chicago Record-Herald,* July 27, 1907.

27. Walter Wellman, "Will the "America" Fly to the Pole?" *McClure's* 29, no. 3 (1907): 241.

28. *Aerial Age,* 169.

29. Ibid., 172.

30. Ibid, 193–194.

31. Ibid., 148.

32. Wellman, "The Polar Airship."

33. *Aerial Age,* 147.

34. "Modèle 1902 de Louis Godard: Dirigeable à double propulseur avec moteurs à pétrole de la puissance de 100 chevaux." Louis Godard file, National Air & Space Museum,. Washington, D.C.

35. David Mondey, ed., *The International Encyclopedia of Aviation* (New York: Crown, 1977), 328.

36. Ibid.

37. Kern, *The Culture of Time and Space,* 214.

38. *Aerial Age,* 124; Wellman, "The Polar Airship," 208.

39. See, for example, Melvin Vaniman, "Revolutionizing Air Travel," *Aircraft,* May 1912, 76–77.

40. "The Fate of Vaniman," *Scientific American,* July 20, 1912.

41. *Chicago Record-Herald,* August 27, 1907.

Chapter Six. Gasbag or Windbag

1. C. D. Chandler, *Balloon and Airship Gases* (New York: Ronald Press, 1926), 4.

2. See, for example, Berton, *The Arctic Grail;* and Francis, *Discovery of the North.*

3. See, for example, Louis C. Gerken, *Airships: History and Technology* (Chula Vista, Calif.: American Scientific Corp., 1990); and Toland, *The Great Dirigibles.*

4. Tom D. Crouch, *The Eagle Aloft* (Washington, D.C.: Smithsonian Institution Press, 1983).

5. Victor Pagé, *Modern Aircraft* (New York: Henley, 1928), 33.

6. See, for example, Bryan Donkin, Jr., *A Text-book on Gas, Oil, and Air Engines* (London: Charles Griffin, 1894); and William Robinson, *Gas and Petroleum Engines* (New York: Spon & Chamberlain, 1902).

7. *Andrée's Story,* 29.

8. Ibid., 29–30.

9. Sven Lundström, *Andrée's Polarexpedition* (Gränna: Wiken, 1988), 62.

10. *Andrée's Story,* 32. The price of supplies must have plummeted in the years between 1896 and 1910, for Wellman records in his memoirs that virtually the same cost, $5,000 (this figure *including* labor), was required to supply his 1910 transatlantic airship with *345,000* cubic feet of hydrogen (*Aerial Age,* 225).

11. Grateful acknowledgments to Susan Barr for this translation from Lundström, *Andrée's Polarexpedition,* 62.

12. C. H. Gibbs-Smith, *Ballooning* (London: Penguin, 1948), 15.

13. Chandler, *Balloon and Airship Gases*, 5.

14. Conway, *The First Crossing of Spitsbergen*, 270.

15. Ibid., 271.

16. *Andrée's Balloon Expedition*, 118.

17. *Andrée's Story*, 42.

18. Ibid., 43.

19. Ibid., 44.

20. Ibid., 47.

21. *Aerial Age*, 131.

22. *Chicago Record-Herald*, August 26, 1907.

23. Ibid., September 14, 1907.

24. *Aerial Age*, 225.

25. Charles B. Boss and Kenneth J. Fredeen, *Concepts, Instrumentation, and Techniques in Inductively Coupled Plasma Atomic Emission Spectrometry* (Eden Prairie, Minn.: Perkin-Elmer Corp., 1989), ix.

26. Ibid., 1–5. Data collected via these scans were analyzed using the software program Excel.

27. *Aerial Age*, 225.

28. Chandler, *Balloon and Airship Gases*, 6.

29. Jules Verne, *Around the World in 80 Days—and—Five Weeks in a Balloon* (Ware, Hertfordshire: Wordsworth Editions, 1994), 195. 30. Sundman, *The Flight of the Eagle*, 127.

31. *Andrée's Story*, 32; Lundström, *Andrée's Polarexpedition*, 62.

32. *Chicago Record-Herald*, September 14, 1907.

33. Robinson, *Gas and Petroleum Engines*, 572–574. Dennis, in his biography of Victor Lawson, the newspaper owner who sponsored Wellman's airship flights, mentions that Wellman in the spring of 1910 "made a trip to Spitzbergen to gather up equipment and supplies that were stored there" (*Victor Lawson,* 307), in order to use them for his attempted transatlantic flight in October 1910. Wellman was in Cairo in late March 1910, and in Atlantic City to prepare for the October flight in mid-June, so it is possible that Wellman made a side trip to Virgohamna in late May 1910, although such a journey so early in the season would not have been simple, and Wellman himself makes no mention of such a trip. On the other hand, Wellman does mention having a special hydrogen-generating apparatus built for him in Paris and brought to Atlantic City, New Jersey, where it was assembled (*Aerial Age*, 225).

34. Susan Barr, "Soviet-Norwegian Historical Expedition to Zemlya Frantsa-Iosifa," *Polar Record* 27, no. 163 (1991): 297–302.

35. Louis Godard file. National Air & Space Museum.

36. Luigi Amedeo of Savoy, *On the "Polar Star" in the Arctic Sea* (London: Hutchinson, 1903), 36.

37. Ibid., 166–167.

38. Anthony Fiala, *Fighting the Polar Ice* (New York: Doubleday, Page, 1907), plate opp. p. 57.

39. Umberto Nobile, *My Five Years with Soviet Airships* (Akron, Ohio: Lighter-than-Air Society, 1987), 31.

Conclusion

1. Riffenburgh, *The Myth of the Explorer,* 166; Herbert, *The Noose of Laurels,* 239; Eugene Rodgers, *Beyond the Barrier* (Annapolis: Naval Institute Press, 1990), 22.
2. *Aerial Age,* 10.
3. Ben Finney, *From Sea to Space* (Palmerston North, New Zealand: Massey University, 1992), 105.
4. Ibid.
5. Ibid.
6. Lord Kenneth Clark, *Civilisation* (New York: Harper & Row, 1969), 346.
7. Edgar Allan Poe, "The Balloon Hoax," *New York Sun,* April 13, 1844.

Select Bibliography

Allen, C. B., and Lauren D. Lyman. *The Wonder Book of the Air*. Chicago: John C. Winston, 1939.

Amundsen, Roald, and Lincoln Ellsworth. *The First Flight across the Polar Sea*. London: Hutchinson, 1927.

Arlov, Thor B. *A Short History of Svalbard*. Oslo: Norsk Polarinstitutt, 1989.

Barr, Susan. "Soviet-Norwegian Historical Expedition to Zemlya Frantsa-Iosifa." *Polar Record* 27, no. 163 (1991): 297–302.

———, ed. *Franz Josef Land*. Oslo: Norsk Polarinstitutt, 1995.

Barr, William. "Wettertrupp Haudegen: The Last German Arctic Weather Station of World War II: Part 1." *Polar Record* 23, no. 143 (1986): 143–157.

———. "Wettertrupp Haudegen: The Last German Arctic Weather Station of World War II: Part 2." *Polar Record* 23, no. 144 (1986): 323–333.

Basalla, George. 1988. *The Evolution of Technology*. New York: Cambridge University Press.

Basberg, Bjørn, and Dag Nævestad. *Hvalfangstminneregistrering På Syd Georgia*. Meddeslelser no. 110. Oslo: Norsk Polarinstitutt, 1990.

Beattie, Owen, and John Geiger. *Frozen in Time: Unlocking the Secrets of the Franklin Expedition*. New York: Dutton, 1987.

Bergengren, Erik. *Alfred Nobel*. London: Thomas Nelson & Sons, 1962.

Berton, Pierre. *The Arctic Grail*. New York: Viking, 1988.

Boss, Charles B., and Kenneth J. Fredeen. *Concepts, Instrumentation, and Techniques in Inductively Coupled Plasma Atomic Emission Spectrometry*. Eden Prairie, Minn.: Perkin-Elmer Corp., 1989.

Capelotti, P. J. *Explorer's Air Yacht: The Sikorsky S-38 Flying Boat*. Missoula, Mont.: Pictorial Histories, 1995.

———. "A Preliminary Archaeological Survey of Camp Wellman at Virgohamn, Danskøya, Svalbard." *Polar Record* 30, no. 175 (1994): 265–276.

———. *The Wellman Polar Airship Expeditions at Virgohamna, Danskøya, Svalbard; a Study in Aerospace Archaeology*. Meddeslelser no. 145. Oslo: Norwegian Polar Institute, 1997.

Carlheim-Gyllensköld, Vilhelm. *På Åttionde Breddgraden (At the 80th Degreee).* Stockholm: AB, 1900.

Carson, Oliver. *The Man Who Made News.* New York: Duell, Sloan & Pearce, 1942.

Chandler, C. D. *Balloon and Airship Gases.* New York: Ronald Press, 1926.

Conway, Sir William Martin. *The First Crossing of Spitsbergen.* London: J. M. Dent, 1897.

Crawford, O.G.S. *Archaeology in the Field.* London: Phoenix House, 1953.

Cross, Wilbur. *Ghost Ship of the Pole.* New York: William Sloane, 1960.

Crouch, Tom. *Bleriot XI, the Story of a Classic Aircraft.* Washington, D.C.: Smithsonian Institution Press, 1982.

———. *The Eagle Aloft.* Washington, D.C.: Smithsonian Institution Press, 1983.

Darby, C. *Pacific Aircraft Wrecks.* Melbourne, Victoria: Kookaburra, 1979.

Deetz, James. *In Small Things Forgotten.* Garden City, N.Y.: Anchor Books, 1977.

Dege, Eckart. "Wettertrupp Haudegen: Forty Years Later." *Polar Record* 23, no. 144 (1986).

Deighton, Len. 1979. *Airshipwreck.* New York: Holt, Rinehart, & Winston.

Dennis, C. H. *Victor Lawson: His Time and His Work.* Chicago: University of Chicago Press, 1935.

Donkin, Jr., Bryan. *A Text-book on Gas, Oil, and Air Engines.* London: Charles Griffin, 1894.

Dymond, D. P. *Archaeology and History: A Plea for Reconciliation.* London: Thames & Hudson, 1974.

Emery, M., and E. Emery. *The Press and America: An Interpretive History of the Mass Media.* 6th ed. Englewood Cliffs, N.J.: Prentice-Hall, 1988.

"The Fate of Vaniman." *Scientific American,* July 20, 1912.

Fermer, D. *James Gordon Bennett and the New York Herald.* New York: St. Martin's Press, 1986.

Fiala, Anthony. *Fighting the Polar Ice.* New York: Doubleday, Page, 1907.

Fisher, David E. *Across the Top of the World.* New York: Random House, 1992.

Fitzhugh, William W., and Jacqueline S. Olin, eds. *Archeology of the Frobisher Voyages.* Washington, D.C.: Smithsonian Institution Press, 1993.

Francis, Daniel. *Discovery of the North.* Edmonton: Hurtig, 1986.

Gerken, Louis C. *Airships: History and Technology.* Chula Vista, Calif.: American Scientific Corp., 1990.

Gibbs-Smith, C. H. *Ballooning.* London: Penguin, 1948.

Gillmor, C. S. "Science and Travel in Extreme Latitudes." *Isis* 85 (1994): 482–485.

Glines, C. V., ed. *Polar Aviation.* New York: Franklin Watts, 1964.

Gould, Richard A. "The Archaeology of War." In *Shipwreck Anthropology,* ed. Richard A. Gould. Albuquerque: University of New Mexico Press, 1983.

———. *Recovering the Past.* Albuquerque: University of New Mexico Press, 1990.

———. *Shipwreck Anthropology.* Albuquerque: University of New Mexico Press, 1983.

Grierson, John. *Challenge to the Poles.* Hamden, Conn.: Archon Books, 1964.

Hacquebord, Louwrens. "Het verblijf van Nederlandse walvisvaarders op de westkust van Spitsbergen in de zeventiende eeuw" (The Sojourn of Dutch

Whalers on the West Coast of Spitsbergen in the Seventeenth Century [with a Summary in English]). Ph.D. diss., Stichting drukkerij C. Regenboog Groningen, 1984.

———. "In Search of *Het Behouden Huys:* A Survey of the Remains of the House of Willem Barentsz on Novaya Zemlya." *Arctic* 48, no. 3 (1995): 248–256.

Harrowfield, David L. "Historic Sites in the Ross Dependency, Antarctica." *Polar Record* 24, no. 151 (1988): 277–284.

Hassel, Bert R. J. *Fish Hassel—A Viking with Wings.* Bend, Oreg.: Maverick, 1987.

Hayes, David. *The Lost Squadron.* New York: Hyperion, 1994.

Herbert, Wally. *The Noose of Laurels.* New York: Atheneum, 1989.

Holland, Clive, ed. *Farthest North: A History of North Polar Exploration in Eye-Witness Accounts.* New York: Carroll & Graf, 1994.

Hughes, Janet. "Mawson's Antarctic Huts and Tourism: A Case for On-site Preservation." *Polar Record* 28, no. 164 (1992): 37–42.

Huntford, Roland. *The Last Place on Earth.* New York: Atheneum, 1985.

Kent, Rockwell. *N by E.* Middletown, Conn.: Wesleyan Univerity Press, 1978. (Reprint of 1930 edition published by Brewer & Warren.)

Kern, Stephen. *The Culture of Time and Space, 1880–1918.* Cambridge, Mass.: Harvard University Press, 1983.

Lachambre, Henri, and Alexis Machuron. *Andrée's Balloon Expedition in Search of the North Pole.* New York: Frederick A. Stokes, 1898.

Lopez, Barry. *Arctic Dreams.* New York: Scribner's, 1986.

Lundström, Sven. *Andrée's Polarexpedition.* Gränna: Wiken, 1988.

Mabley, Edward H. *The Motor Balloon "America."* Brattleboro, Vt.: Stephen Greene Press, 1969.

McKee, Alexander. *Ice Crash: Disaster in the Arctic, 1928.* London: Souvenir Press, 1979.

Meyer, A. C. *The Earlier Years of the Drug and Allied Trades in the Mississippi Valley.* Saint Louis, Mo.: privately printed, 1948.

Meyer, H. C. *Airshipmen, Businessmen, and Politics, 1890–1940.* Washington, D.C.: Smithsonian Institution Press, 1991.

Miethe, A., and H. Hergesell. *Mit Zeppelin nach Spitzbergen.* Berlin: Deutsches Verlagshaus Bong, 1911.

Millbrooke, Anne. *Historic Aviation Properties.* Review and comment draft of National Register Bulletin. Washington, D.C.: U.S. Department of the Interior, National Park Service, 1994.

Ministry of Environment. *Regulations concerning the Cultural Heritage in Svalbard.* Publication T-927. Oslo: Ministry of Environment, 1992.

Mittelholzer, Walter. *By Airplane towards the North Pole.* Boston: Houghton Mifflin, 1925.

Montague, Richard. *Oceans, Poles, and Airmen.* New York: Random House, 1971.

Nansen, Fridtjof. *En ferd til Spitsbergen.* Christiania: Jacob Dybwads Forlag, 1920.

———. *In Northern Mists.* 2 vols. London: William Heinemann, 1911.

Neatby, Leslie H. *Conquest of the Last Frontier.* Athens: Ohio University, 1966.

Nobile, Umberto. *My Five Years with Soviet Airships.* Akron, Ohio: Lighter-than-Air Society, 1987.

Norsk Polarinstitutt. *The Place Names of Svalbard*. Skrifter nos. 80 and 112; Ny Trykk. Oslo: Norsk Polarinstitutt, 1991.

Pagé, Victor. *Modern Aircraft*. New York: Henley, 1928.

Peary, Robert E. *The North Pole*. New York: Frederick A. Stokes, 1910.

Pike, Arnold. "A Winter in the Eightieth Degree." In *Wild Norway*, ed. Abel Chapman. London: Edward Arnold, 1897.

Poe, Edgar Allan. 1844. "The Balloon Hoax." *New York Sun*, April 13, 1844.

Riffenburgh, Beau. "James Gordon Bennett, the *New York Herald*, and the Arctic." *Polar Record* 27, no. 160 (1991): 9–16.

———. "Jules Verne and the Conquest of the Polar Regions." *Polar Record* 27, no. 162 (1991): 237–240.

———. *The Myth of the Explorer*. London: Belhaven Press, 1993.

Robertson, Bruce. *Aviation Archaeology*. Cambridge, England: Patrick Stephens, 1977.

Robinson, William. *Gas and Petroleum Engines*. New York: Spon & Chamberlain, 1902.

Rodgers, Eugene. *Beyond the Barrier*. Annapolis: Naval Institute Press, 1990.

Savoy, Luigi Amedeo of. *On the "Polar Star" in the Arctic Sea*. London: Hutchinson, 1903.

Stevens, George E. "Walter Wellman: Journalist, Explorer, 'Astronaut.'" [Lake County, Ohio] *Historical Society Quarterly* 11, no. 3 (1969).

Sundman, Per Olof. *The Flight of the Eagle*. New York: Pantheon, 1970.

Swedish Society for Anthropology and Geography. *Andrée's Story: The Complete Record of His Polar Flight, 1897*. New York: Viking Press, 1930.

Tenderini, Mirella, and Michael Shandrick. *The Duke of the Abruzzi*. Seattle: Mountaineers, 1997.

Toland, John. *The Great Dirigibles*. New York: Dover, 1972.

Van Dyk, Herman. "The Evolution of the Wellman/Vaniman Airships, Parts One–Three." *Jack Knight Air Log—The Zeppelin Collector*, January, April, July 1996.

Vaniman, Melvin. "Revolutionizing Air Travel." *Aircraft*, May 1912, 76–78.

Verne, Jules. *Around the World in 80 Days—and—Five Weeks in a Balloon*. Ware, Hertfordshire: Wordsworth Editions, 1994.

———. *20,000 Leagues under the Sea*. Annapolis: Naval Institute Press, 1993.

———. *The Voyages and Adventures of Captain Hatteras*. Boston: James R. Osgood, 1875.

"Walter Wellman's Expedition to the North Pole." *National Geographic* 17, no. 4 (1906): 205–207.

Wellman, Walter. *The Aerial Age*. New York: A. R. Keller, 1911.

———. "An Arctic Day and Night." *McClure's* 14, no. 6 (1900): 555–563.

———. "By Airship to the North Pole." *McClure's* 29, no. 2 (1907): 189–200.

———. "The Polar Airship." *National Geographic* 17, no. 4 (1906): 208–228.

———. "Sledging toward the Pole." *McClure's* 14, no. 5 (1900): 405–414.

———. "Where Is Andrée?" *McClure's* 10, no. 5 (1898): 422–426.

———. "Will the 'America' Fly to the Pole?" *McClure's* 29, no. 3 (1907): 229–245.

Westerdahl, Christer. "The Maritime Cultural Landscape." *International Journal of Nautical Archaeology* 21, no. 1 (1992): 5–14.

Whipple, David B. "Aircraft as Cultural Resources: The Navy Approach." *CRM* 18, no. 2 (1995).

Wider, Paul. *Menschen und Ballone.* München: Bechtle, 1993.

Wilkins, George H. *Flying the Arctic.* New York: Grosset & Dunlap, 1928.

Index

Page numbers in italics refer to illustrations.

About the Author

P. J. Capelotti earned B.A. (1983) and M.A. (Phi Kappa Phi, 1989) degrees in history from the University of Rhode Island, and an M.A. (1994) and Ph.D. (1996) in anthropology from Rutgers University. He was elected a Fellow of the Explorers Club in 1993, wrote the introduction to the fiftieth anniversary edition of *Kon-Tiki* published by the Adventure Library in 1997, and was named to the Advisory Board for the Program in Maritime History and Archaeology at the University of Hawaii in 1998. His archaeological research has taken him to Svalbard, Indonesia, and Cuba, and he conducts ongoing fieldwork in modern American material culture in the mudflats and shallows of the eastern seaboard of the United States. He teaches archaeology and American studies at Penn State University, Abington College, in Abington, Pennsylvania.